Table Of Contents

Tarot Unveiled 2021:
The Art of Tarot Reading for Beginners

INTRODUCTION 9

CHAPTER 1: WHAT IS TAROT? 11
    WHAT IS TAROT, EXACTLY? 12
    TAROT THROUGHOUT HISTORY 15
    THE RIDER-WAITE TAROT DECK 19
    GETTING STARTED 21

CHAPTER 2: THE MAJOR ARCANA 25
    INTRODUCTION TO SYMBOLISM IN THE MAJOR ARCANA 27
    0 – THE FOOL 33
    I – THE MAGICIAN 37
    II – THE HIGH PRIESTESS 41
    III – THE EMPRESS 45
    IV – THE EMPEROR 50
    V – THE HIEROPHANT 54
    VI – THE LOVERS 57
    VII – THE CHARIOT 61
    VIII – STRENGTH 64
    IX – THE HERMIT 67
    X – THE WHEEL OF FORTUNE 71
    XI – JUSTICE 75
    XII – THE HANGED MAN 79
    XIII – DEATH 83
    XIV – TEMPERANCE 87
    XV – THE DEVIL 91
    XVI – THE TOWER 95
    XVII – THE STAR 100
    XVIII – THE MOON 104
    XIX – THE SUN 108

XX – Judgment 112
XXI – The World.. 115
The Fool's Journey 119

CHAPTER 3: THE MINOR ARCANA FOR BEGINNERS 123
Numbered Cards of the Minor Arcana.. 124
Suits and Elemental Correspondences 126
Suit of Wands – Fire 128
Suit of Cups – Water 131
Suit of Swords – Air 134
Suit of Pentacles – Earth 136
Court Cards: Formulaic Characters 138

CHAPTER 4: THE SUIT OF WANDS 143
Ace of Wands.. 143
Two of Wands 144
Three of Wands 145
Four of Wands 146
Five of Wands 147
Six of Wands 148
Seven of Wands 149
Eight of Wands 150
Nine of Wands 151
Ten of Wands.. 152
Page of Wands 154
Knight of Wands 154
Queen of Wands 156
King of Wands 157

CHAPTER 5: THE SUIT OF CUPS 159
Ace of Cups 159
Two of Cups 160
Three of Cups 161
Four of Cups... 162

Five of Cups	163
Six of Cups	164
Seven of Cups	165
Eight of Cups	166
Nine of Cups	167
Ten of Cups	168
Page of Cups	169
Knight of Cups	171
Queen of Cups	172
King of Cups	174

CHAPTER 6: THE SUIT OF SWORDS ... 177

Ace of Swords	177
Two of Swords	179
Three of Swords	180
Four of Swords	181
Five of Swords	182
Six of Swords	183
Seven of Swords	184
Eight of Swords	185
Nine of Swords	186
Ten of Swords	187
Page of Swords	188
Knight of Swords	189
Queen of Swords	191
King of Swords	192

CHAPTER 7: THE SUIT OF PENTACLES ... 194

Ace of Pentacles	194
Two of Pentacles	195
Three of Pentacles	196
Four of Pentacles	197
Five of Pentacles	198

- Six of Pentacles ... 199
- Seven of Pentacles ... 200
- Eight of Pentacles ... 201
- Nine of Pentacles ... 201
- Ten of Pentacles ... 202
- Page of Pentacles ... 203
- Knight of Pentacles ... 204
- Queen of Pentacles ... 205
- King of Pentacles ... 207

CHAPTER 8: TAROT READINGS ... 209
- Preparing to Receive a Tarot Reading ... 209
- Selecting a Question ... 211
- Preparing to Perform a Tarot Reading ... 215
- How to Enhance Your Intuitive Sensitivities ... 217
- Memory and Intuition ... 222

CHAPTER 9: TAROT SPREADS ... 224
- One Card Reading ... 225
- Two Card Spread ... 227
- Three Card Spread ... 229
- Horseshoe Spread ... 230
- Romany Spread ... 231
- Celtic Cross Spread ... 233

CHAPTER 10: CUSTOMIZED TAROT ... 235
- Colors in the Tarot Deck ... 237
- Shapes in the Tarot Deck ... 238
- Symbolic Elements in the Tarot Deck ... 240

CHAPTER 11: WHY IT WORKS ... 243
- History of Divination ... 244
- Why Does Divination Work? ... 247

CHAPTER 12: THE SACRED TAROT UNVEILED ... 249

WHAT IS A MYSTERY SCHOOL? 250
TAROT AS A SPIRITUAL PRACTICE 252

CONCLUSION **254**

Tarot Ultimate Guide 2021:
The Supreme Guide for Learning The Art of Tarot Divination and Readings

INTRODUCTION **257**
CHAPTER 1: THE HISTORY OF TAROT **259**
THE MEANING OF TAROT CARDS 261
CHAPTER 2: TAROT AND ARCHETYPES **265**
JUNGIAN ARCHETYPES FOUND IN THE TAROT 268
COMMON ARCHETYPES IN THE TAROT 270
CHAPTER 3: THE MAJOR ARCANA **275**
0 – THE FOOL 276
1 – THE MAGICIAN 278
2 – THE HIGH PRIESTESS 280
3 – THE EMPRESS 282
4 – THE EMPEROR 284
5 – THE HIEROPHANT 286
6 – THE LOVERS 288
7 – THE CHARIOT 290
8 – STRENGTH 292
9 – THE HERMIT 293
10 – THE WHEEL OF FORTUNE 295
11 – JUSTICE 298
12 – THE HANGED MAN 300
13 – DEATH 302
14 – TEMPERANCE 305
15 – THE DEVIL 307
16 – THE TOWER 309
17 – THE STAR 312

 18 – The Moon 314
 19 – The Sun 316
 20 – Judgment 318
 21 – The World 321

CHAPTER 4: TAROT AND THE UNCONSCIOUS 324

CHAPTER 5: TAROT AND NUMEROLOGY 328
 Minor Arcana 329
 Major Arcana 334
 Master Numbers in Numerology 336

CHAPTER 6: TAROT AND THE ZODIAC 339
 The Suits and Their Corresponding Signs 340
 Court Cards 343
 Cardinal, Fixed, and Mutable Signs 345

CHAPTER 7: TAROT AND THE CHAKRAS 347
 The Importance of Balance of the Chakras 348
 Why You Need to Read Your Tarot Cards 351
 The Chakras and the Tarot 353

CHAPTER 8: TAROT AND RELIGION 357

CONCLUSION 360

Tarot Unveiled 2021:

The Art of Tarot Reading for Beginners

By Serra Night

Copyright 2021 Serra Night – All rights reserved.

This content is provided with the sole purpose of providing relevant information on a specific topic for which every reasonable effort has been made to ensure that it is both accurate and reasonable. Nevertheless, by purchasing this content you consent to the fact that the author, as well as the publisher, are in no way experts on the topics contained herein, regardless of any claims as such that may be made within. As such, any suggestions or recommendations that are made within are done so purely for entertainment value. It is recommended that you always consult a professional prior to undertaking any of the advice or techniques discussed within.

This is a legally binding declaration that is considered both valid and fair by both the Committee of Publishers Association and the American Bar Association and should be considered as legally binding within the United States.

The reproduction, transmission, and duplication of any of the content found herein, including any specific or extended information will be done as an illegal act regardless of the end form the information ultimately takes. This includes copied versions of the work both physical, digital and audio unless express consent of the Publisher is provided beforehand. Any additional rights reserved.

Furthermore, the information that can be found within the pages described forthwith shall be considered both accurate and truthful when it comes to the recounting of facts. As such, any use, correct or incorrect, of the provided information will render the Publisher free of responsibility as to the actions taken outside of their direct purview. Regardless, there are zero scenarios where the original author or the Publisher can be deemed liable in any fashion for any damages or hardships that may result from any of the information discussed herein.

Additionally, the information in the following pages is intended only for informational purposes and should thus be thought of as universal. As befitting its nature, it is presented without assurance regarding its prolonged validity or interim quality. Trademarks that are mentioned are done without written consent and can in no way be considered an endorsement from the trademark holder.

Introduction

Congratulations on your purchase of *Tarot Unveiled: The Art of Tarot Reading for Beginners* and thank you for doing so! Within the following chapters, you'll find all of the information that you need to dive deep into the world of cartomancy and divination. You might use this knowledge to entertain, comfort, and inspire yourself, or, with enough practice, you might start offering card readings and guidance to others. Tarot's popularity has skyrocketed in recent years, and many people are hungry for the answers it can provide to their personal questions, as well as life's greatest mysteries. However, you choose to use this book and your Tarot deck. I have no doubt that it will enrich your life in myriad ways and help to open your intuitive eye to the unseen and unknown.

The beauty of the Tarot is that it can be viewed as an art form. No matter how standardized the cards, their illustrations, or recommended interpretations, it is inevitable that each individual will bring something unique to the table when performing a reading or receiving one. That means that once you educate yourself on the Tarot deck and divination methods, your voice and vision will no doubt add a worthwhile perspective to the world of cartomancy. There are no right or wrong answers in Tarot, so there is plenty of room to experiment and try new things, and, above all, trust your intuition. Whether you choose to incorporate Tarot into your daily life, faith, and career, or simply to dabble in card readings from time to time for fun, developing an intimate knowledge of and deep connection to the cards will usher you toward personal growth, empathic understanding, and perhaps even spiritual enlightenment.

This book has been written for beginners and novices, so if the concepts of the Tarot seem wildly unfamiliar, complicated, confusing, or overwhelming to you, have no fear. Together, we'll cover the history and origins of Tarot, the symbolic imagery and interpretations of every single card in the deck, the basics of divination, and the keys to opening your inner eye so that you can access your perceptive and intuitive gifts. Not all cartomancers are clairvoyants or psychics, and many of those who do identify as such started out, once upon a time, just like you—uncertain, inexperienced, but curious and determined. The degree of energy that you put into your divination practice will determine how much you get out of it, so if you are willing to work diligently and remain open-minded, there is no end to what you might achieve or how much growth you might experience with Tarot.

There are many books available on the market concerning this subject, so thank you again for choosing this one! Every effort was made to ensure it is full of as much useful and accurate information as possible. Please enjoy and happy reading!

Chapter 1: What Is Tarot?

The images and language of Tarot are archetypal. Even to those who are unfamiliar with the specific nuances of cartomancy, they often strike a familiar chord upon first sight, stirring up a sense of deja vu or intuitive impulses. That being the case, you may feel that you are familiar with Tarot without ever having learned precisely what it is or how it works. Not to worry—we'll start with the basics in this chapter and build gradually upon that foundation of knowledge, making sure that no stone is left unturned in your study of Tarot and divination. Let's dive in!

What Is Tarot, Exactly?

Tarot is merely one method of divination through card reading, which is also called "cartomancy." Other forms of divination include tasseomancy (the art of reading tea leaves), scrying (divination with the use of a pendulum), osteomancy (the reading of bones), lithomancy (foretelling the future by reading stones), rune casting (an ancient Norse divination practice), geomancy (casting and reading natural elements, such as sand or soil), palmistry (reading the lines on the inside of the palm), numerology (interpreting the meaning of numbers all around you), and astrology (divination through the movements of celestial bodies), among others. Some of the most experienced and talented cartomancers combine their Tarot practice with one or more other forms of divination, gaining an extra dimension to their intuitive perception by noting the universal patterns and themes that exist between them.

Within the world of cartomancy, there are also Oracle Cards, which function similarly to the Tarot, but the decks are not typically standardized, and the number of cards included can range from just twelve to more than a hundred. Tarot decks, by contrast, tend to adhere to certain universal traditions and are more popularly created, published, and used for gameplay, fortune-telling, and even spiritual practice.

The Tarot deck has evolved over the course of centuries, and while there are certainly variations from one deck to the next (different imagery, alternative names, and numbers, sometimes varying quantities of total cards included), most follow the same general structure, with a deck consisting of twenty-two "trump" cards, known as the Major Arcana, along with forty numbered suit cards, and sixteen suited Court Cards, collectively referred to as the Minor Arcana.

Each of these seventy-eight cards carries its own symbolic meaning, or rather, multiple possible meanings, depending on its context. When the cards are laid out in divination spreads, they work together to tell a story, of sorts, which the cartomancer is able to read and interpret with their own unique slant. Most cartomancers believe that the positioning (upright or upside down) and contextual surroundings (which cards are laid beside it) of any card will impact its implications, meaning that there is an infinite number of stories to be found and deciphered in a spread of two or more cards.

That being said, there are very few steadfast rules in the world of Tarot—only guidelines—so you will find that there are always a fair few cartomancers who dismiss certain traditions and decks that defy the norm. In this book, we'll review the most commonly recognized card interpretations and divination methods to provide you with a solid, working foundation of knowledge, but don't let this text limit your understanding of the Tarot! These interpretations and guidelines are just a jumping-off point. You can always build upon your foundational knowledge after finishing this text through further reading and research or by consulting more experienced cartomancers for advice and recommendations. Once you are comfortable with Tarot, you should absolutely feel encouraged to assign your own meanings to certain cards based on the visceral reactions they stir up inside you, design your own spread formats, and even invent new and unique ways to relate to and make use of the deck. The rule of thumb with Tarot is if it feels right or resonates with you, then it can't be wrong.

Tarot Throughout History

While the historical origins of cartomancy as a form of divination are shrouded in mystery, the history of modern Tarot is fairly well-defined. In this section, we'll explore the proven facts alongside the mysteries and myths.

The traditional fifty-two card playing deck that we still use today for solitaire, poker, and other games first came to Europe in the late 1300s, having originated in Islamic countries, popularized by the Turkish card game "Mamluk." The first recorded evidence of Tarot cards—then referred to as "carta de trionfi," meaning "triumph cards" or "trump cards"—came not long after this. In Florence, Italy, in the year 1440, court records tell us of the first commissioned production of a set of these "carta de trionfi," most likely used at the time to trump or overrule the numbered and court cards of the traditional game-playing card deck.

There is overwhelming evidence to point to the fact that Tarot cards were originally used for a form of gameplay, which incorporated some divinatory elements. Card games became a popular pastime for nobility and royalty throughout southern Europe over the following century, and by the 1530s, we see records of Tarot cards being used for a game called "tarocchi" or "triumph," which is similar to modern-day whist or bridge. Interestingly, we also see records of another game called "tarocchi appropriati," in which the trump cards (now known as the Major Arcana) were pulled at random and used to inspire the card-reader to compose a whimsical poem or song about the person sitting opposite them.

This game was most likely played in jest, considering the historical context. Royals and nobles at the time would have been pressured to adhere strictly to a code of conduct as defined by the Roman Catholic Church, which would have condemned any interest in mysticism, including the supernatural practice of divination and belief in clairvoyant gifts. However, as these games gained popularity, we see more and more records of people in positions of power commissioning artists to design unique decks for them, and the possible uses of the Tarot deck began to expand. Many of these designs then became standardized, particularly those that respected the laws and values of the church; these early decks often featured a Suit of Coins or Discs in place of Pentagrams, and Polo Sticks or walking Staves in place of Wands, for example, and some eschewed trump cards like the High Priestess, who represents esoteric spiritual knowledge and aspects of the divine feminine.

This is where historical legend becomes a bit opaque. We know that the name "Tarot" came from these fun card games, which were not originally related to divination or mysticism, but at the same time, records of the name may not tell us the full story of the Tarot tradition. Records usually only capture the activities of royalty, nobility, and clergy in detail, while the activities of commoners would likely have gone unrecorded or viewed as unimportant. Standardized decks were commissioned by the wealthy, but there was nothing to stop those of lesser status from crafting and using their own unique decks for self-determined purposes.

Many believe that the tradition of Oracle Card reading, brought to Europe by the Romany people (also called "Roma" or "Gypsies") from the Middle East during the same time period, was combined with the Tarot deck, explaining the ever-increasing aura of mystical power and esoteric knowledge portrayed in the card illustrations as time progressed. This would be nearly impossible to prove, as these people were shunned throughout Europe, forced to live in a state of constant travel, and their activities would rarely have been noted by record-keepers. Furthermore, their status as eternal refugees would have spurred the Romany people to keep their traditions shrouded in secrecy and mystery, fearing persecution. Finally, even if commoners or nobles *did* allow their curiosity to get the best of them, seeking out fortune tellers to show them their future within the cards, they wouldn't have bragged about these experiences, let alone record them, fearing ostracism or excommunication from the church themselves.

It seems most likely that the Romany people should be credited with the arcane aspects and functions of the Tarot deck, but there are some other popular myths and legends as to these origins. Some believe the Tarot came to Europe with the return of the Knights Templar from the crusades and that the magic of the cards is the reason these knights were able to secure so much success, acclaim, and wealth. Others believe it was the Cathars (a sect of early Christian Gnostics) or the Kabbalists of Jewish or Christian faiths that created the first Tarot decks for supernatural or spiritual practices. Others still believe the arcane knowledge of the Tarot deck originated in unique texts that were destroyed in the fall of the Great Library of Alexandria, preserved by a group of mystics and scholars in Fez, Morocco, who recorded the information in code to protect it from the church.

Whether these legends hold water or not, we can be certain that Tarot became popularized and widely published throughout Europe, marketed as a tool for divination with the rise of the occult and esoteric counter-culture in the late 1700s. Occultist and hermetic groups originally used the most popular standard decks of the middle ages (the Tarot de Marseilles, usually, or the Visconti-Sforza deck) for cartomancy, but Antoine Court de Gebelin and Jean-Baptiste Alliette (also known as Etteilla) changed that in the year 1789 in Paris, France, publishing the first arcane deck with an accompanying manual, allowing anyone with interest to gain access to the Tarot's esoteric secrets and easily decode its symbolism. They claimed that this deck, titled "Le Monde Primitif," was inspired primarily by the ancient Egyptian Book of Thoth, allegedly written by the Egyptian God of arcane wisdom himself. In this deck, we see the four elements, concepts of astrology and alchemy, and valuation of the divine feminine alongside the divine masculine, incorporated into a standardized deck for the first time.

The Rider-Waite Tarot Deck

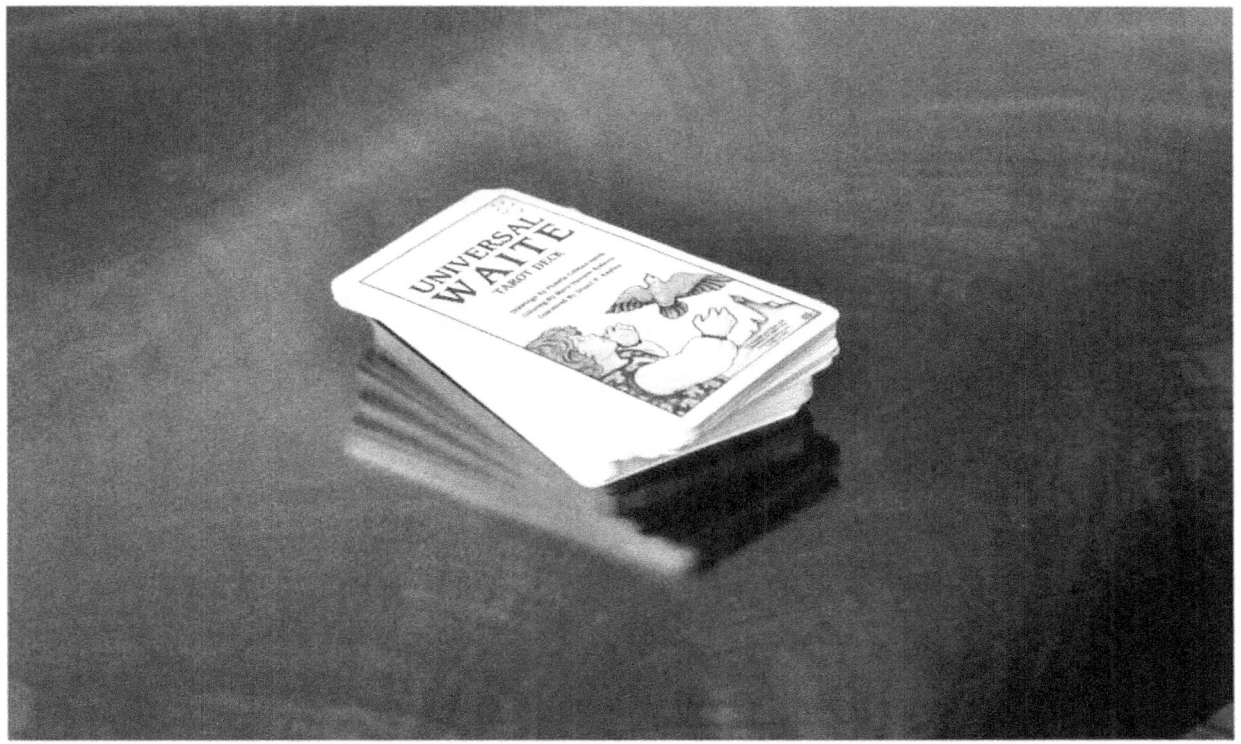

In this text, we'll focus primarily on the imagery, language, and meaning of the Rider-Waite Tarot deck. Originally published in London, England, in the year 1910, published by William Rider and A.E. Waite with illustrations by Pamela Colman Smith, this deck is widely recognized as the modern gold standard for Tarot divination, though it is, by no means, the oldest nor necessarily the most widely loved. It is particularly useful for beginners, as its illustrations are symbolically rich but not overly detailed or cluttered, and the imagery is fairly straight-forward and easy to interpret but not so obvious as to be boring or simplistic. It draws from traditional Judeo-Christian symbolism, but it also incorporates elements of Le Monde Primitif and its ancient Egyptian inspiration, as well as astrological themes, mystical, hermetic, and kabbalistic concepts. It is also believed to elevate the divine feminine in a manner that would have been considered radically progressive at the time of its publication (though designers of modern decks often believe it leaves much to be desired in this area, consistently assigning higher ranks to male figures and including no racial diversity or portrayals of alternative sexual preferences).

What sets the Rider-Waite deck apart from its predecessors is the fact that every single one of the seventy-eight cards features a unique symbolic illustration. Previous decks often included suit cards that resembled those of the fifty-two-card game-playing deck; for instance, the Eight of Wands would simply portray eight identical staves or batons, with no further illustrative explanation. In the Rider-Waite deck, every single card seems to tell its own detailed story. To get the most out of these illustrations, we can learn to decode the symbolism—what do mountains and rivers, and other elements of nature represent? What about animals or celestial bodies or depictions of the four raw elements? And how can we read the color schemes of cards or interpret their numerological values?

We'll answer these questions in detail and outline the specific popular interpretations of every single card. Even if you do not use the Rider-Waite deck you'll likely find that most alternatives are inspired by it to some degree, or if you use an older deck, you'll see many of the same archetypal themes echoed there but stripped of mystical imagery.

Getting Started

Before you dive into the following chapters, I would highly recommend that you work to acquire a deck of your own so that you can build hands-on experience while you read through this book. It isn't necessarily as easy as going out and buying a deck at the store or ordering online, though. Most cartomancers strongly believe that, in order for a novice card-reader to harness the metaphysical and supernatural energies necessary for divination, they should receive their first deck as a gift rather than purchase it by their own hand. This doesn't mean that you couldn't specifically ask someone to do this for you or arrange to exchange first decks with another beginner. Furthermore, you should feel encouraged to purchase alternative decks on your own—as many as you like, and the more, the better—after receiving the first. However, you may find that your first deck will always possess unique and powerful energy, as compared to decks purchased afterward; it may be the most accurate for divination purposes. Once you gain some experience with Tarot, you should make an effort to sustain this tradition by gifting one of your preferred decks to another novice.

Ideally, your first deck should be a classic or traditional design, as you'll then have an easier time deciphering illustrations and researching any questions that may come up in your early divination practice. You'll have an easier time working with decks that offer full, characterized illustrations of the Suit cards, as opposed to those whose Suit cards resemble those of a traditional 52-card playing deck. While minimalist decks can be beautiful and quite useful for experienced cartomancers, their illustrations will leave beginners with a lot of unanswered questions. Also, you'll want a first deck to include as much printed information as possible; avoid decks that eschew numbers or titles for stylistic reasons. Many decks will come with an accompanying guide book; these are great options for novices.

Once you have your first deck, you'll want to take further steps to ensure it is stored properly and regularly cleansed. This will prevent the cards from channeling negative or stagnant energies, and it also ensures the artwork remains pristine. Store your deck inside a silk cloth bag or a protective box with a cover made of natural material (wood or stone are great options; plastic, not so much), and make sure it is kept in a cool, dry, and somewhat dark place. Too much heat, moisture, or sunlight can damage the cards' structure and artwork.

Most cartomancers do not allow other people to handle their decks, even in the midst of performing a reading for them. This protects the cards from picking up negative or invasive energies. Some may be far more lax about this policy in the company of trusted friends and loved ones.

Whether you allow your deck to be touched by others or not, you'll want to get into the habit of regular cleansing. If you're performing frequent readings for yourself or others, this may be done on a weekly or daily basis; if your practice is less frequent, once a month should be sufficient. One great way to cleanse your deck is to leave it sitting on your windowsill under the light of a full moon, which occurs roughly every 29 days—wonderfully convenient timing! Alternatively, you might choose to cleanse your deck with a ritual smoke cleansing, also known as smudging. If you get the sense that your deck has been imbued with particularly negative or nefarious energy, a salt cleansing may be needed. Wrap the deck in an airtight plastic bag and submerge it fully in a dry container of sea salt or rock salt. The deck should remain submerged and untouched for several days before it is used again.

If you choose to store your deck with crystals that harbor protective energies, or those that can diffuse or deflect negativity, you may not need to cleanse your deck as often as you would otherwise. Some cartomancers like to create an altar space on which to store their decks, decorating with crystals, candles, herbs and flowers, and any other materials or props that help to awaken their intuitive minds.

Once you have your deck in hand, I'd recommend spending some time with the images before you read what I, or any other Tarot expert, have to say about their meanings. What do the cards inspire within you? How do they make you feel? Do they stir up emotions or memories? Are there any that you find particularly beautiful or meaningful? Are there any that you immediately dislike?

You may want to start a Tarot and divination journal for yourself and take note of these visceral reactions before reading on. Get in the habit of respecting your gut instincts as authoritative experts in their own right and learn to hold space and reverence for your own intuitive insights, as well as the opinions of professional cartomancers.

Chapter 2: The Major Arcana

Most aspiring cartomancers begin their study of the Tarot with the Major Arcana, which is comprised of twenty-two unique "trump" cards, none of which belongs to a suit. We'll start here as well, for several reasons. For one, the cards of the Major Arcana tend to have the most easily readable illustrations, and their meanings are usually easier for people to memorize than the rest of the cards in the deck. In some decks, the Major Arcana cards are the only ones will full illustrations, while the suited cards will simply display their number and suit (the Seven of Cups, for instance, would simply be an array of seven identical chalices, with no other props or human figures to provide context to the image). The Major Arcana cards are also considered to be heavyweights, as compared to suited cards; in most spreads, these trump cards bear more importance and intensity, shaping your interpretations with greater influence than the other cards. Some cartomancers will even perform readings exclusively with the cards of the Major Arcana, using a deck of only twenty-two cards in total. Personally, I recommend using the full deck once you are familiar with all the cards, as the suits will help to provide more nuances in your readings.

I'll provide highly detailed descriptions and interpretive explanations for all seventy-eight cards in a classic Tarot deck within the next few chapters. Bear in mind, though, that these descriptions, particularly of the illustrations, will be based primarily on the Rider-Waite deck, one of the most popular and widely printed Tarot decks in the world. The Rider-Waite deck is an excellent choice for beginners, with clear archetypal symbolism and a longstanding, widespread fan base. That being said, it is a relatively old design (originally published in 1910), so many modern cartomancers opt to use more contemporary decks, with illustrations that feature more diversity and overtly feminist perspectives or more abstract symbolism. If you are working with an alternative seventy-eight card deck, use the numbers on the cards as your guide, as some titles may be altered (several decks replace the title of the Strength card with the title "Lust," for instance; some may also change the names of the Court Card ranks or even the titles of suits).

Introduction to Symbolism in the Major Arcana

Divine Gender Traits

The Rider-Waite deck is full of symbolic imagery that is heavily tied to contemporary understandings of the occult and pagan religious philosophy; in these traditions, the notion of God or divine power is often conceptualized in dualities, represented by the divine feminine and divine masculine, whose energies feed into one another and, together in cooperative harmony, maintain balance throughout the universe.

The energy of the divine masculine is associated with the sun and sky, daytime, light, and heat, while the divine feminine corresponds to the earth and sea, nighttime, darkness, and cold.

Divine masculine traits include activity, expansion, expression, projection, rationality, forcefulness, stability, virility, opacity, material knowledge, intensity, independence, and cyclical creativity (causing destruction to make space for creation).

Meanwhile, divine feminine characteristics include passivity, contraction, introspection, intuition, emotionality, receptiveness, fluidity, fertility, transparency, mystery and spirituality, calmness, community-orientation, and generative creativity (creating something out of nothing or using creation to fill the void of destruction).

These designations should not be viewed or perpetuated as stereotypes that apply to human men and women. Each of us, regardless of our sexual identities, will embody some traits from both deific genders.

Age, Maturity, and Experience

We can add another dimension to this duality by incorporating the traits of youthful inexperience or mature experience. When the divine masculine is combined with youthful inexperience, it denotes virility, action without forethought, passion, inspiration, vigor, brute force, naivety, and curiosity; combined with mature experience, though, the divine masculine energy becomes rational and wise, more concerned with intellectual and spiritual pursuits than with lustful or sensual actions, and more likely to exude prideful or stubborn energy than a curious one. When the divine feminine spirit is combined with youthful inexperience, it is associated with sensual and material pleasures, fertility, emotionality, safety, security, and abundance; by contrast, when this divine energy is imbued with maturity and experience, it becomes spiritual and intuitive, calm and balanced (rather than emotionally volatile), nurturing, generous, willing to trust in the universe to provide whatever is needed but not personally owned, and more comfortable with change and vulnerability.

It is imperative that you familiarize yourself with these concepts as symbolic of personality types or as illustrations of common dynamics within interpersonal relationships and nature, rather than literal representations of gender and age demographics. An elderly male querent could certainly be represented by the Empress card, for instance, or the Queen of Cups, if he is ruled by nurturing and creative energy, while a young female querent with an authoritative, forceful, and stubborn personality might be represented by the Emperor or Hierophant.

It is also important to stay mindful of the fact that both divine genders embody positive and negative traits in equal measure; neither is better or worse than the other. Furthermore, these divine energies are not right or wrong for any individual; men should not feel ashamed to possess feminine characteristics, nor should women feel uneasy about projecting masculine traits. It is entirely possible—common, even—for some degree of both energies to be present within the same individual, or all four, if you add the dimension of experience and maturity. A person can be wise but young at heart;

inexperienced but emotionally mature; nurturing but volatile; rational but spiritual; authoritative but naive; passionate but calm and grounded; and so on.

Whenever possible, aim to look beyond the cast of characters illustrated in your spreads; when you do so, you'll be better able to focus on the story the cards tell through the dynamics of relationships or journeys of personal growth: action and consequence; risk and reward; cause and effect; revolution and evolution; past, present, and future.

Elements, Timing, and Zodiac Signs

Each card of the Major Arcana is associated with one of the four suits and their corresponding elements, as well as an astrological sign of the Zodiac or ruling celestial body and a suggested timing (which may refer to specific dates or speeds—rapidly, spontaneously, slowly, and so on). This does not mean that the cards belong to their associated suits, but in any complex spread that you're having trouble making sense of, it can help to recognize the connections between trump cards and suit cards in order to trace the thread of a storyline within it. If a spread is dominated by Sword cards and features an upright Magician, it means there is a clear theme of intellectual pursuit, brainstorming, plotting, and planned manifestation throughout the spread.

The Major Arcana cards are first and foremost ruled by the fifth element, usually called "spirit" or "aether," but they'll also have a secondary material elemental correspondence. That means that while a numbered Pentacle card, for example, is connected to the Earth element and speaks to material values, any Major Arcana card connected to the Earth element would speak to the connection between the spiritual and material realms.

The associations of timing can help to give a cartomancer clues as to when or how certain events will take place. For example, the Tower card is associated with abrupt developments, meaning that whatever change it predicts will happen quickly and unexpectedly.

Furthermore, the correlated astrological signs of the cards do not necessarily need to represent a person born under the same constellation or planet (though they sometimes might). Instead, they'll reference the traits of the associated signs or celestial bodies.

If any of these concepts seem confusing or bewildering, try not to worry too much; they'll begin to make more sense and even become intuitive as you read through the following card descriptions. Let's begin!

0 – The Fool

Imagery

The Fool is depicted as a young man embarking on a journey. His stance and facial expression both convey his joy, optimism, and carefree attitude; however, as he gazes up at the sky above, he fails to take note of where his feet are falling and wanders dangerously close to the edge of a cliff, oblivious to his material surroundings. In one hand, he holds his travel sack—a very small pack, a testament to his faith in the universe to provide for him during his travels—while in the other, he holds a rose, a symbol of sexual freedom and sensual liberation. He wears a red eagle feather in his cap, and his travel sack is embroidered with an eagle; both items are symbols of divine guidance and spiritual messages. Close at his heels, a small dog jumps up on its hind legs, representing the Fool's animal instincts; the dog smiles up at him in admiration and urges him forward, but it also appears to be warning him to watch his step, lest he stumbles over the edge.

In the distant background, we see a mountain range: a series of sharp peaks, constantly ascending, warning that the journey ahead may not be easy or quick. Still, the sun shines brightly overhead, a sign that divine powers will smile down upon him throughout his travels.

History

In older decks, The Fool was often portrayed as an elderly beggar or vagabond in tattered clothing. However, in the Rider-Waite deck, and many other modern Tarot publications, he is instead depicted as a young, well-dressed man in sturdy traveling boots and colorful garb. Still, even in the Rider-Waite deck, his tunic has tattered sleeves, a sign that the Fool is not concerned with societal norms and that he values experiences and skills over material possessions. Even when the Fool is drawn in rags, the underlying symbolism remains; his poverty is not a reason to pity him, but rather, a sign that this figure has nothing to lose and everything to gain. His lack of material wealth is a kind of freedom; ahead of him lies nothing but potential for improvement and growth.

Alternative Names

The Madman; Le Mat; Il Matto; Narr; The Lunatic; The Jester. He is usually the first of the trump cards, but occasionally, he will be the last, numbered as XXI (if the Magician is reassigned to the number 0) or XXII (if the Magician is assigned the number 1).

Interpretation

Upright – This card represents curiosity, naivety, spontaneity, adventure, youthful energy, and new beginnings. Though the Fool is drawn as a male in most decks, he most often represents the querent, regardless of their gender identity; alternatively, he could represent a youthful or adventurous figure in their life (their child, sibling, friend, or lover, perhaps). It could easily reference an adolescent's first steps toward independence, or for an older querent, the decision to abandon the structure and safety of their current circumstances (family, social circles, career, faith-based institutions) and forge ahead on their own into unknown territory. It reminds the querent to go against the grain, be bold and daring, and value originality over conformity. His card number, 0, is a reference to the unlimited potential of a blank slate. The sky is the limit, but success isn't guaranteed. The Fool isn't much for planning ahead or paying close attention to details, and his head is up in the clouds most of the time, so there is every chance that he will, in fact, fall over the edge of that cliff, despite the warnings of his canine companion. Still, the yellow sky behind him denotes optimism and divine guidance; even if he falls, the experience will usually be one that defines his identity and trajectory of personal growth. Sometimes, we have to fail in order to learn how to succeed.

Reversed – Upside down, the Fool speaks to a lack of spontaneity, or perhaps a form of spontaneity that is more dangerous and volatile than adventurous. The querent might be overly cautious, frightened of the unknown, or unable to have faith in the universe at large to protect them, like an individual with an unstable root chakra. They might be spending too much time planning and constantly delaying action. Alternatively, they might be too impulsive and daring, perhaps even reckless, asking for trouble. There is a fine line between being carefree and charismatic and being careless and immature.

Contextual – The Fool is beginning a journey, so keep an eye out for other elements that symbolize journeys or paths in surrounding cards. Roads and rivers are the most obvious signs (as in the Moon card, for example, or Temperance), but mountains and cliffs can also connect to this card (in the Three of Wands, for instance, or the Eight of Cups). These cards can help to clarify what direction the Fool is heading in and the ways in which his journey will ultimately shape his identity. His timing implies spontaneity, so if he appears beside any card that represents a choice or crossroads (the Lovers, the Moon, the Two of Wands or Two of Swords), he may be advising you to listen to your gut instincts and just go for it.

Associated Suit: Swords
Correlated Element: Air
Celestial Correspondence: Uranus
Timing: Spontaneity

I – The Magician

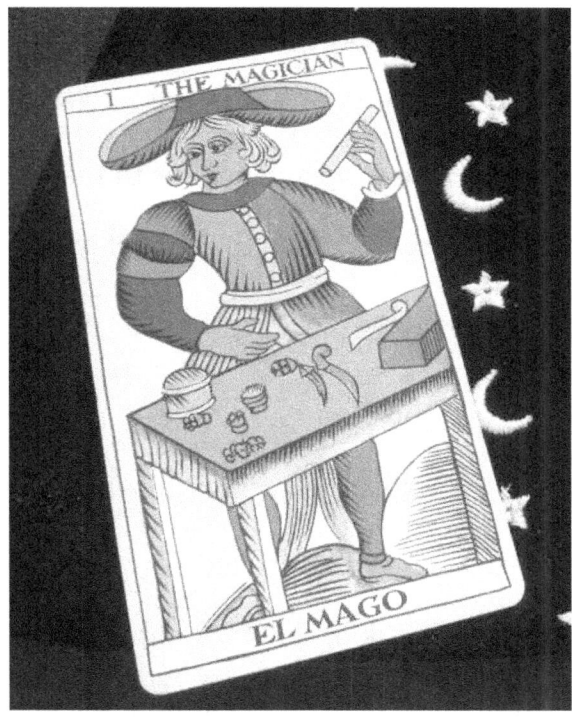

Imagery

The Magician stands alone at his altar, prepared to manifest his desires. He has one arm raised in the air, holding a wand that points up toward the sky, while his other hand points down toward the earth, making himself the conduit between divine energy and earthly, material reality. Above his head, a lemniscate (also known as an infinity symbol) hovers, representing the limitless energy available in the universe that he can tap into, harness, and channel into manifestation.

He wears a long red robe, signifying his passion and empowerment over a white shift, representing the purity of his intent. Around his waist is a belt that is actually a snake, consuming its own tail—another symbol of limitless potential and power and a symbol of rebirth. He is surrounded by flowers, representing manifestation and growth. Four magical tools rest upon his altar: a second wand (brown wood, contrasted with the white wand he holds and points toward the sky), a chalice, a sword, and a pentacle coin. These are representations of the four Tarot suits and the four earthly elements they correspond with (fire for wands, water for cups, air for swords, and earth for pentacles); with these tools at his disposal, there is nothing he cannot achieve once he begins to channel his energy in the right direction.

History

We like to think of magicians as omnipotent wizards these days, but historically, they weren't often revered for their powers. In fact, they were sometimes looked down upon as con-artists or sacrilegious tricksters. The low numerical rank of this card implies that the Magician is more of a novice than a master. Modern decks tend to paint him in a far more favorable light.

Alternative Names

The Magus; The Juggler; Le Bataleur; The Trickster; Mountebank

Interpretation

Upright — Everything you need to manifest your goals and create something new is right here, at your fingertips. The querent is urged to harness whatever energy and inspiration they already have at their disposal and work with it. There is an alchemical theme to this card, so it implies the ability to make something that is more than just the sum of its parts. This could reference an artistic endeavor, a new business venture, an academic development, or the creation of a family. The Magician pushes us to master skill sets, hone talents, express ourselves, and harness the power of will and determination.

Reversed – Have you ever had a boss or teacher who was clearly too inexperienced for the position they held? That is the energy of the reversed Magician. This reversed card usually implies that you have gotten ahead of yourself. You may be failing to manifest due to a lack of adequate preparation, study, practice, knowledge, or resources. It also may be a sign that someone's power, energy, determination, or talent is being misused, or applied to achieve negative ends. As a character, the reversed Magician embodies the trait of narcissism taken to an unhealthy extreme.

Contextual – There are a few cards in the deck that appear to have a direct connection to the Magician. In Strength, for instance, we see a similar color scheme and a lemniscate symbol above the woman's head, pointing to the need to balance willpower, creativity, and passion with calmness, compassion, and emotional balance. In the Three of Wands, we see a figure from behind who could very well be the Magician in a later stage of life. This card has decidedly masculine energy, so if you find it in a spread dominated by feminine cards (the Empress, the Moon, Strength, Justice, the Star, etc.), then there is a clear need for balance between dichotomous traits in order to achieve successful manifestation without causing self-harm.

Associated Suit: Swords

Correlated Element: Air

Celestial Correspondence: Mercury

Timing: Quickly

II – The High Priestess

Imagery

The High Priestess sits upon a square stone, regally (though her seat is not quite a throne) between two stone pillars. One is black, marked with the letter B, while the other is white, labeled with the letter J; these letters stand for the words *Boaz* (meaning "strength") and *Jachin* (meaning "Yah establishes"), which, according to Biblical lore, were the names of the two pillars that stood at the entrance to Solomon's Temple, the very first temple of Jerusalem. These two words are also frequently used in the world of Freemasonry; together, they represent the nature of divine balance and duality, but also serve as a doorway or portal into the realm of the unknown, mysterious, esoteric, and spiritual. Hanging between them, behind her seat, is a curtain decorated with colorful fruits and vines, usually pomegranates cut in half with their seeds spilling out; these are a symbol of fertility but also a reference to the fruit of the Tree of the Knowledge of Good and Evil, as referenced in the Bible (modern and Western translations named this fruit as an apple, but originally, it was a pomegranate). Behind this curtain lies the promise of truth, knowledge, and growth, but there is also a hint of warning, just as there was in the Garden of Eden: once you consume this fruit, there is no turning back and no way to unlearn what you have discovered.

The High Priestess herself wears a solemn, calm expression, confident in her knowledge but with no need to entice, attract, or appease others. She wears a blue robe, similar to that of the Virgin Mary, and a large cross upon her chest, but she also wears a horned diadem for a crown with a globe in its center, which references several spiritual concepts that are usually rejected by the Christian church (this crown is similar to that of the ancient Egyptian Goddess Hathor, and is also reminiscent of the Triple Goddess symbol that is popularly used in Wiccan and Pagan religious traditions). She holds the key to all spiritual enlightenment and embraces varied faiths, knowing they are all different facades for the same universal truth.

With her hands folded upon her lap, she holds a scroll labeled with the word "TORA," which means "divine law," but the word is facing her, not her audience; whatever secrets she holds, she isn't especially eager to advertise or share them, so if you want to know, you'll have to ask her. At the base of her seat, a crescent moon rests, as though pinned down by her foot, showing that she has learned to master change, intuition, illusion, and the unknown. In the far distance behind the pillars and curtain, we can see a body of water, most likely the ocean; this references the Water element and all its associations with emotion, intuition, change, creativity, and femininity.

History

In older Tarot decks, such as the *Tarot de Marseilles*, she may be called the Popess (sometimes spelled as "Papess") or Holy Mother, and illustrated with purely Christian imagery: crowned with a papal tiara (called a "triregnum") in place of the horned diadem, holding a copy of the Bible in place of a scroll, with no moon at her feet and no ocean, pillars, or curtain behind her, seated in a modest indoor setting. Several older decks use portraits of real-life figures for this card, such as the nun Sister Manfreda (found in the Visconti-Sforza deck) or Pope Joan. In some modern decks, published after the Rider-Waite Tarot, she may be depicted and named as the Virgin Mary, the Egyptian Goddess Isis, the Roman Goddess Juno, or the Bride of Christ. Within the Rider-Waite deck and others inspired by it, though, the High Priestess is a representation of Shekhinah, the female body or dwelling of the divine spirit.

Alternative Names

La Papessa; the Popess or Papess; the Holy Mother Church; the Inner Voice

Interpretation

Upright – The keywords of this upright card are intuition, introspection, hidden truths, mysticism, and spirituality. She exudes feminine energy and is passive and receptive. This card may be a clue that the querent can find philosophical or spiritual enlightenment without having to chase after answers; the truth will find you if you remain open and patient. Furthermore, it implies that there is no need to be braggadocious or showy about this knowledge once it is acquired. Those who are truly interested, those who value your thoughts, and those who respect your worth will be naturally drawn to you. Don't waste your power or energy trying to prove yourself or your beliefs to others. The less time you spend speaking, projecting, or performing, the more empowered you'll be to receive divine messages, observe the patterns of truth in nature and the cosmos, and listen to the intuitive voice within yourself.

Reversed – This reversed card usually implies that the querent has begun to value the voices, opinions, and values of others over their own, and to their detriment. Have you ever decided to put your trust in someone, or an institution, despite the fact that a nagging inner voice tried to warn you against it? This card urges you to turn away from external influences and material values and listen to your gut. Otherwise, you may end up regretting it.

Contextual – This card is chock-full of feminine energy, so observe the balance of masculine and feminine cards in your spread. Note the balance of suns and moons in illustrations. If this card is surrounded by upright Cups, it is a clear recommendation for the querent to have faith in their emotional impulses or spiritual beliefs, withdrawing from the material world in search of higher truths.

Associated Suit: Cups

Correlated Element: Water

Celestial Correspondence: The Moon

Timing: Nighttime, or alternatively, the eve of New Moon or Full Moon

III – The Empress

Imagery

The Empress is seated on a plush divan; her posture is regal and authoritative, but she is propped up by a series of pillows. Contrasting the stance of the High Priestess, who faces us directly, the Empress sits at an angle in a slight recline, her knees parted, perhaps hinting at a sexual invitation or the position of childbirth. Her colorful gown is an echo of the printed curtain hanging behind the High Priestess, covered in pomegranates, which represent fertility, forbidden knowledge, maturity, and sexuality. Further testaments to her regality can be found in her crown, boasting twelve stars, one for each sign of the Zodiac, and the golden scepter in her raised right hand, topped with an orb. By her feet, a heart-shaped shield is propped up, decorated with the sign of Venus, reminding us that her powers of love, emotionality, and femininity can be weaponized, if necessary, to protect what she has created.

She is surrounded by nature in bloom. Before her lies a field of wheat, which simultaneously signifies abundance and her reciprocal relationship with the earth itself; if you reap what you sow, it's clear that the Empress has spent a great deal of her energy on planting and nurturing these seeds. Behind her, a lush forest grows, with trees representing male sexual potency. A river flows through the forest and over a cliffside into a waterfall; the flowing water conveys the emotional, creative, and feminine aspects of the Water element, and it flows through the forest into the waterfall and pool as a metaphor for sexual reproduction and cooperative manifestation. The pool itself lies decidedly in her domain, though; while she draws from the male energy in the forest behind her, she is empowered to take care of the resulting product independently.

History

In many decks published before Rider-Waite, the Empress is drawn as a queen, facing straight ahead, wearing a classic gold crown without reference to the Zodiac signs, and holding her shield, which is not heart-shaped, adorned with a painted eagle in place of the Venus sign. In decks where the High Priestess is drawn as a leader in the Christian church, the Empress will often follow in robes of red and blue, signifying her relation to the Virgin Mary. In modern decks, however, she is viewed as an embodiment of mother earth rather than the mother of a single Holy figure.

Alternative Names

The Green Woman; Mother Earth; The Mother; The Grandmother; Aphrodite; Venus Ayizan; Creativity

Interpretation

Upright – While the High Priestess represents the spiritual aspects of the divine feminine, the Empress embodies earthly female energy. She is a sign of material and sensual pleasures, fertility, creation, growth, and abundance in the natural world. At the same time, though, her crown of stars reminds us that her earthly values are overseen by cosmic forces and divine sensibilities, so there is nothing shallow about her value structure. Empowered by the divine, her sensual desires are combined with emotional depth and balance, transforming mere lust into all-powerful love. Since she is adorned with a crown and holding a scepter, we can see she is in a position of power and authority. Furthermore, as she is wearing a pomegranate print on her gown and surrounded by wheat (a symbol of harvest), water (referencing femininity, emotion, and creativity), and trees (symbols of male virility and growth), we can surmise that the Empress is a queen of fertility, maternal instinct, and familial love. There is more wheat than she could consume on her own, which speaks to her desire to feed and nurture her loved ones and her creations, but she sits alone, which illustrates her righteous sense of entitlement to savor the fruits of her own labor. While there is no question that she represents earthly pleasures and motherhood, the Empress may not always point to literal pregnancy or parenthood. She might, instead, signal a form of artistic pregnancy or creative birth. Her plush throne serves to signify the importance of sensual comfort, but she isn't all softness: her heart-shaped shield represents the part of motherly love that is fiercely protective.

Reversed – A reversed Empress card most often speaks to a creative block or lack of productivity. It could signify literal infertility, but it can also point to domestic or social difficulties, stifled maternal instinct, creative exhaustion, or an inability to balance one's personal needs with those of the people they care for. Alternatively, it could serve to warn the querent against a situation in which the positive traits of the Empress will not be useful or appreciated; in a family, workplace, or community where femininity is undervalued and selfishness reigns, the energy of the Empress is wasted and taken for granted. A waterfall cannot flow in reverse, and even the strongest among us can be drained dry by pouring water into a bottomless well.

Contextual – Some cartomancers will always view the Empress as a sign of literal pregnancy or, when reversed, inability to conceive; however, it's important to look to the surrounding cards to see if she might signify another form of creation. If found upright in a spread full of wands and pentacles, for instance, she may very well hint at a growing womb, but she could also easily suggest a creative passion soon to be transformed into a successful business venture. If she is surrounded by a number of Sword cards, she more likely references some form of intellectual growth or spiritual manifestation; surrounded by cups, she could point either toward fertility, stability in a loving relationship, or emotional balance on a personal level.

As counterintuitive as it may seem, the Empress bears a strong connection to the Death card. Whenever you encounter both cards within a spread, they will almost always point to a cycle of life, death, and rebirth, literally or figuratively.

Associated Suit: Pentacles
Correlated Element: Earth

Celestial Correspondence: Venus

Timing: When factors or celestial bodies align in rare formations (eclipses, syzygy, etc.)

IV – The Emperor

Imagery

The Emperor sits squarely on a throne decorated with four ram's heads, which represent the earth-bound aspects of a male divinity, including virility, physical force, action, determination, power, and leadership. The ram is also connected to the Aries sign of the Zodiac; those born under this sign are believed to be intensely passionate, driven, fearless, energetic, protective, stubborn, impetuous, pushy, and sometimes forceful or domineering. Most of the symbolism in this card serves to underline the traits of the ram. The Emperor wears armor beneath his cloak (which also bears a ram's head symbol on his shoulder), a testament to his forceful and protective demeanor, and a jeweled crown on his head, evidence of his power and authority as a leader. He holds a scepter in the shape of the ankh, a symbol of life and death, and a golden globe in his other palm; together, these props illustrate the high degree of responsibility that comes with his authority. His long white beard is meant to illustrate his wisdom, gained through experience. Behind his throne, a tall and rocky mountain range looms in the distance, symbolizing his fortitude, stability, and determination.

History

Illustrations of this card have changed very little throughout Tarot's history. Due to some controversy in which the Christian church mandated the removal of the High Priestess from the deck, he has sometimes been assigned the number III rather than IV in older decks. He is viewed as a secular ruler, and therefore not quite as powerful or authoritative as a religious leader.

Alternative Names

The Green Man; The Rebel; Zeus; the Grandfather

Interpretation

Upright – While the Empress embraces the laws of the natural world, the Emperor rules wherever the laws of man and society are concerned. He is at the top of the secular pyramid of rulership, and therefore, can represent the male ego in the material rather than the spiritual realm. When found upright in a spread, this card signifies structure, order, organization, predictability, and stability. The Emperor can also be viewed as the ultimate father figure, representing the need for firm discipline. Though the querent may yearn for the security and support he can offer, it's important to remember that these benefits may come at a cost; the Emperor desires control and security, so his rules may prove to be quite limiting in the long-run.

Reversed – Upside down, this card often points to either a loss of power and control or an unhealthy obsession with the accumulation of power. It may reference a person who has only been able to establish authority through fear rather than respect or someone whose hunger for power has become destructive to him or herself and others. Additionally, it may point to a false sense of security or stability; perhaps, a character in the querent's life has been led to put their trust in an authority figure or set of rules that, in reality, cannot provide them with the safety or support that was promised. Finally, if the reversed Emperor card does not represent a person in a spread, he may instead represent an institution or set of laws that lack a stable foundation and may soon crumble.

Contextual – To interpret this card correctly in a spread, it's important to discern whether the Emperor represents the querent themselves, an authority figure in their life, or a larger institution. Keep in mind that he is a secular character; if he appears in a spread among more spiritual cards (the High Priestess, the Hierophant, the Hanged Man), this may point to a struggle between knowledge and faith, the laws of man, and the word of God. If he appears in the same spread as another Major Arcana card that depicts a man ruled by determination and drive (the Magician, the Chariot), this can point to a need to maintain faith in the current world order, stay the course, and trust in authority figures to guide you to success. Alternatively, if he appears reversed within a spread with the Wheel of Fortune, Death, or the Tower, the querent should be advised to prepare for a major change: either an internal or societal revolution is coming. Even the greatest rulers can be overthrown.

Associated Suit: Wands

Correlated Element: Fire

Celestial Correspondence: Aries Zodiac sign

Timing: March 21st through April 19th

V – The Hierophant

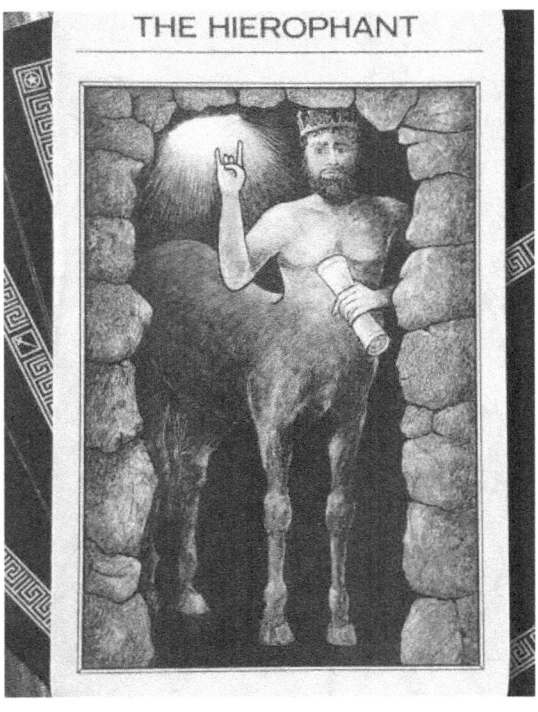

Imagery

The Hierophant sits on a throne inside a church or temple, decked out in regal robes adorned with three crosses. He wears a jeweled triple crown and holds a scepter in his left hand with a triple cross symbol at the top; both of these accessories, as well as the three crosses on his gown, signify his connection to the Holy Trinity. His right hand is raised with two fingers pointing skyward, making a sign of benediction and symbolizing his role as a conduit between the spiritual and earthly realms, similar to the Magician. At his feet lie two crossed keys, representing the keys to spiritual enlightenment. There are two worshippers kneeling before him, as well, hoping to gain access to these keys with his blessing. Behind his throne stand two ornate pillars: one represents law and order, while the other represents liberty and freedom.

History

Historically, the Hierophant card was unquestionably a representation of the Pope, who, for many centuries, was believed to be a literal embodiment of God's will on earth. In the earliest years of standardized Tarot printing, it's important to remember that the Pope's power was not only spiritual but also political; he would even have had influence over military action in some places. His authority and power would then have been seen as obviously superior to that of the Emperor, as the real-life Pope's authority would have overshadowed the rule of kings and queens. He has typically been seen as the male counterpart to the High Priestess, but due to his higher-numbered rank, gender, and depiction of worshippers in the card, it is implied that this character has a greater need for respect, obedience, and prestige. Even in modern decks with heavy feminist slants, the Hierophant is almost always drawn as a male.

Alternative Names

The Pope; The High Priest; The Teacher of Wisdom; Jupiter

Interpretation

Upright – The Hierophant is a leader and ruler, like the Emperor, but also a teacher. When found upright in a spread, this card may serve to recommend that the querent look to their elders or authority figures for guidance and maintain faith in the traditional, standard way of doing things. He urges the querent toward conformity, orthodoxy, and obedience. The rules may not make sense or seem justified to you, but the Hierophant advises you to respect them nonetheless. Have faith; the divine powers work in mysterious ways, and it isn't your place to question them.

Reversed – When you encounter the reversed Hierophant in a spread, it's time to question authority, abandon blind faith, and trust in yourself. Upside down, he usually points to an abuse of power, meaning that the querent will be far better off if they choose to strike out on their own, abandon the traditional route, and forge their own unique path. This card urges the querent to re-examine their values and beliefs, take some risks, rebel, try something new, and aim to walk against the grain. Originality will serve them better than conformity.

Contextual – This card is similar to the Emperor in its contextual role, as it can represent an authority figure or an organized institution. When found beside a card that warns of change (The Tower, Death, The Wheel of Fortune), especially upside down, it usually points to revolution or the overthrow of a powerful leader. It may also speak to a loss of faith for an individual.

Associated Suit: Pentacles

Correlated Element: Earth

Celestial Correspondence: Taurus Zodiac sign

Timing: April 20th through May 20th

VI – The Lovers

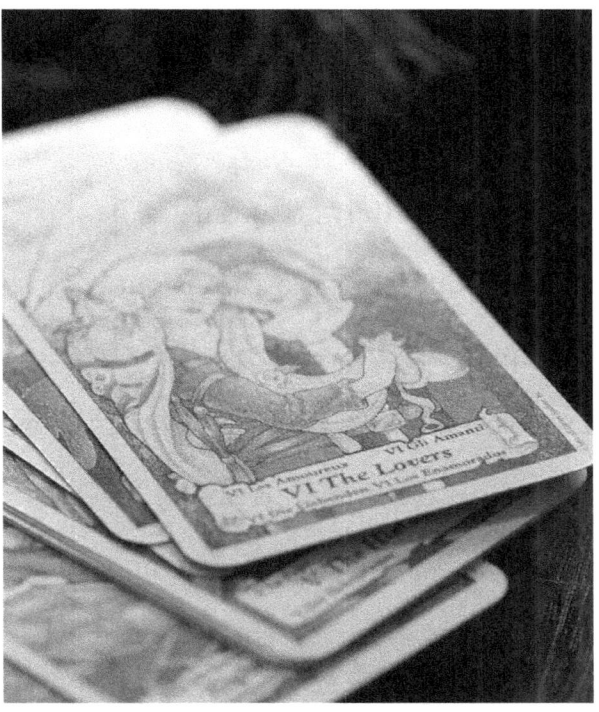

Imagery

Two nude figures, presumably Adam and Eve, stand in the Garden of Eden, their arms open, as if ready to embrace whatever changes may come their way. Their nudity signifies the power of vulnerability and honesty in matters of love. Eve stands before an apple tree, meant to represent the Tree of the Knowledge of Good and Evil, with a serpent coiled around its trunk, enticing her to take a bite of its forbidden fruit. Adam, meanwhile, stands before the Tree of Life, a symbol of immortality, bearing twelve individual flames, one for each sign of the Zodiac. Behind them, a steep mountain looms in the distance, representing the challenges that lie beyond the boundaries of the Garden. However, the archangel Raphael hovers above them, arms and wings spread wide, offering his blessings and the promise of healing. Furthermore, the sun shines radiantly over the scene. Once the lovers are joined together, their journey may be difficult at times, but ultimately, the divines will watch over them, and their love will see them through.

History

Standardized Tarot decks originated in pre-Renaissance era Italy and France. The culture in this time and region was predominantly Catholic, and divorce was not considered an acceptable option. Marriage vows were meant to be eternal. Therefore, these older decks often depicted a much more mundane scene of two young lovers being joined in marriage by a priest. Such an illustration was enough, in those times, to convey the idea of an irreversible decision, but with the popularization of divorce in modern times, the illustration has evolved to reflect our changing values. Alternatively, some older decks would depict one young man being torn between two prospective female lovers or between a young maiden and his mother, while cupid flies overhead, arrow drawn, ready to shoot.

Alternative Names

The Forest Lovers; The Crossroads; Choice; Temptation; Forbidden Fruit; The Twins; Gemini

Interpretation

Upright – This card represents love, of course, but unless the contextual cards mitigate its meaning, it most often references the type of love that Romeo and Juliet had; while it may not necessarily be a star-crossed love that dooms both parties to misery and death, it will be the passionate and powerful kind of love that pushes people to extremes and forces them to make a choice between two people, things, institutions, or passions that they hold dear. It is no mistake that the illustration depicts Adam and Eve in the moments before making the choice that banishes them from the Garden of Eden. Usually, this card speaks to a love that will require a sacrifice of some kind, and once the decision is made, there can be no turning back. The consequences will be serious and lasting, but that doesn't necessarily mean that the sacrifice won't be worth it in the end. The card is more likely to represent a crossroads or temptation than the concept of love in general; however, when upright, it usually urges the querent to make the choice that resonates most with their emotional body. It implies a loss of innocence or stability, but also growth and new beginnings. Follow your heart over your head or your gut. Things may be challenging at first, but love will prevail.

Reversed – Understandably, many assume that a reversal of this card points to the dissolution of a romantic relationship, but its interpretation may not always be so cut and dry. It may instead warn that a relationship in the querent's life, whether romantic or otherwise, will become dysfunctional due to one or both party's dishonesty or inability to follow through on their commitments. Alternatively, it might indicate that the querent is dragging his or her feet, unwilling to dive in headfirst and make the choices or changes that their heart desires.

Contextual – It's easy to associate this card with romance, but depending on the sitter's question and the context of surrounding cards, it could easily apply to a career choice, the decision to follow a passion, familial or friendly love, or even a business partnership. If the surrounding cards seem to be at odds with each other or speaking to oppositional concepts, the Lovers' message is clear: it's time to make a choice, once and for all.

Associated Suit: Swords

Correlated Element: Air

Celestial Correspondence: Gemini Zodiac sign

Timing: May 21st through June 20th

VII – The Chariot

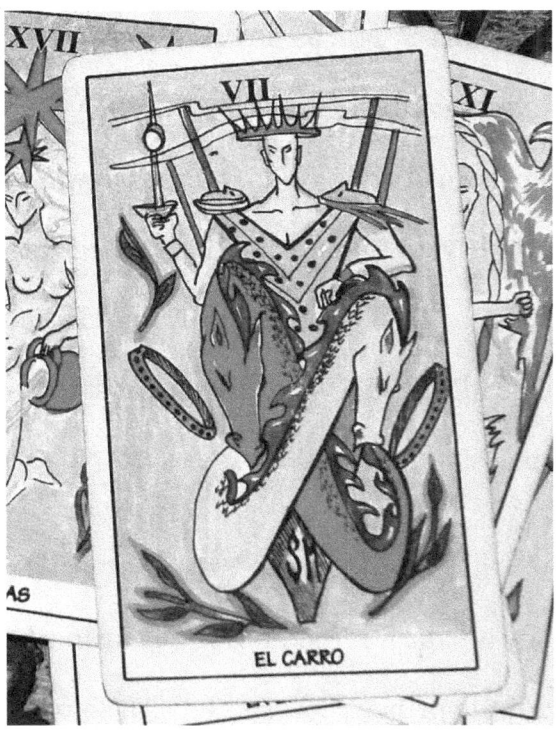

Imagery

A prince stands in his chariot, wearing armor decorated with celestial themes: crescent moons on his shoulder plates and an eight-pointed star upon his crown. There is a square at the center of his breastplate, a symbol of stability, security, fortitude, and grounding in the earthly realm. There is also a crest on the front of his vehicle, featuring a symbol which could be a lingam (a Hindu symbol for the deity Shiva) or perhaps a mallet (a masonic symbol of self-discipline and willpower). It is clear, from his confident stance and determined facial expression, that he is going places and will stop at nothing until he achieves his goals.

His vehicle is pulled by two sphinxes, one white and one black; these mythical creatures represent strength and wisdom, and their contrasting colors signify duality (much like the moons on his shoulders), balance, and the potential for conflict or opposition. It's clear that he has these opposing forces under his control, though, as he drives the vehicle without reins and manages to keep these potential adversaries calm, both headed in the same direction, unified by their purpose. Instead of reins, he uses a wand, held in his right hand, to enforce his will. His chariot drives through a desert landscape, with a vast and towering metropolis, left far behind in the background. He is shielded from the sun's heat by a tented fabric atop the vehicle, decorated with clusters of stars, to convey that his journey is overseen by divine or celestial forces.

History
In older decks, the Chariot was often pulled ahead by a pair of reined horses. It formerly held a connotation to wars, battles, or crusades, with the prince represented as a soldier or knight, whereas modern depictions imply a more personal journey or goal.

Alternative Names
Winged Victory; The Centurion; Transport; The Archer; Mastery

Interpretation
Upright – This card is a representation of determination, focus, momentum, and endurance. The prince drawn in the card is decked out in symbols that serve to convey his resolve and tenacity. For example, crescent moons would normally represent the nature of change, flux, illusion, and deception—all concepts that normally could distract or steer someone off-course. But the moons are pointed away from him as if to illustrate his ability to skirt or shrug off such potential challenges. When this card appears upright in a spread, it usually means the querent has found their rightful path and now needs to

commit to staying the course, not allowing any obstacles to discourage them or alter their trajectory. When you realize your destiny, you can't let anything stand in your way. It's time to charge forward, full speed ahead.

Reversed – A reversal of the Chariot card can indicate a loss of momentum or be a sign that the querent's current path isn't going to take them to their desired destination. It's time to go back to the drawing board, plot a different course, or choose a new goal. Ambition isn't enough on its own to conquer all obstacles. Triumph may lie ahead for the querent, but only if they are willing to try a different route or use a different vehicle.

Contextual – Surrounding suit cards will illuminate the specifics of this card's meaning in a spread. If there are many Pentacles in the spread, the Chariot will often speak to a business venture. Surrounded by Cups, the Chariot references emotional evolution or a journey made for the sake of love. Found among a number of Sword cards, it may represent an intellectual or academic pursuit. Laid beside Wand cards, it usually indicates a long-term or especially ambitious form of creative manifestation.

Associated Suit: Cups

Correlated Element: Water

Celestial Correspondence: Cancer Zodiac sign

Timing: June 21st through July 22nd

VIII – Strength

Imagery

Against the backdrop of a yellow sky, a woman stands in a green field beside a lion. She wears no armor and bears no weapon. Instead, she is dressed in a flowing white gown, symbolizing purity of intent, with a belt and garland of roses, both symbols of triumph and righteous victory. The only weapons at her disposal are her hands and her spiritual energy. She clasps the lion's jaws in her hands, but not with ferocity; her stance and facial expression both appear gentle and calm, as she clearly has the situation fully under control. The lion gazes up at her with admiration and licks her palm. The lion is a multi-faceted symbol of external challenges or predatory characters, and the inner animal instinct that must be understood and managed, and the sense of pride or ego that must be tamed within us all. She manages all of these issues, not through force, but through sensitivity. Like the Magician, she is graced with a lemniscate symbol above her head, referencing the limitless power at her fingertips.

History

Some older decks illustrate a more literal form of physical strength with this card, with a female figure breaking a stone column into two pieces. Others might portray Lady Justice, or Iustitia, blindfolded as she measures out righteous justice with her signature scales.

Alternative Names

Fortitude; Lust; Courage; The Stag

Interpretation

Upright – This card speaks to emotional or intellectual strength rather than physical power. It often indicates that a difficult situation or person in the querent's life can be best handled through sensitivity, with a gentle and empathetic approach. Avoid falling into competition with raging egomaniacs or aggressive antagonists—you'll never beat them at their own game, but if you take a step back to consider your next move, you can certainly outsmart them or perhaps kill them with kindness. This upright card can also reference the immense inner strength and resilience that is needed to face one's internal demons and pursue personal growth.

Reversed – Again, this reversed card does not speak to physical weakness but rather a lack of emotional fortitude. Someone in the querent's life, perhaps the querent themselves, is leaning on cowardice, emotional dishonesty, manipulation, or negativity to protect themselves from external or internal foes. An upturned Justice card can also warn against a literal perversion of justice: an unfair court ruling skirted punishments or rewards offered to those who do not deserve them.

Contextual – Look at the characters in your spread, particularly those who are seated on thrones, wearing crowns, or holding tools of aggression (wands or swords). Who appears the most powerful? The most in control of their surroundings? And who appears to be the most at peace with their degree of power? External power can be taken away as quickly as it is given, but no one can rob you of your inner strength.

Associated Suit: Wands

Correlated Element: Fire

Celestial Correspondence: Leo Zodiac Sign

Timing: July 23rd through August 22nd

IX – The Hermit

Imagery

An elderly man with a long beard and hooded cloak walks alone on a snowy, dark night. His white beard conveys his wisdom, gained through experience, and his cloak is a representation of his desire to shield himself from external influence, protecting and conserving his own energy. He holds a walking staff, which might be interpreted as the "patriarchal staff," symbolizing the authority of a guide or teacher, or it might instead call to mind the properties of the Suit of Wands, which are called "Staves" in some alternative decks. His head is tilted downward, but if you examine his facial features, he appears to be at peace; he accepts his solitude and does not bemoan it but simply focuses on finding the right path. He holds up a lantern to find his way through the darkness; instead of a flame, it contains a six-pointed star, representing divine guidance.

History

This is the era of social media, wherein we determine our self-worth through the opinions of others and our popularity. In the era when Tarot was first popularized, though, this was not the case. Men or women who decided to turn their backs on the material world in favor of quiet lives devoted to service to God were admired and revered. Think of the monks who withdrew from society to live in remote locations, taking vows of silence, spending all of their energy on meditative practices, such as copying religious texts by hand. We are not meant to feel pity for this character; he is someone to look up to.

Alternative Names

The Sage; The Shaman; The Monk; Time, or Father Time; the Wise One; Solitude

Interpretation

Upright – The title of this card may bear negative connotations in modern society, but when the Hermit appears upright in a spread, he usually indicates a positive form of reclusiveness or solitude. Whether it is voluntary or not, this solitude may be necessary in order for the querent to heal, rest, recuperate, or brainstorm next steps. It also may be a good time to devote to personal growth, intellectual pursuits, spiritual enlightenment, or creative progress. Perhaps the querent needs to spend some time alone to get some distance from negative influences in their social circle, workplace, family, or community, or to shield themselves from temptations. Often, the Hermit suggests an abandonment of material values. The querent may be outgrowing their hunger for approval from others, finally learning to look within for the answers to life's greatest questions. At the same time, the Hermit could represent a guide or teacher in the querent's life who is strong enough to walk alone, even if he or she does not have to—think Gandalf from the Lord of the Rings.

Reversed – This card often signifies a return, a comeback, or a re-emergence. However, it does not usually indicate a triumphant return; rather, it may point to a return to the same old cycles that the querent meant to escape by becoming reclusive in the first place. The querent has come out of hiding but somehow failed to learn from past mistakes, falling back into negative patterns or unhealthy habits. Alternatively, the reversed Hermit could signify reclusiveness that is motivated by fear rather than a quest for self-improvement. Are you taking a necessary break from social interaction to care for yourself, or simply hiding from your problems? It's important to recognize the difference.

Contextual – The surroundings cards will offer insight as to what it is that the Hermit needs to accomplish in his (or her) solitude. Wands point to creative pursuits; Cups, to emotional healing; Swords, to an intellectual or spiritual quest; and Pentacles, to physical healing or rebuilding financial security. Take special note if he appears in the same spread as an upright High Priestess, Strength, Temperance, Chariot, or Hanged Man card, as these combinations will usually indicate that the Hermit's solitary journey must be followed through to fruition; don't allow the desire for company, or approval from others, distract you from your personal goals. In the end, the results will prove worthwhile, and you'll be proud to have accomplished them on your own.

Associated Suit: Pentacles

Correlated Element: Earth

Celestial Correspondence: Virgo Zodiac sign

Timing: August 22nd through September 23rd

X – The Wheel of Fortune

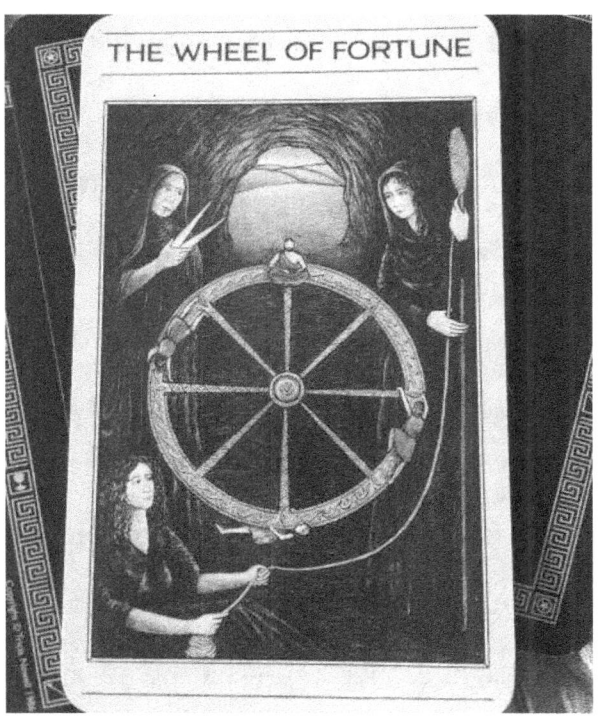

Imagery

There is a great deal of symbolic imagery to unpack in this card's illustration. At its center, we see a large wheel with eight spokes, four of which are crossed with the alchemical symbols for the Earth, Air, Fire, and Water elements. Along the outer edge of the wheel, four letters of the English language and four Hebrew letters, interwoven with one another. The Hebrew letters spell out YHWH, short for Yahweh, the Hebrew name for God. The English letters may spell out T-A-R-O (a shortened version of the word "Tarot") if read clockwise, T-O-R-A (meaning "divine law") if read counterclockwise, and R-O-T-A (the Latin word for "wheel") if the card is reversed and read from the bottom up. The Wheel itself is a symbol of constant flux, karmic cycles, fate, and chance.

There is a sphinx seated proudly at the top of the wheel, wielding a sword and serving as the guardian of divine knowledge. Slithering downward on the left side of the wheel is a snake, a symbol of temptation and transformation. Rising up from the underside of the wheel is a creature with a human body and the head of a jackal; this is Anubis, guardian of the underworld and protector of dead souls. His upward momentum represents the renewed cycle of life after death.

The Wheel floats against a backdrop of clouds to show us that its never-ending cycle is the will of the divine. In the four corners of the card, four-winged figures lounge, each reading through a book. We see an angel in the top left corner, correlated to the Water element and Scorpio Zodiac sign; a griffin in the top right corner, representing Air and the Aquarius sign; a winged lion in the bottom right, connected to the Fire element and Leo sign; and finally, a horned bull with wings, associated with the Earth element and Taurus sign. These are the four fixed signs of the Zodiac (as compared to cardinal or mutable signs), which usually represent stability, grounding, practicality, and tangibility. They also fall in the middle of each of the four seasons, so as a group, they represent the annual cycle of birth, growth, death, and rebirth.

History

This card has a lot of illustrative detail, and thus, a lot of variation from one deck to the next. However, its basic conceptual meaning has remained fairly constant since the fifteenth century. Most illustrations include a wheel and several figures rising or falling with its turning, usually with one seated comfortably at its apex. In older decks, these figures were almost always human, with no hermetic, alchemical, or astrological imagery. Sometimes, the person seated at the top of the wheel, or floating at its center, would be drawn as the blindfolded Lady Justice. Some other historical decks would draw this figure as a religious leader—a pope or saint, perhaps.

Alternative Names
Fate; Chance; Fortuna; Dame Fortune; Change

Interpretation
Upright – When this card appears upright in a spread, it typically indicates that the querent, or some circumstance in their life, is about to undergo a change in station. If the querent is poor, they may soon land a promotion or be blessed with a windfall; if they are wealthy, there may be a major loss of income in the near future. This change does not have to be financial, though; perhaps a single and solitary person will find themselves falling head over heels in love, or someone in a seemingly stable marriage will find it dissolving. The outcast may become popular, while the A-listers are deemed undesirable. The champion may suffer a loss, while the underdog becomes the victor. It's important to keep in mind, though, that the timing of this card is constant: the Wheel never stops turning, so no change in station should be seen as a permanent state of affairs. What goes up must come down, but whatever falls, like a phoenix, will eventually rise again from the ashes.

Reversed – A reversal of this card can represent stagnancy or the illusion of change. Perhaps a new leader has come into power, promising revolutionary change, but in reality, they are an agent of the same regime that was supposedly ousted. The poor may gain a great deal of money but find that it does not provide happiness or fix many of their problems; likewise, the rich may become poor and be surprised to find that this change in station does not change who they are. Alternatively, this reversed card can indicate that the querent is struggling, or flat out refusing, to adjust to fluctuating circumstances or accept a new reality. They should be advised that success and survival come to those who are willing to roll with the punches and adapt. Change is the only constant in the universe; you cannot stop it by planting your feet in the mud or burying your head in the sand.

Contextual – Pay special attention to dichotomies and oppositional forces in any spread that includes this card, particularly if the spread is one that speaks to past, present, and future developments. In a spread dominated by pentacles, expect a change in financial status or a big move; in a spread of Swords, look forward to a major philosophical or faith-based adjustment; if the spread is full of Wands, you can anticipate a change in power status or critical acclaim of creative workings; if the Wheel is surrounded by Cups, prepare for a major change of heart.

Associated Suit: Wands

Correlated Element: Fire

Celestial Correspondence: Jupiter

Timing: Constant and eternal

XI – Justice

Imagery

Lady Justice sits upon her throne, staring you down with an unflinching gaze. She wears a crown with a single square jewel, as well as a cloak with a square button; the squares represent order, structure, stability, and material reality. In her right hand, she holds up a Sword, pointing toward the sky; in her left hand, she holds golden scales, which hang down at her side. These props are the Sword of Truth and the Scales of Justice. One of her feet is hidden beneath the folds of her gown, but the other protrudes slightly; this reminds us that, while some workings of justice remain unseen and mysterious, the important parts will be revealed to us, sooner or later.

As in most Major Arcana cards that feature pillars, the two stone columns behind her represent duality, choice, and balance. They, along with her throne, are made of grey stone with minimal decoration; this is meant to signify rationality and impartiality.

Between the pillars, a purple curtain is hung; its color signifies wisdom, peace, and divine insight.

History

In most older decks, the numerical assignments of the Justice and Strength card are swapped, with Justice following the Chariot as number VIII and Strength following the Wheel of Fortune as number XI. The modern numerical assignments are inspired by the Rider-Waite deck, in which the numbers were switched to better suit the elemental and astrological correspondences of the cards, as well as fit into the story arc of the Fool's Journey (described in greater detail at the end of this chapter).

The concept of Lady Justice, or Iustitia, was popularized in Europe in the 1600s, hundreds of years after the first Tarot decks went into circulation. Some decks from this era will portray her wearing a blindfold, often standing rather than seated.

Alternative Names

Adjustment; Karma; Breakthrough; Law

Interpretation

Upright – This is one of the few Major Arcana cards with a title that conveys its meaning in a straight-forward manner; it's difficult to misinterpret. Absolute and righteous Justice is coming, and it will prevail. Stifled truths will come to the surface; oaths will be honored; debts will be paid; corruption will be exposed; virtues will be upheld; honesty and integrity will be rewarded. This card can often speak to legal matters, but Justice can also be found through karmic retribution. Whatever the outcome, it will represent total fairness and restore equilibrium to the universe.

If the querent is unsure of what matter this card may speak to, it's important to note that it may point to a future choice or decision, wherein options should be considered carefully. In this case, the querent should be advised to set aside personal desires or gut instincts and take some time to meditate on what choice best represents fairness, balance, honesty, integrity, and sustainability in the long-term. It may be tempting to fight fire with fire, but how will you feel months or years from now when you realize that you've allowed an injustice to change who you are on a fundamental level, overwhelming or distorting your values and virtues? This upright card can also be a not-so-gentle reminder to the querent that the consequences of their past actions will come back to them, sooner or later, whether these actions deserve reward or punishment.

Reversed – Again, this reversal is fairly easy to interpret. It warns of an inversion of Justice: an unfair court ruling, dishonest behavior, corruption, or lack of accountability. Alternatively, it may serve as a warning to a querent who intends to exact their own justice through vengeance. Justice is greater than any individual, and an eye for an eye leaves the whole world blind. Trust in the universe, your community, your family to support you and help to restore karmic balance in a way that puts an end to the negative cycle rather than sustaining it. Don't let injustice drag you down to its level.

Contextual – Justice is one of three virtue cards in the Major Arcana, alongside Strength and Temperance. If all three appear in a spread, it is a not-so-subtle reminder to the querent that they are responsible for their own behaviors and life circumstances and that there is no excuse for abandoning one's ethical beliefs or moral values. Stay true to yourself and honor what you believe is right; others will look up to you and feel inspired by your integrity.

Associated Suit: Swords

Correlated Element: Air

Celestial Correspondence: Libra Zodiac sign

Timing: September 23rd through October 22nd

XII – The Hanged Man

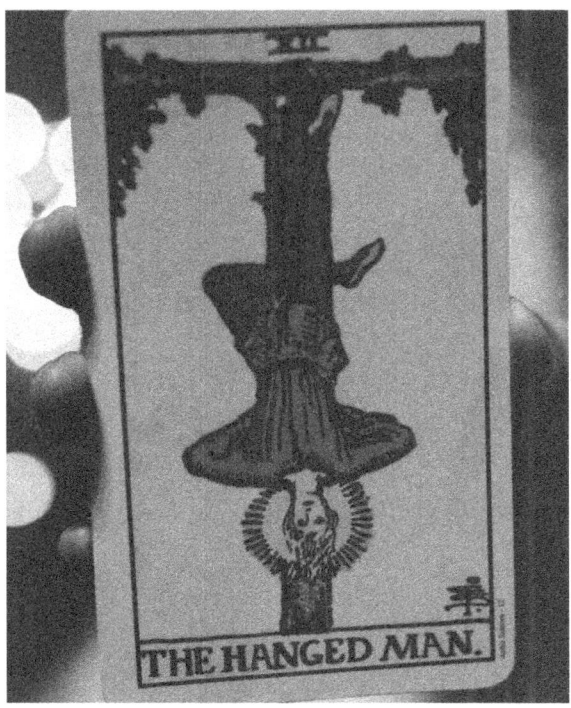

Imagery

The Hanged Man is not hung by his neck with a noose. Instead, he is strung up by one ankle, while his free ankle is bent behind the opposite knee, making the shape of the number four, referencing the four suits, earthly elements, and corners of the globe. His hands are also linked behind his back, and it is unclear whether they are bound or not. His hair hangs down to clarify that he is hanging upside down, and his head is surrounded by an aura or halo, symbolizing spiritual enlightenment. In most decks, he wears either a serene expression or a joyful smile. There is no anguish in his face or posture. However uncomfortable his position may appear, he is happy to be there and, for the time being, determined to stay put.

History

Some see the tree upon which the Hanged Man is strung up as Yggdrasil, also called the World Tree, of Norse Mythology. The legend goes that Odin hung himself upon this tree and stabbed himself in the ribs in order to offer his own blood in sacrifice to the Gods. He refused their help or healing, hoping to earn access to their divine knowledge through this sacrificial offering, and was ultimately successful. Others see the tree as a representation of the cross upon which Jesus Christ was crucified to atone for the sins of mankind. He wears red pants and a blue tunic; these colors are often used in combination to reference biblical or figures in works of art, such as the Virgin Mary.

This form of execution—hanging upside down by one ankle—was commonly used in Italy in the late Middle Ages and early Renaissance era as a form of punishment for traitors. Some older decks with orthodox Christian themes will depict this character as Judas Iscariot, hanging with bags of silver in his hands; in these decks, the Hanged Man's meaning changes to one of betrayal or martyrdom, rather than sacrifices made for the sake of self-improvement.

Alternative Names

The Traitor; Judas Iscariot; Odin; Le Pendu; Suspension; Awakening

Interpretation

Upright – This card is widely misunderstood by those who have not studied the Tarot in depth. Many believe that it references some form of punishment, suffering, or death, calling to mind an execution by hanging; however, the Hanged Man is usually a neutral or positive sign when he appears upright (meaning the card is upright, while he hangs upside down) within a spread. The figure in the illustration is hanging by his own choice. He represents a voluntary surrender, giving in to an unfamiliar or difficult experience in order to learn from it, grow, overcome fears, and free oneself from hang-ups or anxieties. Think of the way one might give in to pain and discomfort during a yoga class in order to increase flexibility, strength, and willpower. This card is all about letting go and becoming stronger, wiser, and healthier for it. He may sometimes reference a sacrifice made willingly to achieve greater gains; apologies or atonement made in order to heal the soul and release feelings of guilt; emancipation from the cage of ego, pride, resentment, or insecurity; learning to trust in the universe to take care of your needs, or submission to the will of the divine. Alternatively, this card can reference stillness or a suspension of time: a meditative experience or retreat into nature, where no progress is made, except the progression of the soul toward fulfillment or enlightenment. Simultaneously, he advises us to be patient and live in the moment, valuing mindfulness over momentum. Stillness can be transformative. The ultimate goal of his suspension is metamorphosis.

Reversed – When this card is reversed, it signifies the inability to let go. The querent, or someone important in their life, has become rigid and controlling, anxious, insecure, distrusting, manipulative, prideful, or resentful, and thus has lost their capacity to handle that which is unexpected or beyond the scope of their dominion. Alternatively, this reversed card may represent time wasted while no lesson has been learned, sacrifices made without consequential gains, or a lack of return-on-investment.

Contextual – There are many different ways in which the Hanged Man can indicate surrender. Look to the surrounding suits for clues. If you find the spread dominated by Cups, he might be advising you to open yourself up and become emotionally vulnerable in order to create a deeper, more intimate bond with loved ones; try to trust them, even if you have been hurt or betrayed in the past. If he is found in the company of Sword cards, he likely is pointing to the importance of suspending disbelief and maintaining faith in order to reach spiritual nirvana or, alternatively, the need to let go of the anger that is no longer serving you, even when a conflict has not been justly resolved. Surrounded by Wands, he urges you to give in to the whims of the creative muse and continue producing, even if critical acclaim or financial rewards have yet to come your way. With Pentacles, he guides you toward a physical healing or restorative experience—perhaps a retreat, rest period, medicinal treatment, or energy healing session—or, in the financial realm, he advises you to hold onto your funds, waiting for the perfect moment to invest or spend them.

Associated Suit: Cups

Correlated Element: Water

Celestial Correspondence: Neptune

Timing: Uncertain, undetermined, elastic, or relative

XIII – Death

Imagery

This illustration in the Rider-Waite deck portrays a busy scene, and its details provide important clues to its true meaning. A skeletal figure, presumably one of the four horsemen of the apocalypse, rides into a field where a battle or coup of some kind has just taken place. He wears black armor, and his horse's reins are decorated with skulls and crossbones—an ominous look, no doubt. But at the same time, he carries a black flag with an emblem of a white rose, and the horse he rides is pure white. Both are symbols of purification, cleansing, and transformation. One of the horse's hooves is raised, demonstrating forward momentum. This illustration of Death includes no stillness, stagnation, or finality.

It's easy to be distracted by the gloomy figure atop the horse, but turn your attention to the background of this scene. The dead figure lying in the dirt below the horse is covered with a sheet, and a fallen crown lies a few feet from his head. The king has been laid to rest, reminding us that death will eventually come for us all, no matter how rich or poor, powerful or insignificant. His death also references the true nature of this card; presumably, under new leadership, everyone's way of life will have to change, henceforth. Meanwhile, all the other figures in the scene are still living, each representing a different manner in which we might process change and death. The pope's hands are raised in prayer, begging the horseman for mercy. The young maiden turns her head away, in denial or fear. The young child looks up at the horseman without fear and offers him a white rose, welcoming the purification and progressive change that he heralds.

Behind these figures, the landscape is dotted with gravestones, but beyond this field, we see a river with a ship sailing in. Finally, in the distance, the sun is cresting the horizon between two tall towers; once we pass through this threshold, a new day is coming, full of brightness and warmth.

History

Older decks typically featured simpler and gloomier illustrations. Often, they would depict the grim reaper on his own, without the horse or surrounding figures, and no promise of sunrise in the background. He would usually hold a scythe, and if there were other figures shown on the card, they would all be corpses or ghouls. These cards were drawn in an era where superstition and fear of death ruled—the Black Plague was a major concern at the time, and most people in Europe had no idea how it had spread or what they had done to deserve its wrath, after all. Therefore, the card was often labeled only with the number thirteen and no name or title.

Alternative Names
Rebirth; The Ending; Transformation; The Card With No Name

Interpretation
Upright – Like the Hanged Man, this card is frequently misunderstood and viewed as a purely negative omen; it isn't always a bad sign, though. It points as much to renewal and rebirth as it does to endings and deaths. It rarely foretells of literal, physical death and more likely is a sign of drastic changes on the way: a break-up, a closing business, or perhaps even the death of a cancerous tumor. Maybe a societal or political revolution is on the way. The end of an era is coming, and afterward, the querent will be given a blank slate upon which to rebuild his or her reality.

Reversed – Which of the figures before the horseman do you most identify with? This reversed card is usually a sign that the querent needs to let go of the old and move forward with the new. Perhaps they are struggling to embrace changes, procrastinating, or stubbornly refusing to acknowledge the writing on the wall. This is a warning not to let yourself get dragged down with the sinking ship—take a leap and swim for shore, and the sooner you do so, the better.

Contextual – Especially for those who are unfamiliar with the complex symbolism of the Tarot deck, this card can stir up panic and dread whenever it shows up in a card reading, so it is extremely important to consider its context before jumping to any dire conclusions about its meaning. Alongside the Wheel of Fortune or Tower, it warns of major societal or structural change which will be forced upon the querent, whether they are ready for it or not. In a spread with the Sun or the Star, the querent can look forward to a far brighter outlook after their current circumstances are dismantled. Besides the Devil, it is time for the querent to give up on a type of addiction, bad habit, or unhealthy relationship once and for all, lest it destroys them before they get the chance. With Justice or Judgment, expect an unjust circumstance or corrupt system to finally be set straight. Alongside the Fool, the Death card may reference the death of innocence or transition from childhood into adulthood.

Associated Suit: Cups

Correlated Element: Water

Celestial Correspondence: Scorpio

Timing: October 23rd through November 21st

XIV – Temperance

Imagery

An androgynous angel stands at the edge of a pool, with one foot solidly planted ashore while the other is dipped into the water; this stance symbolizes both the notion of testing the waters before diving in with both feet and the connection or balance between the water and earth element (between intuition and rationality, emotion and factual knowledge, the subconscious and the evident, the spiritual and the material). The angel's wings are spread wide, and its head is framed by a radiant halo, representing divine inspiration and guidance. The angel pours water from the pool between two golden chalices, a symbol of alchemical experimentation and transformation. On the chest of the angel's white gown is an upward facing triangle (a symbol of the Fire element), encompassed by a square (a symbol of the Earth element, as well as structure, community, and stability); this symbol serves as a reminder that all of the magic in life is bound by the laws of nature, and all passionate, impulsive energy should be tempered with rationality and practicality. Above these shapes is the Tetragrammaton (Hebrew letters spelling out "Yahweh" or "God of Israel") as a reminder that these elements are ruled by the divine spirit. Beside the angel's feet are a cluster of irises in bloom, symbolizing hope, faith, courage, and wisdom.

A path leads away from the pool into the distance, implying that the angel has either completed or is about to embark upon a transformative journey. At the far end of the path is a mountain range, representing challenges and obstacles that have been, or will soon be, overcome. Above the mountains, we see a radiant yellow shape, which could easily be mistaken for the sun, but in reality, it is a divine crown, holding the promise of mastery over alchemical balance and inner peace.

History
The Temperance card was included in even the earliest Tarot decks and has remained a constant presence in the Major Arcana for hundreds of years. Almost all decks feature an illustration of a figure pouring liquid from one cup into another. In orthodox decks, wherein references to alchemical works would not have been included, this act might have been interpreted as the dilution of wine with water in order to moderate the intoxicating effects of alcohol.

Alternative Names
Art; Integration; The Guide; Alchemy

Interpretation

Upright – This card bears a strong connotation to the concept of alchemy and material creativity (cooking, building, and other art forms geared toward crafting a finished product, rather than pure creative expression). While it is popularly associated with sobriety and the process of healing from addictions of many kinds (alcohol or substance abuse, sexual addictions, smoking, and so on), it can also be relevant to queries from those who are not suffering from traditionally recognized addiction. It speaks to the need to find a healthy balance in any aspect of the querent's life, using trial and error and experimentation to achieve harmony and equilibrium. This might reference a balance between work and one's personal life, equally divided attention between different family members or friends, perhaps even a sustainable diet plan to aid in weight loss or management of health conditions. It warns against falling into extremist behaviors or thought patterns and reminds us that anything, in moderation, can be part of a healthy and happy life.

Reversed – When reversed, the Temperance card speaks to extremes. Perhaps a certain behavior or aspect of the querent's life is spiraling out of control, dominating their life, and overshadowing their other values. This could reference addictive behaviors (alcohol abuse, overeating, smoking, risky sexual practices), but it could also point to a tendency to overwork, overspending, extreme dieting or exercise, or a relationship that has become obsessive or unmanageable. Alternatively, it might reference a situation in which there is no middle ground for the querent to stand on; perhaps they are trying to maintain friendships with two sworn enemies or promising to spend equal time with family and at the office when such a balance is not actually feasible.

Contextual – The suits of surrounding cards will help the reader to decipher which aspect of the querent's life needs balancing: their emotional life (Cups), financial matters or physical health (Pentacles), overthinking, rumination, intellectual issues (Swords), or thirst for power and productivity (Wands). If found alongside one or more of the other virtue cards (Strength or Justice), it urges the querent toward introspection, self-care, and personal growth.

Associated Suit: Wands

Correlated Element: Fire

Celestial Correspondence: Sagittarius Zodiac sign

Timing: November 22nd through December 21st

XV – The Devil

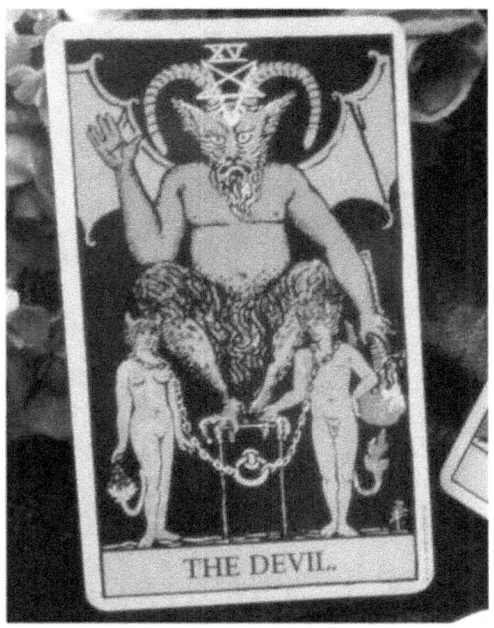

Imagery

The Devil is portrayed as a beastly figure with the horns of a ram, a beard, the body and arms of a man, furry legs, massive bat wings, and a harpy's talons in place of feet. This figure is a representation of a deity known by many different names throughout history, playing a significant role in a number of different religious faiths and mythological traditions; you may know him as Baphomet, the Horned God or Horned One, Cernunnos, Pan, Dionysus, Herne, the Horned Goat of Mendes, Faunus, Lucifer, or Satan. In Christian theology, this deity is the lord of all evil, the antithesis of all that is good, and the arch-enemy of God himself, but it's important to understand that he does not represent evil in many pagan or pre-Abrahamic belief systems. Instead, he most often represents the nature of binary dichotomies (light and dark, good and evil, night and day, life and death, masculine and feminine, etc.), choice, carnal urges, sensual experience, and earthly or material concerns, all embodied in one figure. To illustrate his connection to dichotomies, he has one hand raised up in benediction, while the other holds a torch, hanging low at his side with its flames pointing down toward the ground.

Above his head, there is an inverted pentagram, which is a symbol of the Left-Hand Path—another name for Black Magic that eschews the stigma and connotation of nefarious desires or evil intentions, embracing taboo and chaos in magical practice and believing that absolutely anything goes, so long as it does not cause harm to others. He stands atop a pedestal to which two human figures are chained, one male and one female. If we examine these figures closely, we see that they are no longer entirely human; they have both grown tails and horns of their own. The man's tail is punctuated with a flame, signifying passion, while the woman's tail has a bundle of grapes at its end, a symbol of lust and intoxication. The chains are strung loosely around their necks, and they wear calm, docile expressions, without a hint of anguish. They are not trapped in a hellish, punitive realm where the Devil delights in torturing them. If they wanted to leave, they could; the Devil welcomes their decision to stay or go, without judgment, but he does make it awfully comfortable and easy to stay at his side indefinitely.

History

In the era when Tarot first gained popularity, belief in the literal existence of the Devil was widespread. He was blamed for a great number of things: pride, destructive behaviors, uncontrolled lust, jealousy, corruption, sadness, depression, madness, starvation, illness, and all forms of suffering. People usually believed his influence was ubiquitous, so his appearance in a spread wouldn't necessarily stir up dread, or at least not more so than other aspects of daily, material life.

Alternative Names
The Horned God; Temptation; Pan; Mortal Coil; The Prince of Darkness

Interpretation
Upright — Even if you prescribe to a traditional Christian notion of the Devil as the lord of all evil, it's important to recognize that, in most Christian lore, the Devil is not considered all-powerful, as God is. He is a force to be reckoned with, but in almost every story where his evil prevails, he accomplishes his goals through temptation, not through forceful control. This means that even in his most nefarious acts, he offers his followers a choice. The imagery of this card in the Rider-Waite deck reflects that reality; the chains around the necks of the two followers at his feet are loose enough that they could easily escape if they wanted to, but they don't seem interested in leaving his side.

In the Rider-Waite deck, the Devil represents the notion of being overly invested in sensory experiences or the material world at the expense of intellectual, emotional, or spiritual growth. He also represents the nature of excess, reckless abandon, temptation, addiction, and entrapment. This upright card could reference anything from a bad habit (gambling, smoking, alcohol abuse, gossiping, habitual drug use) to a vice (gluttony, sloth, pride, manipulation) to emotionally risky behaviors (denial, avoidance, sexual addiction, abusive relationships) that the querent is having trouble giving up, despite knowing that these behaviors are no longer serving them. But the Devil does not force them into these situations, nor does he force them to continue participating in negative cycles. He serves to remind the querent that they have the power to escape, though liberation may only come at the cost of some material comforts.

It is time for the querent to seriously consider: what is it that is enticing them to continue holding onto chains that are holding them back? Why is it so hard to let go of these attachments or restraints?

Reversed – When this card appears in reverse, it signals self-liberation. The querent will find the courage, strength, and determination to disentangle themselves from their chains and break the patterns or cycles that are discouraging personal growth. Temptation and dependence are replaced by resolve and transcendence.

Contextual – Keep an eye out for other cards in the spread that signify dualities or dichotomies, as they may illuminate the disparate choices that the Devil is offering the querent. If he is surrounded by Pentacle cards, this is a strong indication that the querent has allowed themselves to be enslaved by material values—wealth, sexual pleasure, consumption of food or alcohol—and will need to look beyond the physical body or earthly realm in order to find true fulfillment.

Associated Suit: Pentacles

Correlated Element: Earth

Celestial Correspondence: Capricorn

Timing: December 22nd through January 19th

XVI – The Tower

Imagery

A tall, grey stone tower stands against a black backdrop, but it may not stay standing for long. Its foundation is precariously built upon a narrow, rocky facade, and an enormous lightning bolt is striking the building, having already knocked off its roof; this lightning bolt is an illustration of a wake-up call, rude awakening, epiphany, or divine intervention. The roof, shown mid-fall, has been built in the shape of a crown; this may reference a literal overthrow of a person or institution in a position of power or the opening of the crown chakra, which allows individuals to free themselves from the cage of ego. The windows of the tower are spitting flames, which fall through the surrounding scene like raindrops; this fire is a symbol of purification and cleansing, destruction for the sake of new creation. There are twenty-two balls of fire in total, one for each of the twelve Zodiac signs and the ten sephiroth of the Tree of Life; even in the face of chaos and catastrophe, divine balance is always at work. Grey clouds fill the darkened sky, representing uncertainty in the future.

There are two figures falling from the burning tower's windows. By their anguished expressions, we can see that they did not jump by choice; they were left with no other option but to burn alive. These figures represent the loss of control or the notion of being stuck between two equally unfavorable options. One of these figures wears a jeweled crown, reminding us that even royalty is no match for revolutionary insurgence or divine will. The falling king also shows us that the higher we rise, the further we may fall without vigilance, support, and the approval of a higher power.

History

Some view this card as a representation of the biblical Tower of Babel story, in which God strikes down a tower built to great heights, with the intention of allowing mortals to reach heaven. In light of this interpretation, you might look at this card as a warning not to overreach or overstep your bounds. Be careful not to develop any sort of God-complex in your career, social life, or religious community; divine powers may see this as defiance, and those below you will be more than happy to see you fall.

Alternative Names

La Foudre (meaning "The Thunderbolt" in french); The Devil's Ladder; The Arrow; Poseidon; the House of God

Interpretation

Upright — This card could be seen as a bad omen, as it points to an upcoming crisis, revolution, insurgency, upheaval, natural disaster, emergency situation, or drastic, sudden change. In particular, it tends to reference an unexpected change or an event that occurs before it is supposed to, throwing the querent's normal routine into chaos.

The silver lining, which can sometimes allow this card to be viewed as a good sign, is that the Tower gives us fair warning and advises us not to wait until lightning strikes to take that leap out of the window. If the querent is willing to embrace the upcoming change and look at it as an opportunity for personal transformation or improvement of the status quo at large, they then have the opportunity to stroll comfortably out of the Tower's front doors on their own two feet, before the fire forces them to jump.

As an example: a house fire is almost always a traumatic and devastating event. But once the flames are extinguished, the aftermath of this fire might leave the homeowner with a large insurance settlement that allows them to renovate the home in ways they otherwise would never be able to afford, empowering them to then sell the property, reap financial benefits that were previously out of reach, and move to a better location.

Sometimes, the universe needs to destroy things or tear them down in order to make space for positive creations and growth.

Reversed — When upside down, this card still signifies an upcoming change, but it may not be unexpected, sudden, or chaotic; think of simmering water gradually heating to a boil rather than a fiery explosion. Perhaps the querent has seen this development in the works for a long while but hasn't taken steps to prepare themselves, procrastinating, or living in denial. On the other hand, the reversed Tower can also indicate a change that has already occurred, one that the querent has been reluctant to accept or embrace. Finally, it might speak to a major societal or political change that actually serves to benefit the querent, a revolution that they've been looking forward to, or a form of chaos that creates new opportunities. Did you know that the inventors of the chocolate chip cookie, the board game Monopoly, and Scotch tape, all started their businesses shortly after the devastating stock market crash of 1929? Destruction and turmoil can sometimes inspire creativity and innovation.

Contextual – The Tower can reference external or internal changes. Look to the surrounding cards for clues. If most of the other cards in the spread feature solitary characters, or if the spread is dominated by Cups, the upcoming change is likely to be something that the querent will have to handle largely on their own: an existential crisis, loss of faith, or emotional upheaval. Alongside the virtue cards of the Major Arcana, it may point to a change in value structure. Besides any card with multiple characters featured in the illustration, look forward to a change that will impact many people at once. The message is clear: however intense these changes, the querent cannot let them become distractions or obstacles that stand in the way of their forward momentum. Followed by the Star, the Sun, or the World, this means that this crisis will actually be an event that changes the querent's life for the better.

Associated Suit: Wands

Correlated Element: Fire

Celestial Correspondence: Mars

Timing: Abruptly, suddenly, without warning

XVII – The Star

Imagery

A nude young maiden kneels at the edge of a small pond below a sky full of eight-pointed stars. Throughout the Tarot deck, stars generally represent hope, inspiration, or divine guidance. The eight-pointed star, in particular, is a symbol of new beginnings, rebirth, salvation, restoration, revival, and abundance. There are eight stars above her; the largest one, in the center of the cosmic cluster, is a symbol of her soul, identity, or internal compass, while the seven smaller stars represent each of the seven major chakras in the body in balance.

She holds two jugs full of water, both upended. One is held before her, pouring water back into the pond, a representation of conscious gratitude, reciprocity, and emotional mindfulness. The second is held behind her back, a symbol of the subconscious mind; this water is poured onto the grassy earth and spills into five separate rivulets, one for each of the five material senses (sight, sound, smell, touch, and taste). There is a tree behind her, with a single bird perched atop its branches; the bird is an ibis, usually associated with imagination, inspiration, creativity, and ambition.

The young woman's stance is similar to that of the angel on the Temperance card, with one foot dipped into the water while the other stays firmly planted on land. This stance represents her balance between dichotomies (the conscious and subconscious, intuitive and rational, material and spiritual, etc.); it also represents the maiden herself as a conduit between these contrasting energies. Using her body as a channel, she allows the water to flow continuously, signifying abundance and infinite potential. She is illustrated in the nude to reference her willingness to be vulnerable and honest, trusting in divine powers to protect, support, and inspire her.

History
The meaning of the card has remained fairly constant throughout the centuries. Some illustrations might depict scenes from the bible, wherein the three kings followed the Star of Bethlehem to the manger in which Jesus, a symbol of renewed hope himself, was born into the world.

Alternative Names
Hope; Faith; Silence; Belief

Interpretation
Upright – Following the Tower in the Major Arcana's numerical sequence, this card references the first hint of optimism that comes after a low point. It represents renewed

hope after a loss or crisis, restored faith, reinvention, and rejuvenation. Perhaps the querent has suffered through a tumultuous ordeal but now feels a deeper connection to the universe as a whole and is inspired to transform the negative energy of the past into something positive for the future, for example, being robbed of all your possessions, only to discover that a minimalist lifestyle provides you with a greater sense of peace, creativity, and fulfillment. This upright card can also signify trust in higher powers or a renewed sense of personal significance. The querent understands, now, what their purpose is; those stars represent a higher calling, and the querent is empowered to follow them toward contentment, peace, and fulfillment. Usually, this card is considered a sign of good luck, forward momentum, growth, and blessings just around the corner.

Reversed – When this card is upright, it represents positivity following negativity and hope prevailing after a catastrophe; therefore, when it is reversed, it often indicates that a negative event in the querent's life hasn't been fully overcome or left in the past. Perhaps an injury, illness, or emotional scar is still being carried, and healing will not be possible until the querent works to adjust their outlook. The reversed Star can signify depression, pessimism, discouragement, cynicism, stagnation, negativity, skepticism, and a loss of convictions, hope, or faith. The querent should be advised to look up at the stars, immerse themselves in nature, and try to remember the bigger picture. Suffering is often a tool for learning, growth, and transcendence, rather than a sentence of condemnation; it's all about how you look at it.

Contextual – Look for symbolic themes running throughout the spread. Other cards that feature stars, such as the Chariot or the Hermit, will underline the message that the querent must keep their eyes focused on their goals and pursue their ambitions, no matter what obstacles they may encounter; their quest will prove to be worth the effort, in the end. If the surrounding cards also feature flowing water (as in Temperance or the Empress), this may indicate that hope can be found through artistic creativity, or maybe the birth of a child. It is always a good sign when this card follows a bad omen card (the Tower, Death, Five of Pentacles, Nine or Ten of Swords), foretelling that a loss will be followed by an even greater gain.

Associated Suit: Swords

Correlated Element: Air

Celestial Correspondence: Aquarius Zodiac sign

Timing: January 20th through February 18th

XVIII – The Moon

Imagery

At first glance, this illustration may seem counterintuitive; it's titled as The Moon, after all, yet the scene appears to take place in daylight, and the moon's face is drawn within a larger sun. This is purposeful. Everything in this image serves to illustrate the concept of hidden meanings, dualities, deception, illusion, mystery, and cognitive dissonance.

The landscape is bisected by a river which flows into a pool at the base of the card. There are two towers in the distance, one on either side of the water. They represent a choice or crossroads. One tower houses positivity, honesty, goodness, and truth, while the other harbors negativity, deceit, falsehoods, confusion, and evil, but the towers are identical. How can we decipher which option is preferable or which path to follow when they appear so similar on the surface level?

In the forefront of the scene, we see two animals on either side of the river: one is a domesticated dog, while the other is a wolf. Both howl at the moon, and together, they represent the dichotomy between the tame and the wild, animal instincts and human values, safety and risk, the natural and supernatural, the past and the present (canines have evolved from wolves, after all), the transparent and the mysterious.

At the base of the card, where the river feeds into a body of water, we see the only symbolic character that isn't doubled: a lone, blue crayfish emerging from the depths of the water. This creature is associated with the Cancer Zodiac sign, and in this context, it represents the surfacing of repressed emotions or forgotten memories, as well as the subconscious mind. The only way to navigate this confusing scene is to trust in your intuition, as your material senses will offer little in the way of guidance.

History
While the illustrative themes of this card can be traced back to some of the earliest standardized decks, such as the Tarot de Marseilles, there are two common alternative images in some older European decks. One alternative features a lone woman seated beneath the Moon opposite a single tree, holding a distaff and spinning thread. The other depicts two astronomers standing beneath a moonlit sky, each using a different tool to try and read the cosmos. Very few historical decks illustrate a Moon Goddess figure on this card (Diana with her hunting dogs, for instance).

Alternative Names
Illusion; Luna; Selene; Hecate; Artemis; Past Lives; Memory

Interpretation

Upright – The Moon card can serve to warn the querent that things in their present or future reality aren't quite what they seem. It symbolizes the fear of the unknown, hidden truths, uncertainty, illusion, secrets, and mysticism. Someone in the querent's life is two-faced and harboring ulterior motives, or maybe, an institution they've been led to trust turns out to be built upon a lie. This card can also signify the importance of trusting in one's gut and extrasensory perceptions, valuing intuition over rationality. In this situation, only half of the querent's reality is visible or fully understood, while the other half remains shrouded in darkness and mystery.

This all may sound quite negative and frightening, but much like the Tower, this upright card offers advice as to how the querent can navigate their way through these murky waters and emerge unscathed. The Moon has powerful feminine energy, so it recommends that we put our trust and esteem in the traits of the divine feminine (emotionality, passivity, intuition, creativity, complexity, discretion, flexibility, receptiveness, introspection) in order to survive the darkest of nights. The Moon is also a symbol of constant and cyclical fluctuation, so it can symbolize recurring nightmares, old memories or emotions resurfacing repeated patterns, or the return of something the querent lost long ago. Finally, as the various phases of the moon are often associated with supernatural energies, this card may reference an event in the past or future that is inexplicable, uncanny, or otherworldly, whether it is miraculous or disturbing in nature.

Reversed – When the Moon is reversed, secrets are exposed, mysteries are unveiled, disguises are dismantled, the fog dissipates, and illusions fade. Truths surface, but they may not always lead the querent to immediate happiness or fulfillment; the face behind the smiling mask might be monstrous, and the mystery may be far more comforting than the distasteful reality that hides behind it. This card points to an awakening, which may be painful initially, but will ultimately lead to growth and healing.

Contextual – Surrounded by Cups cards, the Moon points to emotional dishonesty and the need to get fully in touch with one's intuitive powers. Among Swords, it can reference a flawed academic, philosophical, or spiritual belief system. Besides Pentacles, it may indicate that material senses or values are overshadowing what is truly important or clouding the querent's judgment. It is difficult to think clearly under the influence of alcohol, in the throes of sexual desire, numbed by gluttony, or sheltered from the outside world by thick, secure walls. Surrounded by Wands, the Moon warns the querent not to put their trust in those who are too charming, overly passionate, or extremely powerful, as these traits may prove dangerous in the long run.

Associated Suit: Cups

Correlated Element: Water

Celestial Correspondence: Pieces

Timing: February 19th through March 20th, or on the night of any full Moon throughout the year.

XIX – The Sun

Imagery

The Sun looms bright and large overhead, dominating the upper half of the card's illustration. It is anthropomorphized, wearing a serene expression, reminding us that the Sun is a representation of the masculine deity, just like the Moon is the celestial embodiment of the divine feminine. Below him, a young naked child rides upon the back of a white horse, smiling and spreading his arms wide. His nudity, young age, and open-armed posture represent freedom, expression, vulnerability, and optimism. He wears a floral wreath, signifying abundance and victory, as well as a feather in his cap, a symbol of whimsy, playfulness, and joy. He also holds a large, bright red banner: this is an announcement of victory, the message of change, or the heralding of a new day. The white horse represents purity and forwards momentum.

Behind the child and horse is a stone wall, representing structure, stability, and safety. There is a garden of blossoming sunflowers behind it, though, all popping their heads over the top of the wall. This indicates that abundance, optimism, and joy are overwhelming the need for caution, protection, and rationality. It may also reference past obstacles that have been overcome.

History
The symbolism and significance of this card have changed little over the centuries; has anyone ever been disappointed to see the Sun shining overhead?

Alternative Names
Innocence; Freedom; Joy.

Interpretation
Upright – One glance at this card's bright colors and cheery elements makes its meaning clear. Happiness, satisfaction, triumph, new beginnings, growth, success, abundance, and joy are all on the way. Some view it specifically as a sign of mastery over a skill or acquisition of long-sought-after knowledge. It is generally rooted in material sources of pleasure rather than spiritual nirvana. It also signifies growth, the loss of doubt, eradication of stress or anxiety, and the ability to let go of inhibitions. The querent has something to look forward to, even if they don't yet know what it is. They'll soon be walking with a spring in their step.

Reversed – Many cartomancers call this the best card in the Tarot deck because even when it is upside down, it still implies positivity, success, and happiness. In reverse, though, the Sun usually implies a muted sense of joy. Perhaps the querent is having trouble feeling gratitude for their myriad blessings or still viewing the glass as half-empty rather than half-full. Alternatively, this might reference a situation wherein the querent has accomplished all of their goals, only to realize, in the end, that this reality isn't what they really want for themselves. If you've ever fought hard to win a promotion, only to discover that the job isn't really all it was cracked up to be, you'll understand the energy of this reversed card. Everything is in its right place, but something is still missing.

Contextual – Try to spot all of the celestial bodies in your spread. The Sun often points to illumination or enlightenment when found alongside cards with moons or stars in them (The High Priestess or The Hermit, for example). Due to this card's inherent optimism and high numerical value, its promise of positivity can trump almost any bad omen card in the deck (Death, The Tower, etc.). If it appears reversed, though, in a spread with a number of upright feminine cards (The Moon, High Priestess, etc.), it might point to a situation in which the belief in traditional values is overshadowing the querent's true desires. Perhaps you've been told that success means getting rich and starting a family, but in reality, you want to buy a van and travel across the country on your own, doing odd jobs for cash. Why not? You get to determine what happiness means to you.

Associated Suit: Wands

Correlated Element: Fire

Celestial Correspondence: The Sun

Timing: Summertime, or high noon

XX – Judgment

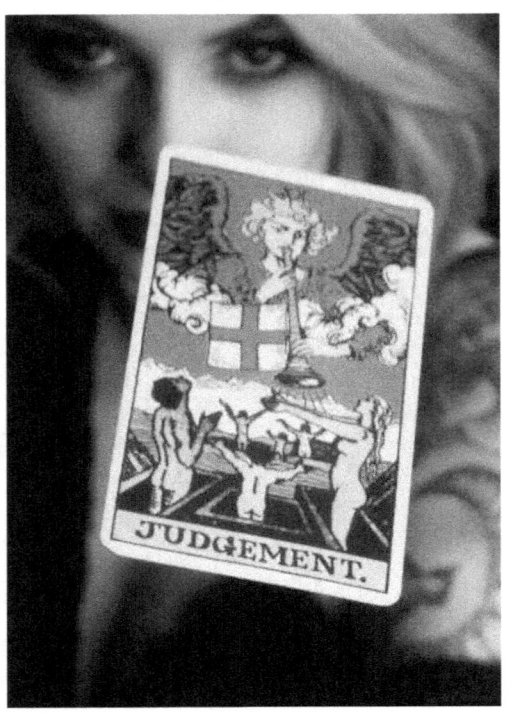

Imagery

In the Rider-Waite deck, this card is inspired directly by the biblical description of the Last Judgment in the Book of Revelation. We see an angel (most likely Metatron) overhead, with wings spread wide, blowing a horn to send a message down to the earth. The horn bears a flag with a red cross on it, referencing the four elements, four corners of the earth, and four suits; it also represents a choice or crossroads and is seen by some as a symbol of protection, peace, and healing (as in the Red Cross Logo used in times of war to symbolize the rules of the Geneva Convention and the motto: "In War, Charity").

Down below, on earth, we see a number of grey-skinned bodies emerging from opened coffins and the sea. These are figurative, not literal, representations of the undead being granted a new chance at life. The coffins they emerge from should be seen as cages that they are escaping; they are abandoning material values and turning toward the spiritual realm. Those who are emerging from the sea are escaping repressed feelings or emotional entanglements that formerly made them feel trapped (social anxieties, for example, or fear and shame). In the distant background, we see snow-covered mountains; winter, representing death, has passed, but still, they rise.

History

Since this illustration is based on a biblical scene, it hasn't changed much between the 1400s and 1910 (the publication year of the Rider-Waite deck). Many modern decks abandon biblical themes entirely with this card, though. For instance, in Aleister Crowley's Thoth Tarot deck, it renamed the Aeon and portrayed three different deific figures layered upon or within one another; this interpretation is thought to reference the cyclical nature of time and evolution or the end of one era leading into the birth of a new one.

Alternative Names

Karma; The Aeon; Atonement; Resurrection; Absolution; Prudence; The Lifted Veil

Interpretation

Upright – This upright card can point to a wake-up call that is impossible to ignore. Has the querent been drudging through life, falling into routines and comfortable patterns, losing sight of their ultimate goals or values? Have they been asleep at the wheel or phoning it in? They won't be allowed to continue in this way for much longer. Often, this card signifies a spiritual calling or cosmic sign. Will you open your arms up to the angel overhead and heed the call? Or stay asleep in your coffin?

This card can also point to an upcoming event that will separate the strong from the weak and the righteous from the undeserving. That could be something as simple as a company merger or as intense as a war.

Reversed – Upside down, this card points to fear of change and denial. All the signs are right in front of you, but still, you insist on ignoring them, clinging to the stability of your routine. How loud does the horn need to be for you to admit to yourself that you hear it?

Contextual – Look for other angels and messengers (Pages, Sword cards) in your spread. The universe is trying to tell you something, but it's up to you to listen. Alongside the Devil, there is a strong indication that it's time to move past addiction of some kind before it destroys you. Beside Death, the Tower, or the Wheel of Fortune, major changes and rebirth lie ahead. Alongside the Moon, it's time to stop buying into the facade and name the truth that lies beneath it; no more lies, no more illusion.

Associated Suit: Wands

Correlated Element: Fire

Celestial Correspondence: Pluto

Timing: Winter or stormy seasons

XXI – The World

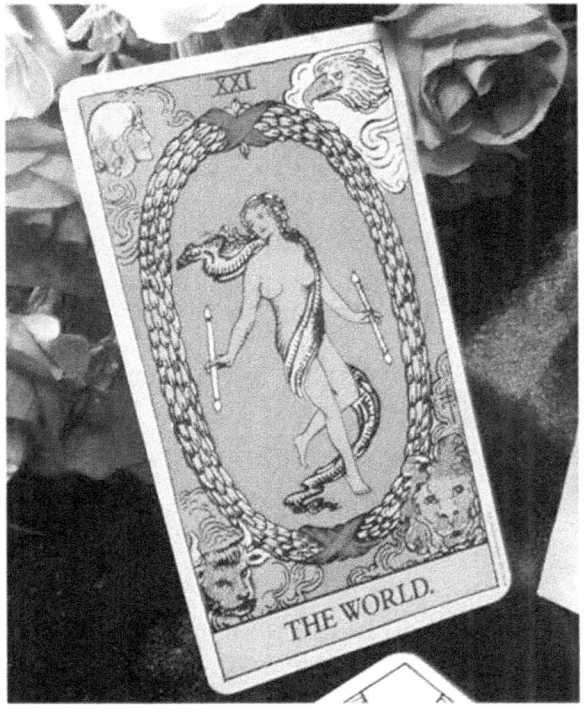

Imagery

A frolicking woman appears to be floating on air, with a clear blue sky behind her. She is naked, meaning she is vulnerable, open, and free, but a purple sash is draped across her torso, held on by the wind. The color of the sash is a reference to wisdom, insight, regality, and spiritual guidance. Her legs and feet are a reversed mirror image of the Hanged Man's posture; she is at a crossroads but appears confident about her next steps, despite the fact that her head is turned back, reflecting on how far she has come, rather than focused exclusively on where she is going. She holds two wands by her sides with a gentle grip, one in each hand, as contrasted with the Magician, who holds one overhead; this shows us that she has found balance, and while all the powers of the universe are at her disposal, she doesn't feel the need to grip them too tightly or fear to lose them, nor does she need to lord over others or prove herself to anyone.

Her figure is framed by a green laurel wreath, decorated with a red banner; this is a symbol of victory, accomplishment, constancy, eternal cycles, and completion. In the four corners of the card, we see four figures, known as the evangelicals, who represent the same characters that we see in the corners of The Wheel of Fortune card, though their faces are larger and closer now. She has come closer to reaching the divine or spiritual plane, ready to meet them at their level.

History
Some older decks depict this character as Jesus Christ himself, seated upon a heavenly throne, still surrounded by the four evangelicals, as described in the Book of Revelations.

Alternative Names
The Universe; Completion; Nirvana; New Jerusalem; Heaven

Interpretation
Upright – This is the final card of the Major Arcana, and therefore, when facing upright, represents a sense of completion or wholeness. The querent has reached (or soon will reach) a place of both material fulfillment and spiritual enlightenment and now feels at peace with their surroundings and at one with the universe as a whole. Whereas the Sun card points to a material sense of joy or optimism, this card usually signifies a sense of unending peace and belonging, as well as liberation from material values. Whatever comes their way next, whether it is joy or suffering, they will be able to handle it with acceptance, serenity, and undying hope for the future.

Reversed – The querent is oh-so-close to the finish line, but an unforeseen obstacle has popped up to stand in the way of successful completion. This could be interpreted literally (perhaps graduation is next week, and they've just discovered that they're missing a required credit) or figuratively (they thought they tasted nirvana in a meditation session last week, but their insecurities and hang-ups are still weighing them down, now—what gives?), but either way, it points to an unexpected setback at an inopportune moment. Having gotten their hopes up, the querent is now overwhelmed by disappointment. Alternatively, this card could imply that the querent is struggling to move on from a negative experience, cannot find closure after a heartbreak or major loss, or that they have not learned from their past experiences. It's important to work on a resolution so that you don't become stagnant or stuck in the past. Heaven is mindfulness and acceptance in the present.

Contextual – This is the ultimate trump card. Whenever it shows up in a spread, regardless of context, pay special attention to it. It overshadows all other cards, whether they are positive or negative. As an example, if you see a reversed Sun beside an upright World, it means that you'll find peace and fulfillment through nontraditional avenues or that prosperity and abundance aren't necessary in order to find joy. By contrast, an upright Sun with a reversed World means that material success, no matter how great, cannot provide you with lasting or true happiness. This card can serve to either amplify or undermine the meaning of other omens in the spread.

Associated Suit: Pentacles

Correlated Element: Earth

Celestial Correspondence: Saturn

Timing: Gradually, in the long-term, constantly, and eternally

The Fool's Journey

The illustrations of the Major Arcana cards each contain powerful archetypal images and symbolic meanings that can stand well on their own. At the same time, though, you may notice that these cards, when laid out in numerical order, appear to tell a developing story that expands in scope as the numbers ascend. This story is known as "The Fool's Journey." Many novices find it to be a helpful part of the memorization process because it illustrates the meanings of the cards in a way that resonates with their own life experience.

The Fool begins his saga as a carefree but naive wanderer. Soon, he begins to encounter other characters, usually grouped in dichotomous pairings, which represent different ways of dealing with situations or stages of life. The Magician and High Priestess represent different ways of handling power and knowledge; the Empress and Emperor represent two different takes on parenthood or leadership; the Hierophant encourages conformity and respect for a higher power, while the Lovers embrace risk and rebellion. The characters, concepts, and institutions he finds along the way also mirror the progressive stages of his growth in life. By the time he finds the Chariot, he feels empowered as an adult and charges forward, but then, meeting Strength, he is reminded that his physical maturity doesn't necessarily make him emotionally capable of handling life's difficulties. He then retreats, either becoming or following the Hermit, once again searching for answers, but this time, he turns within to find them.

The Wheel of Fortune is a turning point, where he begins to expand his perceptions and starts to see the bigger picture. He is confused, at first, at how the mighty can fall just as easily as the weak. He then encounters Justice, though, and is reminded that there is a natural balance to the universe, and all of this chaos and flux is merely a part of the divine plan. So, he decides to surrender himself to a higher power, as the Hanged Man does, relinquishing his need for control, comfort, and rational understanding. Through this experience, he reaches a point of ego Death and is able to be reborn as someone who accepts the loss and embraces life's unexpected changes. The next stage of his journey is ruled by Temperance, as he has grown tired of this constant seesawing; he wants to find balance and stability, and he's willing to put in some hard work and make sacrifices to achieve this end.

Soon, though, this desire for stability and routine becomes overly comfortable, seductive, even. He meets the Devil and begins to realize that, although he thought he had reached enlightenment, he's actually gotten stuck in a rut and become too firmly rooted in material sensations. He sees no way out of this comfortable bondage, so divine forces strike the Tower with a lightning bolt to make him decidedly uncomfortable and force him out of those chains.

It's a traumatic experience for him, but he finds inspiration, serenity, and renewed hope in the Star, allowing him to keep moving forward. He continues the work that he began with Temperance, but this time, he shares his creations with the world around him, rather than keeping it all confined to his own cup; this seems to be the key to true balance and fulfillment. Now that he is so happy, though, he is also vulnerable; his intense optimism makes it hard for him to see past illusions, as he wants to see the good in everyone, feeling universal empathy, and hoping to continue being as generous as possible with others. The Moon reminds him that truth is not found through blind trust or faith; that there is a good and bad side to everything, including divine power; and that he must trust in his intuition, rather than presuming that things are just what they appear to be.

When he finds the Sun, he feels that he can see everything clearly, and it is a joyous sensation. He is ready for anything, now, and enthusiastically rides on, reborn, ready to face a new day. As he journeys on, though, he can't help but meditate on his past mistakes. He has achieved material success and comfort but still longs for something more—perhaps forgiveness or guidance from a higher power? A sense of purpose or universal connectivity, maybe? He wants to offer forgiveness and guidance to others, as well, and help them to see the light that it took so long for him to discover.

With the World, he has come full circle and understands that his journey never truly ends. It isn't meant to; life itself is a journey, and even after death, the journey continues. He has learned from his experiences, though, and found balance, harmony, and fulfillment in the act of moving forward. Perhaps the next leg of his journey will be dedicated to helping another Fool follow in his footsteps. He recognizes, now, that all of the elements of the earth and cosmos are working together, in concert, to hold him up, teach him lessons, and help him grow. He has faith that whatever comes next will be exactly what he needs, at the perfect time and place. He is now one with the universe.

Chapter 3: The Minor Arcana for Beginners

Every single card in the Tarot deck carries its own unique meaning, but memorizing seventy-eight different images and interpretations can feel like an overwhelming or nearly impossible task for many beginners.

It may be easier to start by memorizing some of the symbolic values that remain constant throughout the deck. Each of the Minor Arcana cards has a suit and number, or court rank. When we combine their meanings in a formulaic fashion, we can usually decipher a fairly accurate interpretation for these cards at only a fraction of the effort. For instance, a card's numerical value + suit/elemental meaning = interpretation; or, for Court cards, suit/element + court rank = character. I'll provide more specific examples throughout this chapter to help you get the hang of these formulaic readings.

Numbered Cards of the Minor Arcana

- **Aces**: new beginnings; fresh starts; new opportunities; potential; renewal; originality; raw energy; independence; individuality. Aces represent their suits and the energy of their corresponding elements in their purest forms; the Ace of Wands conveys the raw energy of Fire; the Ace of Cups represents the element of Water; the Ace of Swords signifies the nature of the Air element; the Ace of Pentacles embodies the energy of the Earth element.

- **Twos**: dualities; choices; a fork in the road; partnership; cooperation; union or peaceful compromise between two disparate characters or concepts; mergers; balance

- **Threes**: creativity; growth; expansion; creative expression; manifestation; community; family; teamwork; completion of a first stage or achievement of the first phase of a long-term task

- **Fours**: security; stability; rationality; a steady foundation; stagnation; permanence; strength; structure; formalized institutions; organization; reliability; a plateau in progress or growth

- **Fives**: changing circumstances; instability; challenges; obstacles; volatility; conflict; fluctuation; movement; motivation to evolve; action; momentum

- **Sixes**: balance; cooperation; community; harmony; conflict resolution; celebration; abundance; healthy communication; finding solutions to problems; fairness and objectivity; reconciliation; overcoming obstacles and challenges; owned responsibilities; finding peace

- **Sevens**: intuition; struggle; major choices; knowledge; cataclysmic changes; challenges; assessment; provoked reflection or introspection; revolution; sudden or rapid developments; adjustment; forced movement; transition; transformation; reevaluation

- **Eights**: accomplishment; manifestation; results; major achievements; milestones reached; mastery of skills or talents; graduation; advancements; forward momentum; abundance; successful activity; sometimes, they can point to the manifestation of negative expectations, fears, and doubts, for instance, you see something like a disaster waiting to happen, and your fears are then realized, just as you predicted.
- **Nines**: completion; attainment; works coming to fruition; wisdom; intellectual or spiritual enlightenment; endings; fulfillment; earned rewards
- **Tens**: endings leading into new beginnings; completion of a cycle; fulfilled or sustained traditions; things coming full circle; final results; rebirth; perfection

Some Tarot novices find it difficult to distinguish between the symbolic meanings of fives and sevens or between nines and tens. Keep in mind that these numbers signify increasing intensity with increased value. While fives and sevens can both represent changes and challenges, the seven cards will always signify more extreme struggles because they have a higher numerical value. If both a Five and Seven of Cups appear in the same spread, you might interpret the Five of Cups to point to dissatisfaction in a relationship, while the Seven of Cups would point to the ultimate decision to either make it work or cut ties. To further clarify the difference, note that Sevens often indicate an internal or personal struggle: a crisis of faith, a change of heart, or a need to transform and evolve as an individual. They also usually point to introspection or reflection. Meanwhile, Fives tend to refer to the first visible cracks in the facade of an organized and seemingly stable structure or organization (this is especially true whenever a Five follows a Four of the same suit in a spread). Therefore, a Five of Swords in a spread might point to your frustration with a competitive and flawed academic institution, while a Seven of Swords could signal your decision to change your field of study, fight back against the flaws in the institution, or abandon it entirely, striking out on your own.

The same logic of increasing intensity applies to Nines and Tens; both point to endings and completion, but Tens will always bear a greater sense of finality and ultimate achievements. For example, the Nine of Pentacles would likely point to the achievement of career goals, or the chance to finally enjoy the fruits of one's labors, while the Ten of Pentacles might indicate a major windfall (lottery winnings, inheritance, the sale of a company for a large sum) or successful retirement.

These numeric values can also be used to help decipher the meanings of Major Arcana cards in spreads where they seem not to make sense. For any cards with numeric values greater than ten, you can add the digits together to find their numerological meanings. For example, the Tower card is the 16th in the Major Arcana; its numerological value is 7 (1+6), and it indeed signifies intense changes, struggles, revolution, and transformation, as well as the need to re-evaluate one's personal values and future goals.

Suits and Elemental Correspondences

Each of the four suits in the Tarot deck can be associated with one of the four earthly elements (fire, water, earth or air), while the cards of the Major Arcana will represent matters of the fifth element (often referred to in western esotericism as "spirit," "void," or "aether," though in other cultures it may be called a "universal life force," "vitality," "kundalini," "spiritual energy," or "divine will," among other possibilities).

Each element, in turn, connects the suits to their own corresponding geographic dimension, the season of the year, representational color scheme, and perceptive sense. The elements have their own meanings and traits, like personality types or flavors, that can lend an extra dimension of symbolism to any Tarot spread. As an example, the Suit of Pentacles is connected to the Earth element, which is associated with financial and practical matters; therefore, when interpreting a confusing spread that contains more cards from this suit than any of the others, you might discern that the cards are trying to convey a message concerning a practical issue in the querent's life—career matters, housing, nutrition, physical health, fertility, or safety—rather than speaking to something emotional, artistic, intellectual, or spiritual.

On the other hand, if a spread is dominated by one suit, but all of its cards are reversed, this may indicate that the associated element will present a challenge to the querent; for instance, a spread with several reversed cards in the Suit of Cups, which is connected to the Water element, emotion, and intuition may imply that oversensitivity or a lack emotional balance will pose the greatest threat to the querent's desired outcome. Or, this may imply that their intuitive sensibilities will betray them in the matter at hand.

Suit of Wands – Fire

This suit was historically called the Suit of Staves, Suit of Clubs, or Suit of Rods, so you may find some illustrations in alternative decks that depict them as walking sticks or battering clubs. It is now more popularly known as the Suit of Wands since this item more easily calls to mind the creative and powerful energy of the suit, which is primarily associated with manifestation, aggression, empowerment, determination, and vitality.

While each card in the suit has its own specific meaning, all cards in the Suit of Wands speaks to the energy of the Fire element. Fire is associated with youthful male energy; this does not mean that Wand cards represent actual young men, only that they reference traits that have historically and traditionally been seen as masculine and attributed to youth or a lack of significant experience. In particular, the Fire element is assertive (rather than receptive, which is considered a feminine trait) and active (rather than passive, another traditionally feminine elemental characteristic).

Fire can be both creative and destructive; it is powerful, physically, and spiritually but also volatile and difficult to predict, control, or extinguish. This element connotes passion, lust, virility, inspiration, motivation, enthusiasm, creativity and manifestation. On the other hand, it may also represent a hot temper, short-sighted plans, actions taken without forethought, violence, or destructive behaviors. It is externally focused energy, meaning that it implies action over contemplation, introspection, or reflection; cards within this suit will generally signify that the character described in the spread will take action upon someone or something else, rather than turning their energy inwards, whether the impact is positive or negative.

This is a transformative element that points to rapid change and excitement—nothing about Fire is slow-moving, stagnant, or dull. Much like the Magician card of the Major Arcana, it represents the sheer force of willpower and the channeling of divine spirit into earthly matter. This is the only one of the four earthly elements that mankind has learned to create, harness, and control (to some extent, at least) by our own hands, but it is also the element that separates us from the rest of the animal kingdom, bringing us one step closer to the divine but also attracting the wrath of the Gods for its defiant nature. It contains more spiritual energy than earthly energy; therefore, a Wand card in a spread that implies creative manifestation is more likely to signify creation for the sake of artistic expression or spiritual enlightenment, rather than financial gain, material rewards, or physical security—the kind of creative energy that takes hold of a person and overwhelms logic, practicality, or rationality.

The Fire element corresponds with the South; the summer season; the colors red, orange, white, and black; and the sense of sight.

Formulaic Example: The Four of Wands

Four means structure, stability, permanence, and a strong foundation. Wands speak to creativity, enterprise, and action. The Four of Wands represents something lasting and solid built with passion and creativity—through innovation, determination, and hard work, you have been able to create a thriving business, a happy family, a literal building, or a rewarding career.

Suit of Cups – Water

In alternative decks, the Suit of Cups might be called the Suit of Chalices, Bowls, or Hearts. Cards within the Suit of Cups are connected to the elemental energy of Water, which is considered feminine. It is receptive (a traditionally female trait) but also active (usually considered a male trait). The receptive trait should not be mistaken for weakness or apathy. Anyone who has seen oceanic waves crash upon a rocky shoreline knows that water can be gentle and soothing, but also wrathful and extremely powerful. At some times, Water will allow you to wade or dive in, happily supporting your weight as you displace its mass with your own; at other times, though, the receptive trait might mean that violent waters will swallow you whole. It may help you to replace the term "receptive" with "open" or "accepting," though the word "receptive" will be more commonly used in metaphysically oriented communities to describe the energy of the divine feminine.

Water is transparent and internally focused; while it can easily consume, it rarely produces externally or allows things to emerge from it, and its surface hardly conveys a fraction of what's going on in its depths. That being said, it is still a creative element associated with the uterus or womb and birth. Though few things emerge from the water, occasionally, it generates magic and produces miraculous creations; it is the original source of all life on earth, after all.

The Water element speaks to matters of emotion and intuition. It can be moody and easily influenced by the movements of the wind (Air represents matters of thought and intellect, so this elemental metaphor works on multiple levels). It can also work to extinguish Fire, just as emotions and introspection can stand in the way of action or manifestation. Combined with Earth (representing practicality and that which is grounded in reality), it is healing, nurturing, and fertile. Unlike the other elements, it is imperative that we all keep our bodies full of Water, or we become sick and die; this points to the central importance of emotion and love in life. What is the point of living if we cannot feel deeply?

Like Fire, it can be seen as a transformative element, used for cleansing, purification, and rebirth. However, just as all the earthly elements encompass dualities and contradictions, Water can be just as destructive as it is creative, and in many cultures, it is associated with death and the afterlife as well as birth and spiritual rebirth.

The Water element corresponds with the West; the autumnal season; the colors blue, green and white; and the sense of taste.

Formulaic Example: The Five of Cups

Fives are points of instability or change. Cups represent emotional issues, introspection, and relationships. The Five of Cups points to a change of heart or dissatisfaction in a relationship.

Suit of Swords – Air

Perhaps the most frequently misunderstood of the four suits, Swords in Tarot are connected to the Air element and primarily concern matters of intellect, thought, rumination, communication, conflict, and truth. Beginners often struggle to grasp the difference between Wands and Fire and Swords and Air since Swords seem like an obvious representation of violence and aggression; in truth, though, Wands and Fire are more connected to singularly aggressive behaviors, while Swords and Air correspond to dualities and conflict. When all else fails, remember the phrase "a double-edged sword"—if there are two sides to a violent conflict—that may be represented by Swords, whereas an individual or group that imposes violence upon an innocent other would be represented by Wands. As counterintuitive as it may seem, Wands are more often indicative of physical aggression, while Swords typically speak to intellectual conflict or a battle of wits.

The energy of Air isn't all bad; it can represent intellectual, philosophical, or spiritual wisdom and the power of knowledge. The mind plays an integral role in most aspects of life, allowing us to analyze, plan, communicate, and understand one another, as well as the universe as a whole. At the same time, overthinking can be a dangerous habit, as it turns to obsession, rumination, doubt, skepticism, negativity, suspicion, and, if left unchecked for long enough, narcissism and closed-mindedness. Think of the difference between a gentle summer breeze and a tornado or maelstrom. Thoughts that aren't grounded in reality or expressed through manifestation can spiral out of control, gaining enough momentum to become violent and destructive. At the same time, Air is able to influence the movements and functions of all other elements, making waves in the ocean, feeding or extinguishing flames, and spreading seeds over the earth, as well as helping to distribute rainfall over fertile patches of ground. It is invisible but ubiquitous and permeates all aspects of life on earth.

The Air element corresponds with the East; the spring season; the colors yellow, white and grey; and the auditory and olfactory senses.

Formulaic Example: The Two of Swords

Twos usually reference choices or crossroads, though they can sometimes point to balance and partnership. Swords speak to matters of the mind. This card is about a difficult choice between two equal but opposite forces or paths.

Suit of Pentacles – Earth

The Suit of Pentacles has also been named the Suit of Discs or Suit of Coins in some earlier decks, and in many illustrations within this suit, the cards depict the Pentacles as actual currency. Therefore, it should be fairly easy to remember, as you begin to interpret spreads, that Pentacles and the Earth element are both associated with matters of finance. The symbolism goes deeper than just money, though, as the Earth element is connected to all aspects of material comfort, security, safety, and stability. It often signifies prosperity and wealth, but depending on the querent's values and the context of the card spread, this might refer to abundance in another material realm; for example, upright cards in this suit might point to the growth of a garden or a successful harvest yield, an expanding collection of items that only have value to the querent, matters of physical health, or even fertility, rather than financial advances.

The Earth element is youthful and feminine, meaning it is receptive, passive, cool, and calm. It is solid, opaque, reliable, and predictable, but without the warmth of the sun (Fire energy) or moisture of rain (Water energy), it can become rigid, impenetrable, unforgiving, and downright cold rather than cool. Under ideal conditions, though, Earth is fertile, nurturing, and provides sustenance and stability for us all. It concerns matters of tradition, community, responsibility, patience, structure, and the natural order of the world. It is often overlooked and undervalued, which is ironic and pitiful because, without it, there would be no life.

The Earth element corresponds with the North; the winter season; the colors green, brown, and black; and the sense of touch.

Formulaic Example: The Eight of Pentacles

Eights imply success, achievement, progress, satisfaction, momentum, manifestation, and expected results. Pentacles concern practical matters, finance, structure, stability, and materiality. This card is about rewarding hard-work, craftsmanship, and productivity.

Court Cards: Formulaic Characters

The four ranks of Court Cards each possess their own traits across the four suits, so while the King of Cups and the King of Swords will carry different meanings, they will also have some characteristics in common. We can apply our understanding of the four suit's overarching themes to these Court Cards, using a formula to combine these meanings with their ranks to decipher their characters: rank + suit = character type.

I should clarify that the Court Cards are representative of personality types, not physical or demographic identities. A Queen of Cups card might represent the behavior of a young man; a Page of Swords might represent an elderly woman. Kings and Queens are symbols of experience and maturity, not biological ages, so they might represent teenagers or even children. The gender identities of Court Cards do not need to be interpreted literally. Some people see a correspondence between these sixteen cards and the sixteen different Myers-Briggs personality types; this theory might help you to let go of stereotypical associations with gender and age as you get to know the characters.

Pages are characterized by their inexperience, naivety, and youthful energy. They are often connected to matters of communication or represent messengers or heralds. Regardless of the suit, they are connected to the Earth element and all of its implicated connotations; this means they are usually representative of characters that are level-headed, humble, responsible, reliable, calm, and in touch with their feelings but not overly emotional. They are rational and receptive but ambitious and geared toward growth. Usually, they will not shy away from hard work; they are eager to learns and recognize that progress takes time and consistent effort. The Earth element is considered feminine, so the Page is associated with youthful feminine energy, even if he is illustrated as a young man. In some decks, this rank's title may be named "Princesses" or "Apprentices."

Knights, meanwhile, are more experienced than Pages, but not yet masters of their realms, nor do they denote high authority. In some decks, they may be referred to as Princes; their energy is decidedly masculine, but they do not necessarily represent men in real life. They are known for their determination, bravery, strength, and ambition. Most are seen as protectors. Regardless of the suit, they are connected to the Fire element. This means they may reference characters in the querent's life who are charismatic, vivacious, passionate, lustful, and bold. They are active, creative, courageous, and love a new adventure. Sometimes, though, Knights can be difficult to deal with, as their energy is volatile and unpredictable. They may be easily irritated, impatient and might turn to violence or destruction as the quickest means to their desired ends.

Queens represent feminine experience and authority, though they are generally seen as one step below Kings in terms of their authoritative power. They are mature, intuitive, emotional, but wise. They are nurturing, devoted, and extremely capable. Regardless of the suit, they are associated with the Water element. This means they are patient, compassionate, and understanding; passive and receptive, but not weak; most often cool-tempered, but capable of wrathful actions when provoked. They are usually introspective but kind and selfless with others, perhaps even to a fault. Often, they are able to display empathy and mercy to those who may not deserve their benevolence. At the same time, they are not ruled by rationality, so their behaviors may at times appear flighty, moody, or capricious.

Finally, Kings can be interpreted as the masters of their suits. They harness the ultimate degree of wisdom and authority, though their power can sometimes become controlling or domineering. They have the highest degree of experience. Regardless of the suit, they are ruled by the elemental energy of Air; therefore, you can expect them to be intellectually and philosophically sharp-minded and concerned with matters of communication, rationality, and truth, above all else. Despite their love of rationality, they may come across as eccentric kooks, exhibiting truly bizarre behavior; this is usually because of their supreme authority, where their behavior goes unchecked, and they have no motivation to modify their actions due to the judgments of others. When things are working in their favor, they will often seem jovial, carefree, generous, and charming; however, when the going gets rough, they can quickly turn selfish, apathetic, insensitive, and perhaps even cruel. These characters are independent, clever, capable, sometimes controlling, and their tempers can flip at the drop of a hat, much like the turning of the wind.

Let's try a few combinations for practice.

Say you draw the Page of Wands. Pages are inexperienced but ambitious and dedicated. They are great communicators. They are ruled by the Earth element, so they are patient, reliable, productive, and figuratively fertile. Wands speak to passion, creativity, innovation, and enterprise. This card likely describes a young student, apprentice, or new hire, who shows great promise. They have a good relationship with their teachers or bosses, know how to ask for the tools and knowledge that they need, and are willing to put in a lot of diligent hard work before seeing results. They will accomplish great things one day, but they are in no hurry to reach this point; they want to become masterfully skillful before they apply their talents to manifestation of personal goals. Their greatest flaw is perfectionism.

Now, let's look at the Queen of Swords. Queens are wise, intuitive, and emotionally mature but, sometimes, moody. They are empathetic, usually serene, but like the Water element, deceptively powerful. They can be generous, but this generosity may be manipulative; they expect kindness, respect, and gratitude in return, and if it is not offered, you may incur their wrathful side. Swords represent thoughts, philosophies, rationality, and intellect. This card describes a character whose mind is their sharpest tools or weapon; they feel emotions deeply, and they are incredibly smart. They may have trouble distinguishing between emotions and tangible realities since they spend so much time in their heads. They have learned a great deal from their experiences but may have a tendency to ruminate on negative events of the past, obsess over moral or philosophical quandaries, or use their intellect to justify gut feelings or emotional impulses rather than analyze the tangible evidence.

These formulas can be used to interpret any card in the Minor Arcana in a pinch if you cannot remember its designated meaning. In the following chapters, we'll detail these cards one at a time to provide further guidance and clarity.

Chapter 4: The Suit of Wands

Ace of Wands
Imagery
A large hand, presumably belonging to a deity or divine power, reaches out from the clouds to offer us the Wand in all its glory. It points straight up toward the sky, and the phallic imagery is no mistake—this card bears decidedly masculine energy. The wand itself looks like a living tree branch, sprouting leaves, some of which are already falling to the land below; this shows us that the wand is a tool of creation and manifestation, though some of its workings will be successful while others fail. In the landscape below, we see a castle built atop a hill, a representation of ambition, hard work, and fortitude. There is also a river, symbolizing motion and progress, and trees, symbolizing growth.

Interpretation

Upright – This card can be viewed as a big green light. Whatever ambitions you've been harboring or creative endeavors you've been brainstorming, now is the time to go for it. Start taking steps to manifest your dreams into realities. The universe will have your back.

Reversed – Have you ever been stopped at a traffic light, only to have your engine stall out as soon as the light turned green? That is the essence of this card. Be wary of a false start, loss of momentum, or failure just after the beginning of a new project. It may also be a warning that your passionate energy has become too intense, too early—more preparation, planning, rationality, and focus are needed to achieve success.

Two of Wands
Imagery

A man stands atop a parapet, gazing over the landscape beyond the castle walls. One wand is planted in the ground behind him, while the other is held in his hand; they represent what has already been achieved and what is still anticipated or desired, respectively. He also holds a globe in his other hand to show us that the world is his oyster, with endless possibilities at his fingertips. In the distance, we see mountains, symbolizing challenges, obstacles, and fortitude, as well as an oceanic bay, representing emotional desires and intuitive feelings. We can tell by his boots, hat, and cloak that he is ready for an adventure. Atop these stone walls, he is safe and secure, but something deep inside him is longing for the risks and unpredictability of a journey into the unknown.

Interpretation

Upright – Success has been achieved, but this accomplishment has only left you wanting more. External forces may be trying to convince you that your safest bet is to capitalize on what you already have created, but you feel ready to move on to bigger and better things. Will you heed their advice, and stay put, where moderate success is all but guaranteed? Or will you listen to your gut and take a risk?

Reversed – Upside down, this card tells you plainly that you've got to keep moving. The success you're enjoying now will be short-lived or ultimately unfulfilling if you don't take steps to expand upon it. Strike while the iron is hot because if you wait too long, you may miss your chance.

Three of Wands
Imagery

Similar to the figure in the Two of Wands, a man in a cloak and traveling sack stands on the edge of a cliff, looking over the ocean. Two wands are planted in the ground behind him, representing past achievements, while he appears to be using the third as a walking stick, planning to journey forth. There are several ships sailing on the bay, each a symbol of forward momentum, new opportunities, and risks; he has a number of options available to him. The sky over the bay is a golden yellow, a sign of optimism.

Interpretation

Upright — Your past experiences and successes have empowered you to journey on. You can feel comfortable turning your back upon these accomplishments and letting them be; they've been built on a sturdy foundation and can stand on their own without your assistance now. This means you are free to try something new and step outside of your comfort zone. This card often urges a querent to seize any travel opportunities on the horizon, as it is a good omen.

Reversed — This may indicate that your aspirations are a bit too lofty for your current level of experience or that you have not yet accumulated the resources you'll need to achieve success. It is also considered a bad travel omen; don't leave home until you've adequately prepared yourself for the journey ahead!

Four of Wands

Imagery

Four wands are propped up like tent stakes with garlands of flowers strung up between them, like a canopy. Behind them, we see a scene of obvious merriment: figures holding bouquets and wearing floral wreaths, dancing for joy in front of a castle. This is a victorious celebration, enabled by creativity, innovation, manifestation, and passionate energy.

Interpretation

Upright — The number four and the castle both represent structure and stability, while the flowers and dancers are symbols of abundance and victory. Here we can see that your consistent and organized work on manifestation has finally paid off, enabling you and your loved ones to take a break from all the hard work and revel in the fruits of your labor. Your efforts have resulted in established success and lasting rewards; you can afford to kick back and relax for a while now.

Reversed – You've accomplished your goals and earned your rewards, and you should be dancing for joy—but for some reason, you can't, or you don't want to. Perhaps something is distracting you or tainting your ability to feel contented. It may be your ego, anxiety, or the need for constant forward and uphill momentum that is stopping you from standing still and appreciating what you already have at your disposal or how far you've already come. Ask yourself: if you're not happy now, with all that you have achieved, then when *will* you be satisfied? How much achievement will it take for you to feel proud of yourself?

Five of Wands
Imagery
Five young males, each with a wand in their hands, are battling one another for power and supremacy in a chaotic scene. The battle isn't particularly violent, and some of the participants even appear to be enjoying themselves. None of these wands is planted in the ground; they are all raised up in the air, symbolizing ambition, but with a lack of grounded energy.

Interpretation

Upright – This card is about healthy competition pushing you to be more creative, innovative, aggressive, and diligent. It's not exactly teamwork, but you are able to draw on and become inspired by the energy of your strongest competitors. Try to remember to have fun in the midst of it all, and stay gracious; these competitors could become your partners or greatest supporters one day.

Reversed – Competition isn't always healthy. Here, your competitors have become true adversaries, and the environment, which was once creative and inspiring has become cut-throat, possibly even corrupt. If you have to tear someone else down in order to prop yourself up, is winning really worth the cost to your moral conscience? This reversed card can also represent counterproductive avoidance of conflicts or passive-aggressive behaviors.

Six of Wands
Imagery

A triumphant figure rides a white horse in a yellow shroud through a celebratory parade. The horse references forward momentum and purity of intent, and his yellow jacket is a symbol of optimism. The rider wears a wreath on his head and carries another at the top of his Wand, both signifying victorious achievement.

Interpretation

Upright – The illustration makes it fairly obvious that this card references a major win or accomplishment. The querent's hard work has paid off, and now, they are being celebrated. They have earned respect, critical acclaim, and elevated status.

Reversed – This points to a lot of hard work done in vain. The querent feels like a loser. Maybe they've been humiliated; people were expecting great things from them, but now, they are disappointed. This reversed card may indicate that your biggest fans have suddenly become your harshest critics, or perhaps your steepest competition. It could also reference a leader whose followers have become mutinous.

Seven of Wands
Imagery

A young man is balanced at the edge of a cliff, with his back to the ledge. There are six wands pointed at him, threatening to drive him over the edge. He holds the seventh wand in both hands, ready to use it as both a weapon and a shield. On one foot, he wears a low-topped shoe, while he wears a boot on the opposite foot. The mismatched shoes could represent an inability to choose one path or the other, which is perhaps how he got himself backed into this corner; alternatively, they might be worn for the sake of misdirection or distraction, or they could represent his originality and refusal to conform to societal norms.

Interpretation
Upright – Your passion and creativity have set you apart from the crowd, but now, you find yourself having to defend your values, beliefs, or personality. Being original, innovative, talented, and independent won't always make you popular. Stay strong, focused, and proud of what you've achieved; your critics can only drive you over the edge if you allow them to.

Reversed – You've been working and fighting for so long that you've become exhausted and weakened. You've allowed the voices of your critics to get inside your head, and now, you doubt yourself. This doubt is stifling your creativity or productivity. You might even be thinking about throwing in the towel. You'll have to ask yourself: did you start this venture for yourself or to gain approval from others?

Eight of Wands
Imagery
This is one of the rare cards without any human figures in its frame. We see eight wands spread diagonally across the page, all parallel with one another. They seem to be flying through the air, soon to be staked in the earth, like arrows shot up toward the sky, completing their natural arc. There is a river flowing behind them, representing momentum and flow.

Interpretation
Upright – You've aimed well; now, your arrow is about to hit its target. This card speaks to progress, momentum, and sitting on the cusp of a major achievement.

Everything seems to be in order; stay focused, keep moving forward, and you'll be sure to accomplish your goals.

Reversed – When upside down, this card implies reversed progress, a delay or setback, or losing sight of your true goals. Have you ever been lost while driving and kept hitting the gas pedal, moving forward without consulting a roadmap, only to carry yourself further away from familiar roads and your ultimate destination? Progress for the sake of progress can actually be counterproductive, not to mention a waste of energy.

Nine of Wands

Imagery

Eight Wands are planted in the ground in a row, like a fence. The ninth is held in a man's arms. He should be lining it up with the rest, but instead, he's leaning on it, plainly exhausted. There is a bandage around his head, signifying a psychic wound. He glances back at the other Wands with an expression of resentment. In the background, there is a mountain range, representing challenges and uphill battles.

Interpretation

Upright – You are inches away from the finish line but so worn out, you don't even want to think about taking another step forward. You should be looking back on your past achievements with pride, but you are so tired and hurt that all you can wonder is why you ever undertook this project in the first place. What has it brought you, thus far, besides pain and suffering?

This voice in your head is irrational—a result of overworking yourself. Try not to listen to it or let it get the better of you. Take a quick break to rest and restore your energy, but don't lose sight of your goal. You're almost there! Resilience is key. Once you see the finished product, you'll feel foolish for ever having doubted this project's potential or in yourself.

Reversed – This card usually indicates defeat, paranoia, resentment, or disrespected boundaries. You feel that all your hard work has been in vain, and you don't even want to try and redeem yourself. You just want to give up, walk away, and never look back. This card may also point to a situation in which you've been working tirelessly, on your own, with no support from others, and this lack of support has led you to feel taken for granted or unappreciated. Perhaps you're building this fence for someone else's sake, and now you realize they are not, or will they ever be, grateful to you. Are you being forced to put up boundaries due to someone else's lack of respect for your personal space? This situation feels unfair, exhausting, and disheartening. Maybe this project isn't worth your time, after all.

Ten of Wands
Imagery
A man carries ten wands in a bundle as he treks across a field. In the distance, we see a house, presumably one that he is in the process of building, as well as a series of trees, representing virility, potency, and growth. The house is a symbol of stability, security, permanence, and rewards. His eyes are fixed on the ground, though. Success is within

reach, but he worries that if he keeps his eyes on the prize, he'll rush it and trip over his own feet.

Interpretation

Upright – This is the final push. After this, you'll be able to set your Wands down, prop your feet up, and enjoy the fruits of your labor. But that can only be done if you stay focused right now. It's a heavy burden and a lot of pressure, but the rewards will be worth it in the end. Don't look at the finish line; focus on maintaining your form to be sure you won't falter at the last minute. Believe in yourself, but don't allow pride, anxiety, or anticipation to distract you.

Reversed – This can be an especially cruel card, implying that everything is about to fall apart just before reaching a state of completion. Think of a structure collapsing under the weight of its own roof. Perhaps you've been taking on too much responsibility, not delegating tasks or sharing the burden, and now that all of the weight is on your shoulders alone, you can't carry it anymore. You may have lived by the motto: "If you want to see things done right, you'll have to do them yourself." It's clear now that this philosophy isn't sustainable. Maybe everything won't be perfect if you pass responsibilities to other members of your team, but if you don't share the load, there won't be any finished product to speak of.

Page of Wands
Imagery
The Page stands alone in a desert landscape with mountainous slopes in the background. He uses his Wand as a walking stick, planting it in the ground, but turns his gaze up toward the sky; he is grounded but ambitious. He wears a feather in his cap, denoting youthful naivety and carefree attitudes, but he also wears a cloak, symbolizing protection and preparation. His tunic is covered in a salamander print; salamanders are the animal representation of the Fire element.

Interpretation
Upright – This character is ambitious and bold but rational and hard-working—a highly effective combination. He has a lot of inspiration and passionate energy, and he's ready to channel these things into a new project or career. Success is more than likely, but it may take some time for him to get there.

Reversed – Upside down, this card may speak to action without forethought, or alternatively, obsessive planning without action. Either a lack of confidence or confidence that is unwarranted. There is a lack of balance here. You can't let yourself get too bogged down in the details, but you also can't overlook them entirely, either.

Knight of Wands
Imagery
The Knight rides a red horse, charging through the same desert landscape where we found the Page of Wands. He holds his wand up in place of a sword or weapon, rearing

his horse up on its hind legs. He wears an armored helmet, elbow pads, and boots, but his torso is unprotected, perhaps because he wants everyone to see the ornate print on his yellow tunic. He also has a cluster of red feathers protruding from his helmet, and the faceguard is displaced, so you can see how handsome he is. The yellow tunic is a symbol of optimism, and the red horse and feathery plumage reference passion and boldness. He looks determined and fierce, ready to play the hero in some kind of battle. But if he's so focused on forward momentum and victory, why is his horse rearing instead of charging? Why isn't his armor more secure? It's possible that this display is more about bravado than it is about action.

Interpretation

Upright – This card references a character who is charming, charismatic, and swoon-worthy, but also probably a bit too arrogant for his own good. He is aiming to impress and willing to play the hero in order to do so. But there may not be much substance beneath the surface. If you're feeling lustful, go for it; he'll be sure to show you a good time, for a while at least. But if you're looking for emotional fulfillment, intellectual depth, or long-term stability and growth, you'd be wise to keep moving.

Reversed – This reversed card points to a lack of follow-through or a false promise. There may be a character in the querent's life that has promised them the world but can't deliver much at all. Be wary of people who oversell themselves; they are masking profound insecurities and trying to distract from their shortcomings.

Queen of Wands

Imagery

The Queen sits comfortably upon her throne with her legs parted, like the Empress, in a sexually inviting position. She holds a Wand in one hand, like a scepter, and a large sunflower in the other; both items are symbols of manifestation, though one speaks to magical creation, while the other references growth in the natural realm. Her throne is adorned with lions, displaying her bravery, power, and inner strength (remember the imagery of the Strength card in the Major Arcana—this illustration echoes the same themes!), and a black cat sits obediently by her feet, serving as a familiar and protector.

Interpretation

Upright – This character has found a nearly perfect balance between youthful masculine energy and feminine intuitive experience. She is totally empowered, confident in her abilities, and loves the life she's created for herself. She exudes confidence but isn't too full of herself. She appreciates the material beauty of the world but also has a mind that wanders into spiritual and mystical realms frequently. She may defy prescribed gender norms, but she is still proud of her traditionally feminine qualities.

Reversed – The empowered queen has become domineering, attention-seeking, temperamental, and overly ambitious. She wants to have it all and doesn't see any reason why she shouldn't be able to take what she wants from others, by force or manipulation if necessary. She is talented but thinks herself better than everyone else, which makes her personality noxious. You do not want to get in her way, nor should you ever rely on her to look out for anyone but herself.

King of Wands
Imagery
The King of Wands sits on a throne decorated with lions and wears a lion-head pendant, symbols of courage, royalty, strength, and power. The points of his crown are in the shape of flames, and he wears a red robe with a yellow cloak to show that his heart is full of passion while his outlook remains inspiring and optimistic. He holds a wand as a scepter and nothing in his other hand; his powers of manifestation are all that he needs to secure and hold his position of power. There is a salamander at his feet, a symbol of the Fire element and alchemy; through his leadership, he aims to create something that is greater than the sum of its parts.

Interpretation
Upright – This character has passion, charisma, experience, and authority. Think King Arthur or Martin Luther King. He is well-suited to leadership, as he is easily able to inspire others to action. He may not have much in the way of wisdom, strength, or emotional depth, but it almost doesn't matter. His intensity and motivation are infectious, and he is able to make you feel like he believes in you, so in the reflection of his gaze, you start to believe in yourself, too. He is persuasive, and with enough support, his words and ideas could move mountains. If you want to maintain faith in him, though, don't prod too far below the surface. His passion makes him a great leader, but

in his personal life, you may find that he is a heartbreaker, two-timer, irresponsible parent, or someone who lacks substance outside of the context of leadership.

Reversed – The King of Wands thrives when he is inspiring others, but what happens when his followers start to question his motives or authority? His egomaniacal motivations start to reveal themselves as he becomes impatient, controlling, contradictory, and dictatorial. You once believed in his mission and passion; perhaps you even thought that he saw something special in you and recognized your potential. Now, you start to wonder if you've been duped. Was it all just an act? A show he put on to get attention, or feel a sense of dominion over other people? This King has developed a God complex, and it is clouding his judgment, as well as revealing an underlying character that isn't much fun to be around.

Chapter 5: The Suit of Cups

Ace of Cups
Imagery
A hand reaches out of the clouds, palm faced up, offering a golden chalice; this cup is the Holy Grail, representing divine love, belief in perfection, and faith in the unknown. The chalice is overflowing, spilling water into a pond below, dotted with lotus flowers, which symbolize renewal, growth, and delicate beauty generated from the tough and mundane (lotuses often grow in the mud). There is a white dove ready to dive into the cup, holding a wafer in its beak. The dove signifies hope, healing, and peace, and the wafer is a Communion wafer, a representation of the Body of Christ that, when consumed, is believed to have transformative powers.

Interpretation

Upright – This card is urging you to keep your heart open and believe in the power of love. This might reference a romantic relationship, but it could also speak to family or friendship, creative endeavors, or spirituality. Swallow your cynicism; true love is real and far more powerful than lust. Somewhere out there is a person, idea, or thing that is so wonderful, so perfect for you, that you would travel to the ends of the earth to find it. But if you don't believe this is possible, it may pass you right by. How can you find something that you're not looking for?

Reversed – Your emotions are repressed, stifled, or blocked, and even if there is love all around you, you can't feel it. Your ideal mate might be trying to flirt with you, but your fear and distrust have become walls built around your heart. You may not even realize that they're working on trying to win you over; you're so closed off. If this reversed card doesn't speak to a relationship, it may imply a creative blockage or inability to see the divine light, even as blessings are illuminated all around you.

Two of Cups
Imagery

A young couple stands, facing one another, each with a cup in one hand, while their free hands are intertwined. They both wear floral wreaths on their heads, symbols of victory and abundance. Over their heads, a winged lion and Caduceus symbol hover. The lion represents passion, courage, and spirit. The Caduceus represents healing. Once these two join forces, there are sure to be good times ahead.

Interpretation
Upright – This card is always a good sign for a querent who is falling in love, as it represents partnership, balance, compromise, and commitment. It carries the same meaning in spreads concerning matters of family or business. The querent will soon join forces with another party, and together, their strength, power, and joy will be more than doubled.

Reversed – This card speaks to a severed connection, broken promise, uncooperative attitude, or conflict. Some form of union in the querent's life, be it romantic or otherwise, is doomed to fall apart. Cut your losses, grieve appropriately, and move on.

Three of Cups
Imagery
Three women in colorful gowns are dancing in a harvest scene, each with a cup raised up for a celebratory toast. The ground around them is littered with pumpkins and ripe fruits, symbols of abundance and gratitude. They all wear wreaths to represent a victory won through cooperative effort.

Interpretation
Upright – This card references a community celebrating the rewards of their cooperative and harmonious efforts. Teamwork makes the dream work! It also reminds us that women can accomplish incredible things when they work together, instead of seeing one another as competitors. There is more than enough to go around here. Now

it's time to let loose and enjoy the fruits of your labor together. Be sure to express your gratitude to one another so that this party can become an annual tradition.

Reversed – Too much of a good thing is sometimes worse than nothing at all. This might speak to daunting levels of excess (gluttony, alcohol abuse, and materialism), social connections getting in the way of productivity, or the reverse: too much work and not enough time to play. Harmony turns to discord, and your social circle may be on its way to disintegration.

Four of Cups
Imagery
A young man sits with his back against the base of a tree, symbolizing male sexual energy and virility. His arms are crossed over his chest, blocking his heart chakra. There are three golden cups on the ground before him, laid out in a row. A fourth cup is offered by a divine hand, reaching down from the clouds, but he won't even look at it. His gaze is fixed on the ground; maybe he thinks this new offering will just be more of the same old song and dance, and he's already had enough.

Interpretation
Upright – By the formulas described in Chapter 3, this card should signify emotional stability, but the figure in the illustration does not appear to be interested in that or open to it. Maybe he's been hurt by past loves and doesn't want to take another risk. Or, perhaps he was hoping for something more exciting—a passion-filled, volatile, melodramatic romance, maybe. But the fourth cup is being offered by a divine hand,

implying that this new emotional connection might be exactly what he needs. Don't dismiss a potential mate or creative opportunity for its lack of flashiness or excitement; those kinds of thrilling relationships are rarely sustainable and usually end in fiery, violent explosions. Don't close yourself off to new experiences out of a sense of fear, either. Later on, you may regret having passed up this chance.

Reversed – The querent is ready to open their heart and seize the next opportunity that comes their way. In fact, they may be a bit *too* eager. In matters of love, emotion, and creativity, you can afford to be a little picky. Don't let yourself feel rushed into a relationship that you have lukewarm feelings about. You don't want to spend the rest of your life with someone you just settled for because you were worried they might be your last shot at love.

Five of Cups
Imagery
A figure in a black mourning cloak stands at a riverbank, gazing down at three cups that have toppled over, spilling their contents; these cups represent failed emotional connections or creative endeavors. She is so focused on her heartbreak that she doesn't even notice the two cups behind her, still standing upright. Across the river, in the distance, there is a castle, representing her ultimate desire for something secure and permanent. We can also see a bridge in the distance that could take her to it if she is willing to pick up the pieces and move on. The river references forward momentum and is a literal illustration of letting past heartbreaks become water under the bridge.

Interpretation

Upright – We all experience heartbreak, loss, and emotional grief from time to time. But we can't allow ourselves to lose sight of gratitude or drown in our own sorrows. However sad or dejected you may feel, try to take stock of all the love and opportunity that you still have at your disposal. Regret and rumination aren't worth much; to find true and lasting happiness, you'll have to pick yourself and keep moving forward.

Reversed – This usually indicates that the querent has hit their low point, and they are ready to start turning things around. This heartbreak has been painful, but they've managed to accept the loss and start healing. Perhaps they're even starting to feel hopeful and motivated to gear up for that journey across the bridge. It is also a sign of forgiveness; the querent was deeply hurt at first, but now sees that their past relationships were never meant to last, and they're better off on their own, now.

Six of Cups
Imagery
Two young children, a boy and a girl, stand in a garden outside a castle's walls. Four cups are planted in the ground as vases, holding flowers. A fifth cup is placed upon a pedestal behind the boy's back, while the sixth is in his hands, being offered to the little girl. The castle walls and guard on patrol in the background contribute to a sense of security and safety. These children are sheltered and happy, but it isn't clear what they're doing or where they're headed next.

Interpretation

Upright – This card refers to joy and abundance but particularly speaks to feelings of nostalgia or youthful idealism. Remember how you used to see the world through rose-colored glasses as a child? You can still capture some of the spirit as an adult. Try to keep yourself young at heart when it comes to matters of love and creativity. Be playful, optimistic, trusting, and open. Love can't thrive without emotional vulnerability.

Reversed – Are you having trouble letting go of the past or over-idealizing it? When a relationship is over, some of us tend to focus on all the good things about it that we miss, forgetting all the misery and conflict that led the relationship to end. Memories can be seductive, but you don't want to get trapped in them. Be mindful; be present; be here, now; and stay open. Nostalgia isn't nearly as fun as looking forward to what lies ahead.

Seven of Cups
Imagery

A figure stands with his back to us, overwhelmed by all the options before him. We see seven golden Cups floating on clouds, each holding the promise of something. One holds a serpent (temptation or lust); another holds a wyvern (strength, power, and vengeance); another, a laurel wreath (victory and acclaim); the next is overflowing with gold coins and jewels (riches and material wealth); the following Cup holds a towering castle (power and authority); the next holds a young maiden's head (love, beauty, and youth); the last Cup has a shrouded figure protruding from it, arms open wide, with a holy aura (spiritual enlightenment). Some see these Cups and their contents as representations of the seven deadly sins. The figure is cast entirely in shadow, leading us to believe that he sees himself as a blank slate and finds all of these options equally enticing.

Interpretation

Upright – At this point, the querent feels overwhelmed by the number of options or opportunities available to them. Perhaps they have several suitors and can't figure out which, if any of them, to give their heart to. Or, maybe these options represent creative opportunities or chances for personal growth. Either way, the querent has to stay mindful of the fact that all these options look great from a distance, but in reality, any path they choose will have its ups and downs. Every choice requires some sacrifice.

Reversed – The querent is in awe of the possibilities laid out before them, but the clock is ticking. If they don't make a choice soon, the decision will be made for them. Opportunities this good don't last long. Take a moment to listen to your gut and figure out what you really want, but don't take too long. Once you identify your heart's desire, it's time to make a move!

Eight of Cups
Imagery
Under a crescent moon, a man walks along the seashore toward the mountains in the distance. The moon references cyclical change and fluctuating emotions, while the mountain represents hurdles or challenges. He leaves a stack of eight golden cups

behind him. The structure he's built is solid; he isn't worried about its stability or longevity, so he moves on, not feeling the need to look back.

Interpretation

Upright – You've built something beautiful and stable, but now, you're feeling a bit bored. Luckily, the relationship or creation you've made is strong enough to stand on its own without your constant presence or vigilance. You can afford to wander off on your own for a while to do some soul-searching and reinvigorate yourself with some challenging experiences. Most likely, whatever you've built will be able to withstand the tests of distance and time apart.

Reversed – This is a sign that you've outgrown your current relationship or circumstances, but you can't bring yourself to walk away. Or, alternatively, it might mean that you're jumping ship at the first sign of trouble. One of the greatest keys to happiness is knowing when to let go and when to stick around and fight it out.

Nine of Cups

Imagery

A plump-faced man with a plush feathered cap sits on a bench by a banquet table. Nine golden cups are set upon it, creating a semi-circle around him. His arms are crossed, but not in defiance; his posture implies satisfaction, and they also make him look a little smug. What could one man want with all of this abundance, sitting all by himself? He has far more than he needs, and he appears to be loving it.

Interpretation

Upright – This card speaks to emotional fulfillment, success, gratitude, satisfaction, and wishes coming true. If it falls in a future position in your spread, it implies that you will soon find yourself with more success and happiness than you ever dreamed possible. Since this is a Cup card, it may foretell a lasting love that seems almost too good to be true (but isn't—this is the real thing), or a period of emotional stability and joy after a spell of depression.

Reversed – The reversed Nine of Cups embodies the spirit of a popular idiom: "Be careful what you wish for." Too much of a good thing, like sugar or alcohol, can leave you feeling sick, and love is no exception to that rule. Maybe you thought you wanted a lover who would focus all of their attention on you and show total honesty and emotional vulnerability; in reality, though, that lover turns out to be obsessive, overly sensitive, too honest, and high maintenance. Overindulgences should be tempered, and goals carefully considered before they are pursued. Aim to restore a sense of balance in your life.

Ten of Cups

Imagery

Four figures stand in a golden field, overlooking a river, trees, and a small house in the distance. The two adults, a man and woman, stand with one arm, each wrapped around the other, while their free hands stretch up toward the sky in jubilation, awe, or perhaps gratitude; through their love, they have been able to manifest a glorious and rewarding existence for themselves. Meanwhile, their two children hold hands as they dance in circles, representing innocence and the continuation of the cycle of life. There is a rainbow arc overhead made of ten golden Cups, symbolizing divine blessings and the power that love has to bridge the gap between heaven and earth.

Interpretation

Upright – This card often points to a feeling of true contentment. The querent may be approaching a state of domestic bliss, creative fulfillment, financial stability, or an abundance of love in their family, social circle, or a spiritual community—perhaps they're even lucky enough to have all of the above. This is their "happily ever after" moment; life is peaceful, and the future holds promise. They no longer feel the need to search for something more.

Reversed – The querent has created a life that they thought would bring them lasting happiness, but instead, there's trouble brewing. This card often points to family drama, dysfunctional romantic or business relationships, financial strife, or personal dissatisfaction. Maybe things look great on the surface, but true happiness comes in all kinds of shapes and sizes. If there's a persistent nagging voice inside, telling you this situation isn't working, it might be time to listen and think about making some major changes.

Page of Cups
Imagery
The Knight of Cups stands on a platform with his back to the ocean. He holds a golden Cup and makes eye contact, and smiles at the fish who is poking his head up over its rim.

The fish, like most sea creatures in Tarot, is a symbol of subconscious emotions and knowledge rising up to the surface. The Page isn't afraid or doubtful of these subconscious messages; instead, he welcomes them.

Interpretation

Upright – The Page of Cups is inexperienced, but his youthful energy allows him to be deeply in touch with his emotions without having to make much of an effort. He is naturally insightful and might have a habit of speaking profound truths in a casual manner or seeming to read people's minds just by looking at them. Though others may not value his intuitive wisdom due to his lack of authority or whimsical nature, he has a knack for telling people, even his elders, exactly what they need to hear at the precise moment that they need to hear it. Maybe he's never been in love but somehow manages to offer advice on your marriage that saves you from the brink of a messy divorce. He is curious and empathetic, sensitive, creative, and emotionally wise beyond his years, though he may not be conscious of his peculiar talents. Whatever his biological age, he is young at heart and idealistic.

Reversed – Sometimes, childlike qualities aren't terribly charming. This card might represent a character who is inexcusably emotionally immature and has no intention of growing up. Maybe his refusal to grow or conform to societal norms stems from an unaddressed past trauma or deep emotional wound; you'd like to feel sympathy for him, but his melodramatic, selfish, oversensitive, and defensive attitude makes it darn near impossible. Pages are often seen as messengers, so this reversed Page might symbolize a person who lacks tact and hurts people's feelings casually, without even noticing or someone who takes perverse pleasure in being the bearer of bad news.

Knight of Cups
Imagery
The Knight of Cups rides on the back of a white horse (symbolizing forward momentum and purity of intention) with his back straight and a golden chalice held up in one hand, ready to offer or receive love. He's headed toward a river, and once he crosses it, he'll reach a rocky mountain range covered in trees. The trees symbolize male sexual potency, and the mountains speak of challenges ahead. His quest for love may not be easy, but he is prepared for the journey and unintimidated.

He bears no weapon, and he doesn't spur his steed to hurry. He wears a suit of armor with his face exposed and a blue tunic covered in a red fish pattern; again, the fishes represent subconscious feelings being acknowledged and expressed. His helmet and boots are adorned with the wings of Mercury, the god of eloquence. He has a soldier's poise and resolve but the heart and mind of a poet.

Interpretation
Upright – If any of the Knight cards can be characterized as a true Prince Charming, this is the one. The Knight of Cups is more experienced and emotionally mature than the Page of his suit but still a romantic, empathetic, and sensitive soul. He is able to accurately identify his emotions and communicate about them in a healthy, effective manner, recognizing that unexpressed feelings tend to stew and turn sour the longer

they are held inside. If he has any faults in love, it is perhaps that he acts on emotions without considering the practical side of a matter. This is the type who might show up at your place of work the day after your first date with a bouquet of roses and a box of chocolates, not understanding that, while you appreciate the generosity of this gesture, you find it somewhat inappropriate and embarrassing. His heart's in the right place, though.

Reversed – With this card, we find a character whose romantic idealism has become formulaic or manipulative. Are you in a romance with someone who, despite ticking all your boxes and seeming to be committed to the relationship, treats you a bit too much like a paper doll? Do you get the feeling that the love notes and gifts you're receiving from him are somewhat generic, pulled straight from a one-size-fits-all romance manual? Perhaps things are feeling too lovey-dovey and sappy sweet all the time; there's no real emotional depth or a refusal to acknowledge unpleasant realities. Or, maybe you're starting to realize that he turns passive-aggressive when he feels undervalued or doesn't get what he wants. It's time to work on lifting the veil and figuring out who this person really is, below the surface. You're not playing house here; real love can't be sunshine and roses all the time.

Queen of Cups
Imagery
The Queen's throne is built upon the seashore, so close to the water that it's hard to tell where folds of her gown end and the ocean begins. Her throne is adorned with cherubs, water nymphs, and seashells, showing us that her emotional and intuitive depth

provides her with access to the spirit world and metaphysical plane. Her gown is white (representing pure intent), and her cloak is blue with red trim; the blue represents the Water element and all its connotations, so the cloak's design tells us that she values her emotional and intuitive knowledge as power and a shield but keeps her passionate nature reigned in, somewhat privately, only showing it to a select few trusted individuals.

The Cup she holds is more ornate than any other depicted in this suit, including the Holy Grail portrayed on the Ace card. It looks more like a trophy than a chalice, covered in jewels and decorative carvings. The King of this suit may have more authority or experience, but in terms of emotional wealth and psychic ability, there is no question: the Queen reigns supreme.

Interpretation

Upright – This character is perhaps the most traditionally feminine in the entire deck. She is deeply sensitive, intuitive, nurturing, creative, and emotionally focused. Her heart seems to be overflowing with love, empathy, and generosity of spirit. Whatever you're going through, no matter how complex or difficult it is to explain, she understands. She's not happy all the time; in fact, she believes that all emotional experiences are equally valuable. When she's happy, she's downright gleeful, but if she's sad, she may have a tendency to wallow, enjoying the catharsis of a good long cry. You'd do well to treat her with reciprocity and respect, though, and be careful not to take advantage of her time or attention. Anger is another emotion that she doesn't shy away from, and if you provoke her, you may live to regret it.

Reversed – This character is the queen of melodrama. She feels her own emotions deeply—too deeply, as some might say—but doesn't seem to have much compassion or patience for other people's feelings. She might burst into tears at the drop of a hat, unable to handle even the slightest criticism or spot of miscommunication. If you're having a bad day and don't offer her a smile or hug, she may be deeply hurt. Her emotions are often used to manipulate people, too; she might exploit sympathy to get attention, use false kindness to win someone over, or sob to avoid being held accountable for her actions. She tends to take up all of the emotional space in any room, romantic relationship, or social group, leaving others exhausted, stifled, and frustrated.

King of Cups
Imagery
The King's throne sits upon a platform floating in the middle of the ocean. In the water behind him, we see a ship sailing, representing the ability to navigate through a vast sea of emotions, and a leaping fish, representing subconscious feelings being expressed. His throne has a minimalist design, signifying his ability to rest upon a foundation of rationality and stability. He wears a blue robe, signifying a core of emotional wealth, under a yellow and red cloak, signifying optimism and passion, respectively. He holds a golden chalice, but also a scepter; his emotions are kept in balance with his power and responsibility.

Interpretation

Upright — This card represents a character who has mastered emotional balance and understands their power without letting them run his life. He feels things deeply, but he also knows that it isn't always constructive to express his emotions or dwell in them. Furthermore, he is able to keep emotions inside when necessary, without allowing them to fester or become repressed. He probably values his romantic partner, family, friends, or religious community above all else and is able to teach them the true nature of unconditional love by leading through example. Even if his lover has been unfaithful, or his child throws a temper tantrum and says that they hate him, he is able to hold love in his heart for these people in the midst of an argument. He is deeply compassionate but also a master of maintaining emotional boundaries. He can empathize with someone in grief or fury without letting their emotions drag him down. This is the kind of partner or father figure (or mother figure, if the card represents a female in the querent's life) that we all wish we could have. His greatest flaw is his tendency to put the needs of others before his own. He might be the type to try and stay strong at a funeral in order to support others in grief, only to break down in tears the moment he gets home to a private space.

Reversed — Upside down, this King is the worst kind of emotionally immature person. He fancies himself an expert in matters of love and life, but in truth, all of the love he offers is conditional. His internal motto is: "If you love me, I will show you kindness. If you hurt me, I will hurt you back, and worse." The worst part is he isn't self-aware of this defensive emotional instinct and refuses to acknowledge the problematic aspects of his behavior. He might have ten failed relationships under his belt, all of which followed a similar trajectory and ended in the same way, but he'll refuse to acknowledge the pattern in his behavior; instead, he'll just blame everything on his ex-lovers.

He also has trouble keeping his emotions in check, flying into rages or tears of anguish or hysterical laughing fits at wildly inappropriate times. He is stuck inside his own emotional cage and has a very hard time empathizing with others or recognizing that they might feel things just as deeply as he does. One easy way to identify this character is this: he can't apologize directly to anyone that he may have hurt or treated unfairly, even if he is able to acknowledge his wrongdoings and admit them to other, uninvolved parties. That kind of emotional vulnerability terrifies him. Still, he expects you to grovel at his feet if you've offended him. His emotional hypocrisy could drive you mad, especially because you may feel that it's far easier to indulge his absurd behaviors than it is to stand up for yourself or establish boundaries. He may look like an adult, but inside, he's basically a toddler.

Chapter 6: The Suit of Swords

Ace of Swords
Imagery
A divine hand reaches out of the clouds to offer a sword, with its blade pointing straight up—again, a pointedly phallic symbol, much like the Ace of Wands. This sword is topped with a crown, however, and a strand of a green leafy vine, which the sword has pierced and cut in two pieces. The crown simultaneously represents regal authority, as well as the crown chakra, a portal to divine insight and wisdom. The vine symbolizes the earthly element; the sword, representing thought, has broken through, or overcome, material reality.

There are six golden sparks hovering above the sword's hilt, representing inspiration or the moment of intellectual breakthrough—the "eureka!" moment. The landscape below is stark, with a collection of grey mountains, symbolizing rigidity and rationality. The clouds hint at an uncertainty or a lack of mental clarity.

Interpretation

Upright – The Ace of Swords heralds the message of truth. This card embodies the raw energy of the entire suit concerning matters of communication, philosophy, intellect, and spiritual wisdom. Aces often represent beginnings, so this card might point to the flash of inspiration or curiosity that leads you to a new intellectual or academic path. But the Sword suit, more so than any other, is often double-edged. This card can also warn of an upcoming conflict or difficulty in communication. The truth will prevail, but that doesn't mean that everyone will be happy about it. A lot of people resent the power of the Sword because it forces them to confront realities they'd rather not see.

Reversed – Upside down, this card points to confusion, intellectual lethargy, or mental anguish. The querent may be feeling that their brain has become their own worst enemy, or wishes that they could escape their thoughts for a while. Past dishonesty may be nagging at their conscience, or a source of cognitive dissonance might be giving them a headache. Alternatively, they may be growing tired of banging their head against the wall, trying to work out a problem that seems to have no logical solution. The desire to numb the mind with substance abuse or material distractions is powerful. Try to find a way to give your brain a break without killing too many brain cells in the process; your mind is your most powerful tool and weapon.

Two of Swords

Imagery

A woman sits on a platform, turning her back to a large body of water under a crescent moon. The moon and the water symbolize flux, intuition, and emotional depth. Not only has the woman turned away from these elements—she wears a blindfold as well, aiming to be entirely rational, unswayed by her feelings. She holds up two swords with her arms crossed over her chest, forming an X shape, symbolizing a choice or crossroads. In this stance, she is blocking her heart chakra, representing the fact that she is not open to considering emotional motivations in whatever decision she must make.

Interpretation

Upright – This card points to a choice that the querent must make between two seemingly equal, but opposite, paths. The woman's blindfolds indicate not only a desire to be impartial, like Lady Justice but also her lack of willingness to look for a way to move forward. The querent might be delaying action, hoping that patience will eventually serve to clarify which option is preferable; however, they may also be in denial or stuck on the fence, not wanting to take sides or commit to one path over another.

Reversed – This card either indicates a lack of balance between two choices or the need to choose quickly, lest the decision is made for you. Either the answer is obvious, or one option has already been taken off the table. If the upright card symbolizes being stuck at the crossroads, the reversed Two of Swords represents the point at which the querent knows for certain which path they will take.

Three of Swords

Imagery

A large red heart hangs in the sky amidst a sea of grey storm clouds and rainfall. It is pierced by three swords, each crossing the others to form a sort of asterisk shape. These symbolic elements tell us that the heart is under attack; thoughts, uncertainty, and anger are all working against feelings of love and emotional vulnerability.

Interpretation

Upright – This card most often points to heartbreak or spell of depression. Whether the querent's sadness is justified or not, his or her thought patterns have become ruminative, cynical, and irrational. Whatever circumstance is inspiring this mood, it isn't serving you. It's time to look for a way out—find a new path that will lead you to a brighter outlook.

Reversed – The reversed Three of Swords speaks to emotional healing and mental recuperation. The querent is finding effective ways to stop negative thought patterns in their tracks and balance the needs of the heart with the needs of the head. The storm is passing, the mind is clear, and the heart will soon be open to love once more.

Four of Swords

Imagery

Inside a church, below a stained-glass window, a man is laid to rest atop a platform that could be a coffin or a stone bed; this figure isn't necessarily dead. He may simply be resting. His hands are arranged in the position of prayer, symbolizing his need for divine guidance through his healing journey. There are three Swords hung on the wall above him, blades pointing down toward his body, possibly signifying past victories in hard-fought battles. The fourth Sword is laid beneath him, parallel to his spine, inside the coffin, representing the defeat which he is now recovering from.

Interpretation

Upright – This card may be viewed as a representation of recovery from a serious physical injury, but it is more likely to speak to recuperation from a mental wound or breakdown. This is often a situation in which the querent has been forced into a rest period, rather than taking a break voluntarily. Perhaps they've become addicted to some form of stress and learned to normalize it. The body and mind can only work in harmony when both are well-fed and well-rested, though. It usually recommends meditation, contemplation, and self-reflection. There is a reason you ended up in this position; think carefully about how you can avoid repeating this unhealthy cycle.

Reversed – Your rest period has come to an end, and you are ready to get back into the swing of things. You are now well-rested, and hopefully, you've learned something valuable from this forced time-out. You feel mentally energized and ready to jump back in with both feet. Make sure you have a game plan, this time, to avoid burnout. Your mind and body will both thank you for it.

Five of Swords

Imagery

On a platform beside a body of water, under a grey clouded sky, three male figures stand in the aftermath of a battle. There are five swords represented on this card, but two lay fallen upon the ground, while the remaining three are all in the hands of one individual. The apparent victor has turned his back to the water, representing an abandonment of emotion and empathy, though he does glance over his shoulder at the defeated figures with a smug smirk. The defeated men face the water. Heads bent low in sorrow and humiliation. The victor seems pleased with himself and looks down on his former adversaries. He appears to feel no remorse about the fact that he only won by rigging the game in his favor.

Interpretation

Upright – This card speaks to a situation in which someone has decided that they will prevail by any means necessary—even if they have to cheat, lie, steal, or harm someone else. It implies callousness, betrayal, indifference to emotion, and calculated cruelty. It also usually indicates that these attitudes will secure a victory—but at what cost? The important question is: does this figure represent the querent? Or someone else in their life who intends to screw them over? In certain contexts, this card specifically warns that someone close to the querent will betray their trust in order to take what is not rightfully theirs.

Reversed – The reversal of this card doesn't change its underlying meaning by much; it mostly alters the timeframe. It points to the experience of recovery after a betrayal. The querent is learning to trust again, both in their own judgment and in the inherent goodness of others. They are also likely learning a difficult but important lesson: you cannot win in a fight against a brick wall. Cruel and merciless people don't regret the pain they've caused to others, and you can't convince them to change, no matter how hard you try. Best to pick up the broken pieces and move on; otherwise, you'll just keep giving them further opportunities to rub salt in your wounds.

Six of Swords

Imagery

Under a grey sky, a man stands in the back of a boat, helping to ferry a cloaked woman and child through a body of water. Six swords are planted in the front of the boat, positioned as if to shield or hide them. On one side of the boat, the waters are choppy, but on the other side, they are calm and flat as polished glass. Expect smooth sailing ahead.

Interpretation

Upright – This card is about moving on from a period of loss, grief, or strife. The querent is navigating their way out of a bad situation, finding a new path or perhaps even a new home. There is still a sense of shame or fear, though, as implied by the arrangement of the Swords; physically, you're moving on but still carrying some damage from the past with you. It also implies heroism and supportive action; the three figures in this card are all in the boat together, though it appears as though the woman alone has her head bent low in mourning. It's okay to lean on others when you don't feel strong enough to stand on your own.

In a more literal sense, this card may be interpreted as a good omen for travel by water, particularly as a means of mental recovery from depression, heartbreak, or betrayal. Getting over a loss is always hard, but doing it on a cruise ship may help to ease the process a great deal.

Reversed – This implies that the querent is stuck in a destructive pattern and can't seem to break free. Perhaps they are swimming against the current, going nowhere fast, and exhausting themselves. They are trying their best but can't move forward. Alternatively, it may be viewed as a bad travel omen—avoid boats, for the time being.

Seven of Swords
Imagery
A man sneaks through a military camp on tiptoe, stealing a bundle of Swords. There are five Swords slung over his shoulder and two more within reach. He smiles at them, considering how much he can get away with taking without slowing himself down. There is a cluster of soldiers in the distance, but they don't appear to see the thief in action.

Interpretation
Upright – Traditionally, this card speaks to theft and stealth. Since Sword cards often represent matters of the mind, this may particularly warn against an intellectual theft or

a stealthy betrayal. Has your best friend managed to seduce your lover and done so right under your nose? It's important to note that the thief in the card seems quite pleased with himself. Whatever will be stolen from the querent, the thief isn't likely to feel guilty about it. Or, perhaps the thief represents the querent in this case, in which case, they'll have to carefully consider: how much can you get away with before you are caught? Is it worth the risk?

Reversed – If the querent has been robbed of something, this card usually implies the return of stolen goods. If the querent is the thief, this is a warning: someone is onto you, and you'll soon be caught red-handed.

Eight of Swords
Imagery
A woman stands on a sandy shore amidst puddles of water, blindfolded and bound with her hands behind her back. She is surrounded by eight Swords planted in the sand. At first glance, we are moved to feel sympathy for her, but then we realize that she is standing still, despite the fact that her legs are not bound. This is perhaps a prison that she created for herself. In the distant background, we see a lone castle built atop a high mountain range: another representation of self-imposed restraint.

Interpretation
Upright – This card often speaks to a conundrum or sense of captivity, which the querent can blame on no one but themselves. It may reference a mental prison or a cyclical problem. For instance, perhaps the querent feels a sense of obligation to

someone whose values fundamentally contradict their own and is repeatedly asked to do things that betray their morals. Or, maybe they are feeling overloaded and run down but they are too proud to ask anyone for help. There is an easy way out of this situation, but the querent is blind to the possibility of escape. Deep introspection is recommended here in order to find a way to self-liberation.

Reversed – This card is about freedom and relief. It might be about quitting an unnecessarily stressful job, leaving a bad relationship, escaping an abusive situation, or maybe just a major attitude change. You may not even have realized how constricted you were before, but now that you're liberated, you can't imagine ever going back to those restraints.

Nine of Swords
Imagery
In the dark of night, a female sits upright in bed, her face buried in her hands. Nine swords hover above the bed, parallel to her mattress. The bedframe is engraved with illustrated scenes, one of which clearly depicts a duel or battle.

Interpretation
Upright – This card frequently refers to nightmares or a disturbance of conscience that is preventing healthy sleep. It might describe obsessive rumination over a past betrayal, in which the querent was either the victim or the traitor. It could also point to mental anguish over fears and anxieties.

Reversed — Worries and fears have been put to rest, and now the querent is able to get a good night's sleep. This card may also indicate that someone who has caused harm to the querent is now riddled with guilt, unable to sleep at night. In some contexts, it may speak to someone's inability to wake from a nightmare or extract themselves from a damaging situation.

Ten of Swords
Imagery
A man lies face down in the sand, with ten Swords staked in his back like fence posts. Despite his many wounds, there is no blood spilled on the shore; furthermore, his body is half-covered in a blanket, which the Swords also pierce. He did not struggle against this attack; it seems like he laid down, put himself to sleep, and accepted this defeat willingly. His head is turned toward the distant landscape: a large, calm body of water, a shallow mountain range, and the hint of a sunrise.

Interpretation
Upright — People often view this card as a depiction of an ultimate betrayal or injury, but by observing the illustration closely, and remembering the element + numerological value formula, we can see that its meaning isn't quite so simple. The man in the card isn't physically wounded—it's his mind that's truly causing him pain. This card may reference guilt, atonement, or acceptance of a punishment that is deserved. If it does reference a betrayal, it might be one that the querent should have seen coming a long time ago—maybe they didn't deserve this suffering, but, in some sense, they did ask for it. There is definitely a silver lining to this card, shown in the distant sunrise; the

querent will undoubtedly learn and grow from this experience. Sometimes, we have to hit rock bottom before we can see the light. Suffering can be transformative.

Reversed — This reversed card indicates that the querent is on the road to recovery and lasting change. They've been given a chance at a fresh start, and they are ready to make the most of it. Mistakes have been made, but they have learned their lesson, and now it's time to turn over a new leaf.

Page of Swords
Imagery
The Page stands on a grassy hill with a Sword held over his shoulder and feet in a dancer's position as though ready to strike at a moment's notice. Behind him, we see a partially cloudy sky and a flock of birds overhead; the clouds are parting, and clarity is on the way. He wears yellow tights, representing his optimism, and a red tunic and boots, representing passion and boldness.

Interpretation
Upright — This character is inexperienced, but his mind is sharp. He has a curious and decisive nature, so he tends to set to work on solving problems that most others just shrug their shoulders over. If he deciphers a potential solution, he sees no reason not to put his ideas into action straight away. He is intelligent and independent, and though his words usually ring true, they may not be delivered tactfully. Unfortunately, not everyone appreciates this tendency; his comments and advice may sometimes be seen as presumptuous or impertinent. He has likely been called a smart aleck a few times in his

life. He may also be a touch defensive, unable to admit when he is wrong. He speaks the truth religiously, though, so his honesty may be a breath of fresh air in circles where bravado and false fronts have become the norm.

Reversed – This character believes himself to be far smarter and more capable than he actually is. He tends to speak and act without much forethought and confuses his opinions, beliefs, and feelings with proven facts. He has a tendency to get in over his head a lot, especially in competitions or conflicts with those who are far more experienced than he. He might even have a particularly mean streak, too, using cruelty to overrule others when his wits fail him. Furthermore, he may be reluctant to submit himself to guidance, instruction, or education. He's a know-it-all who doesn't actually know that much.

Knight of Swords
Imagery
Beneath a stormy sky, the Knight of Swords charges full steam ahead on the back of a white horse, sword raised in the air, ready to strike. His intention is pure, but his attitude is fierce; we can see by his facial expression that he means business, and mercy isn't on his agenda. He wears a full suit of armor, prepared for a true battle, and a red cape, as well as red feathers in his helmet; passion is what spurs him forward, as well as duty and honor.

Interpretation

Upright – This card describes a character who is determined to do the right thing, even if it is hard and even if the situation doesn't concern them. The Knight is a true hero: the kind of person who regularly stands up against injustice and works to defend the weak against bullies and autocrats. He also believes strongly in truth, so if he hears someone telling lies about you, he won't think twice about speaking up to defend your honor. He is brave, bold, assertive, honest, and direct. He's also someone who acts quickly, rather than waiting around to see if a situation will settle down on its own. He is a protector and may be looked up to by many. The trouble is, he doesn't appear terribly friendly to the casual observer; instead, he's probably a bit intimidating. He also may have trouble seeing the error in his ways if he misreads a situation and immediately inserts himself into it. He is probably no stranger to the phrase: "Mind your own business!"

Reversed – The reversed Knight of Swords represents someone who talks a lot about doing the right thing, but when push comes to shove, they usually rest on their laurels or run away and hide. He may feel a sense of impotence, unable to act on his beliefs. Or, if he does take action, his behavior is largely misunderstood. Perhaps, in an attempt to defend someone from an oppressor, he allows himself to be more violent or domineering than is necessary, and suddenly, he becomes the bully that everyone fears. This character would do well to spend a bit more time working to balance their thoughts and actions. No one likes to take advice from a hypocrite; make sure your rhetoric matches your behavior.

Queen of Swords

Imagery

The Queen sits in profile on a throne decorated with cherubic faces. She wears a crown of butterflies and holds her Sword upright, echoing the stance of Lady Justice, while her free hand is raised in benediction. Her lips are set in a stern expression.

In the background, we see clouds settling while a lone bird soars through the clear skies overhead. Behind her throne, in the distance, we see trees, representing masculine sexual energy; some cartomancers infer that this symbolizes her identity as a widow or a woman who has learned a great deal from the loss of a past love. Others see this as an implication that her rulership is supported by men.

Interpretation

Upright – This is a character who is ruled by rationality and values truth above all else. She is professional, knowledgeable, and a bit perfectionistic. Some see her as a visionary; she isn't swayed by the whims of emotional flux but still has a creative mind. She is a fair judge of character and believes that honesty and integrity should be rewarded. She has a level-headed demeanor, a cool temper, and a sharp mind. See those tightly sealed lips? She isn't one to speak before thinking, nor does she like having to repeat herself, so when she does open her mouth, you'd be wise to listen carefully. She can be generous-minded, but she won't suffer fools gladly.

Reversed – The reversed Queen of Swords represents a character whose judgmental attitude is manifested in bitterness, manipulation, derision, and perhaps even cruelty.

Her experiences have turned her into a cynical and stingy person who isn't willing to give most people a first chance, let alone a second. She is still a seeker of truth and justice but has lost sight of the fact that all humans err from time to time, and nobody is perfect. All her energy is directed toward her mind, and she is out of touch with her emotional body.

King of Swords
Imagery
The King sits, facing us squarely, on a tall throne decorated with butterflies, which symbolize growth and transformation, as well as the Air element; he believes that his mental prowess as a leader will allow him to foster change. He holds a Sword in one hand while his other hand rests in his lap; truth and knowledge are the only tools he needs to rule effectively. He wears a cloak and headdress under his crown so that the only flesh exposed is on his face and hands; he is well-protected and uncomfortable with vulnerability.

Interpretation
Upright – The King of Swords is an intellectual or philosophical leader who is known for his high level of intelligence. He has mastered the realm of logic and is often someone that people turn to for answers to complex quandaries. He is highly rational and rarely emotional, even around friends and family. His authority resides in his ability to make fair and balanced decisions that are not swayed by sympathy or compassion; this is the sort of person who believes that laws must serve one as they serve all and that exceptions to rules should rarely be made for the sake of mercy. There is a spiritual

element to his wisdom, as well; he believes his primary responsibility is to discover and advance the truth, leaving matters of karmic justice up to a higher power.

Reversed – This card represents a person whose mind is sharp enough to use logic and philosophical reasoning to manipulate others. He is a master of gaslighting, trickery, logical fallacies, and intellectual cruelty. Think, for instance, of a scientist who uses the study of eugenics to justify the sterilization or extermination of another race. He can be condescending and callous but defends his unsavory attitudes by eschewing personal responsibility for them. "It's not me," he might say, raising his hands in a feigned gesture of innocence, "these are just the facts!" He has no integrity, so don't bother engaging in an argument with him; you'll likely only end up infuriated and defeated because he will never admit that he could be wrong. As a leader, he has a tendency toward tyrannical behavior.

Chapter 7: The Suit of Pentacles

Ace of Pentacles
Imagery
A hand reaches out the clouds, offering a golden Pentacle coin: financial and material blessings are in store. The landscape below is a lush, green garden with a trellis gateway, through which we glimpse mountains in the distance. These material gifts will transform you and take you places, but they may become burdensome or challenging at times. Are you ready to receive this abundance and all the potential blessings or curses that may come with it?

Interpretation

Upright – This card is considered a sign of good luck and new beginnings. A new business venture or financial opportunity is on the horizon. It can also be a sign that a dream is about to materialize; that could apply to prosperity, creativity, or fertility.

Reversed – The reversed Ace of Pentacles is a sign of an anticipated opportunity that never materializes or works that never come to fruition. You may have been promised the world, but this card warns you not to hold your breath. It may be some time before you see results if you ever see any at all.

Two of Pentacles
Imagery
A young man in a jester's costume juggles two Pentacles within an infinity loop, but his feet are not grounded, and he looks worried; he is trying to maintain balance but he can barely manage the load. Behind him, in the distance, we see an unrealistic representation of the ocean with a topsy-turvy surface, like a series of hills, with trade ships rising and falling on its slopes; this represents the difficulty of handling the unpredictable ups and downs of the financial market.

Interpretation
Upright – This card represents a situation in which the querent is trying to have it all, as they are unable to make a choice between two disparate elements, but the workload is almost too much for them to handle. This might represent the balance between work and home life, juggling two jobs or career tracks, trying to please too many people with

your work, or stretching your money too thin. The Pentacle suit and Earth element are both concerned with financial matters, but also with rationality, practicality, and physical health; this card is urging you to choose one path or slow down before you burn out. You can't keep juggling if your body gives out.

Reversed – This card is a warning that you have to set aside one of your tasks or responsibilities before you end up dropping the ball. The current situation isn't just unsustainable—you've already gone past your limit, and the overload is going to catch up with you soon. Time to make a serious change, or failure and ruin lie ahead.

Three of Pentacles
Imagery
Three figures stand in a church; a member of the clergy and a member of the nobility stand together to confer and advise a painter who is working on a painting installation. Over their heads, we see three Pentacles built into the interior roof of the building. Together, they'll work cooperatively to create something beautiful, inspiring, and permanent.

Interpretation
Upright – This card represents cooperative creativity in its highest form. There is a creative passion, divine inspiration, and financial support; what more could you need? This card also references apprenticeship, guidance, and learning; the painter on the card is quite young, but he's being offered an incredible opportunity. Talent can only go so far

on a theoretical level; if you want to achieve great things someday, you'll have to start with hands-on experience.

Reversed – Talent isn't everything. This card speaks to talents misused or underdeveloped, a failure to pay attention to details, or an inability to manifest a finished product. It can also represent poor quality work or a problem collaborating with others. Don't get ahead of yourself; talent is one thing, and skill is another. You'll need a balance of both elements in order to find success.

Four of Pentacles
Imagery
A man sits on a high platform with his back to the sprawling metropolis behind him. He wears a crown with a Pentacle atop his head. There are also two Pentacles on the ground, pinned down by his feet, and a fourth Pentacle in his arms. It's hard to tell whether he is proud of these golden coins or worried about letting them slip through his fingers; his grip seems a bit too tight for him to feel secure in his wealthy status. There are so many options available to him, but he appears uninterested; all he wants to focus on is holding onto his gold.

Interpretation
Upright – With all this success and prosperity, you should be feeling secure enough to let loose, relax, take some risks, and live a little. But for some reason, you're reluctant to take your eye off your purse strings. This card represents selfishness, greed, stinginess,

and irrational hoarding. You can afford to be generous at this point. The only reason we make money is to spend it, so spread some of that wealth around!

Reversed – This card is a call to let go of some wealth, material possessions, or irrational fears. Karma will ensure your generosity is returned to you and magnified. Try to have some faith in the universe to look after your material needs, rather than trying to control everything yourself.

Five of Pentacles
Imagery
Outside a church, two vagabonds trudge through a snowstorm, their faces anguished. One uses crutches and wears a bell around his neck—a sign of leprosy. People are too busy fearing contagion to feel any sympathy or offer charity to these poor, unfortunate souls. Most keep their distance when they hear them coming. But the stained-glass window of the church, decorated with five Pentacles, offers a sliver of hope, warmth, and shelter. They may be able to survive the winter if the Church takes them in.

Interpretation
Upright – This card is usually a sign of misfortune or ill health. Help is available, though, so long as you aren't too frightened or ashamed to ask for it. It may feel undignified to appeal to those who look down on you, but what else can you do?

Reversed – This reversed card is a sign that the querent has already hit rock bottom. Things can't get any worse; the only way forward is up now. If someone is offering you a hand, take it now, and get yourself back up on your feet.

Six of Pentacles
Imagery
A nobleman stands before two kneeling beggars. He holds a scale in one hand as he drops coins from his opposite palm, offering charity. It seems he is only interested in helping one of the men kneeling before him; the scales tell us that he is concerned with fairness and justice, so he is selective about whom he shares his wealth with.

Interpretation
Upright – This card is about giving or receiving acts of generosity, charity, or mercy. It also speaks to the karmic aspects of economic growth. By giving to others, we can enrich our own lives. There is no shame in accepting help when you need it, either.

Reversed – This card might indicate that you have the power to help someone in need, but for whatever reason, you are reluctant to open up your wallet or offer a supportive hand. Perhaps you are placing judgment upon those less fortunate than yourself. It might also indicate that the querent is the one in need, stubbornly refusing to ask for assistance in spite of their desperation. Whichever position you're in, make an effort to reach across the divide and establish a connection.

Seven of Pentacles

Imagery

A young man stands in a garden, leaning on a rake, admiring the results of his hard work. He's compiled six Pentacles into a statue, of sorts, along with lush green vines. There is one Pentacle left on the ground that still needs to be added to the pile. He'll complete his task soon, but for now, he's happy to stop and smell the roses. He's earned a break.

Interpretation

Upright – This card represents growth and progress toward material goals and the ability to feel proud of your work before the finished product is fully manifested. Enjoying the work is half the battle; happiness isn't only found through completion. This is also a reminder that slow and steady wins the race: working slowly usually means you're focusing on detail and quality.

Reversed – Upside down, this card speaks to impatience in productivity. Perhaps the querent is unable to maintain a vision of the finished product or ultimate goal and has started to lose interest in the work. Or, maybe they are losing stamina due to an absence of rewards or praise. Try to keep your eyes on the prize; it's tough to sell an unfinished piece.

Eight of Pentacles
Imagery
A young carpenter sits at his bench and hammers an engraved Pentacle shape into a golden disc. There are six finished Pentacles hung on the wall ahead of him, and an eighth on the ground by his feet, next in line for the workbench. His gaze is focused on the hammer, representing attention to detail and due diligence, and he wears a serene smile. It's hard work, but he seems to be enjoying himself.

Interpretation
Upright – This card represents progress, focus, productivity, and determination. It also calls to mind the mood of a proud and contented artisan. When you enjoy your work, the hours can fly by, and creative energy flows easily. Furthermore, your skills and talents are enhanced with every passing day.

Reversed – You've made quite a bit of progress, but now you're growing tired or distracted, and the quality of your work is slipping. This might reference sloppy craftsmanship or careless mistakes made at the office. You yearn for new creative inspiration, a change of scenery, or an entirely new career path. Something needs to change soon because you're on the verge of burning out or dropping out.

Nine of Pentacles
Imagery
A woman in a long yellow robe stands in her lush flower garden, surrounded by ripe grapevines and golden Pentacles. A hooded falcon is perched on her fingers, a symbol of

discipline and determination. She has worked hard to get to this level of prosperity. Now, she is entitled to enjoy the fruits of her labor and get some relaxing time to herself.

Interpretation

Upright – This card holds the promise of luxury, success, financial independence, and an abundance mindset. Particularly if you are a woman, don't let anyone tell you that you're selfish or overindulgent for wanting to treat yourself. You've worked hard to get here; you deserve some satisfaction and peace.

Reversed – You've got it all, but you still feel that something is missing. This reversed card represents the "grass is always greener on the other side of the fence" attitude. It's time to ask yourself: are you working toward a goal that will satisfy you in the end? Or have you become addicted to the feeling of forward momentum, seeking higher and higher achievements continuously? Material wealth may prove unfulfilling. Maybe it's time to set your sights on a different goal or find some friends and family to share your spoils with.

Ten of Pentacles

Imagery

A family is gathered in celebration outside the entrance to a walled city, under a grand archway. We see family members from each generation: the venerated grandfather, loving parents, young toddler, and even a pair of pet dogs. The archway represents a journey, as well as cooperative structure. The scene is rich with color, and the theme of abundance is evident. The grandfather looks over his family with admiration and gratitude, knowing that, as he nears the end of his life's journey, this was his higher purpose all along: family, community, and love.

Interpretation

Upright – This card speaks to completion of cycles, material comfort, stability, gratitude, success, and familial harmony. The querent has reached a point where they feel that all their hard work has paid off in spades. They have been able to see their dreams manifest into realities. They now feel ready to pass their blessings forward and share their wealth with loved ones.

Reversed – When reversed, this card is a warning against the false promise of a happy ending. A large sum of money may be lost overnight; a family structure may crumble; a temple or fortress may be torn down. Security and safety can no longer be taken for granted. Try not to count your chickens before they hatch; it's always a good idea to have a back-up plan.

Page of Pentacles

Imagery

The Page stands in a meadow with trees and mountains in the distant background. He gazes in awe and anticipation at the floating Pentacle coin before him, ready to receive it in his open palms. The future is ripe with opportunity; he needs only to reach out and grasp it.

Interpretation

Upright – This card represents an eager but inexperienced entrepreneur. He has a mind for business and innovation but may need some support or guidance to help get his brilliant ideas off the ground. He is determined and diligent, ready to put in some hard work, but inspired mainly by material rewards; he doesn't want to create or produce just for the thrill of it. He takes a focused and methodical approach to his work and aims for constant growth; in his opinion, "good enough" isn't acceptable. He may be overly ambitious and easily distracted by the temptation of material luxuries. Ultimately, though, he is someone you can count on to produce results. Outside of characterization, this card might represent a new financial opportunity or an unexpected windfall, like a winning lottery card or inheritance.

Reversed – This character desires financial success but lacks the focus, drive, or direction to find it. He has trouble organizing his priorities and managing his time and money effectively, so he has a tendency to oversell himself, make promises he cannot keep, and spread himself too thin. Think of the masterminds behind Fyre Festival or the Theranos company. The vision is there, but the necessary skill set is lacking in this individual. Beyond characterization, this card might warn the querent of bad news on the way: a sudden loss of a job or an unexpected financial setback.

Knight of Pentacles
Imagery
The Knight sits on the back of his black horse, gazing over the landscape before him, in no hurry to move. He wears a full suit of armor and holds up a Pentacle coin. The

ground before him is a tilled field; soon, it will be time to start planting seeds. The sky above is yellow, a sign of optimism and good things to come.

Interpretation

Upright – The Knight of Pentacles is concerned with practical action inspired by an ambitious vision. He is pragmatic, goal-oriented, level-headed, patient, and reliable. While others may be better suited to brainstorming, he is the one who ensures the work gets done and all the details are taken care of. He is great at delegating tasks and motivating a team to work with him in cooperation. He is also focused on security, stability, and sustainability.

Reversed – This character desires productivity and manifestation but lacks focus. He may be a bit too scatter-brained or distracted to oversee the projects he's agreed to take on, and progress is therefore slow. His methods are disorganized, which means sometimes, he ends up having to do a lot of extra work to make up for careless errors. He may also have a tendency to lose steam and plateau halfway through the process. He means well, but he may not be able to manage his responsibilities effectively on his own.

Queen of Pentacles

Imagery

The Queen's throne is found amidst lush greenery and vegetation, adorned with ripe fruits, cherubs, and goat's heads. She sits beside a river that symbolizes flow, progress, and creativity. She holds a Pentacle coin in her lap, and its round shape implies the fullness of a womb. There is a brown rabbit hopping near her feet, a symbol of fertility, abundance, and the promise of spring.

Interpretation

Upright – Similar to the Empress, this Queen is the ultimate earth mother, skilled in both the domestic realm and the business world. She is nurturing and protective of her loved ones, with a practical mind and the ability to provide whatever they might need, whether that is food, shelter, money, or the simple comfort of her understanding smile. She can be emotional but never allows her moods to stand in the way of her ability to take care of her family or business. She knows that creating a stable environment is the first step to helping her loved ones thrive in love, creativity, spirituality, and emotional fulfillment.

Reversed – This card represents a character who is stressed and insecure by nature. The fridge might be stocked full, but she constantly worries that there isn't enough to feed her family. She may be overprotective, perhaps even clingy, with her loved ones, and her anxiety is almost contagious. Her tendency to worry about every little thing that might go wrong leaves her scatter-brained, unfocused, disorganized, and sometimes forgetful; she's so focused on keeping the first-aid kit stocked with emergency provisions that she forgets to pay the light bill. She feels stretched too thin, but the only person pressuring her to juggle so many tasks at once is herself.

King of Pentacles

Imagery

The King sits on his throne, admiring the evidence of abundance all around him: ripe fruits, flowers, green vines, a sturdy castle behind him, and of course, plenty of gold. His throne is decorated with horned bull's heads, representing stability, virility, stamina, strength, confidence, and determination. He holds a Pentacle coin in one hand and a golden scepter in the other, signifying his authority and capability as a ruler. His crown is decorated with flowers, and his robes are covered in a grape print. Any material desire he could ask for is well within reach.

Interpretation

Upright – This card represents a character who is down-to-earth and humble despite his authority and wealth. For him, the best thing about prosperity is being empowered to share the wealth. He has a benevolent spirit and a level-headed demeanor, ruled by generosity first and rationality second. This kind of leader or father figure looks at most members of his community as if they were his own children, so he is protective, forgiving, and supportive. He has found wealth, success, and authority by earning the respect of others, rather than demanding it. He is an easy figure to look up to and is well-liked, even by those who envy him.

Reversed – The reversed King of Pentacles is not fit to be a leader because he has trouble putting anyone else's needs before his own. He might have more money than he'll ever be able to spend, but he'd rather hoard it in order to feel powerful and invincible than share it, even with his own family members. If he runs a business or works in politics, he's likely to secure the success he desires through corruption, bribery, strong-arming, perhaps even theft. Greed is his primary motivator, and he believes all means can be justified to satisfy his ends. There isn't a selfless bone in his body, and he may lack empathy for others. Money is the ruler of his universe, and he answers to no other God or calling.

Chapter 8: Tarot Readings

Preparing to Receive a Tarot Reading

Many people presume that it's entirely up to the cartomancer to make the most of a card reading, buying into the false belief that Tarot readers are psychics who should be able to predict the future, accurately and in full, without their assistance. In reality, though, a Tarot reading should be viewed as a joint effort between the querent and the card reader, regardless of their clairvoyant abilities. The moods and mindsets of both individuals will influence the energy of the deck and impact the way the cards fall, so skepticism, negativity, or a lack of emotional investment on the part of the sitter are never ideal. On the other hand, a querent can enhance the experience and encourage greater accuracy for the fortune teller by taking steps to prepare themselves emotionally, intellectually, and spiritually before the reading begins.

Though this is far easier said than done, it's best to clear your mind and try to let go of any particular expectations or even hopes before your cards are drawn. When a querent wishes to see something specific in the cards, their hopeful energy will often blind them to the true message of the card spread. In turn, this energy can also impact the cartomancer's ability to read the cards truthfully, distorting their interpretation of the spread.

One great way to do this is to meditate before receiving a reading. Acknowledge your hopes, fears, expectations, and desires, but allow yourself to detach from them. The universe may have some great surprises in store for you, but you'll need to keep yourself open in order to receive such unexpected gifts.

Another easy way to facilitate this mindset is to bring your mind to a passive, rather than active state, through entertainment media or activity. I don't recommend using movies or television, but reading can work wonderfully, especially if you choose a book or story that has some fantastical, unpredictable, and metaphorical elements. Books about magic can help, whether it's the Harry Potter saga or a work by Gabriel Garcia Marquez—a master of magical realism. Lyrical prose is also helpful, as well as poetry. You might also choose to close your eyes and listen to some music or an audiobook that helps you to feel relaxed, open, and connected to the world.

Creativity is also a wonderful portal to the open mind, especially if it is done freely, without pressure, stress, or the aim of reaching a particular goal. Freewriting and free drawing are easy tasks to perform almost anywhere if you have a pen and paper with you. Painting, playing music, dancing, and singing are also great choices. Some forms of exercise can help to achieve the same ends, such as yoga, swimming, or running. Alternatively, you might work on a coloring book designed for adults, a crossword or sudoku puzzle, or any game that helps to put you in a trance-like state without encouraging anxiety (so video games with guns or combat might not work so well). Gardening and spending time in nature will almost certainly help, too.

Any task that helps you to reach a mental state where you feel that you're "in the zone," so to speak, can help to dismantle the rigid, ego-centric state of mind that most of us are forced to embrace in modern daily life, at least temporarily. These methods are all useful in helping to awaken the intuitive mind, as well, but I'll provide further advice on that subject later in this chapter.

Selecting a Question
Divination through cartomancy is often thought of as a means of predicting the future. In truth, though, Tarot readings can reveal as many truths about the past and present as they can decipher what lies ahead for the querent. Most of us think we already know where we've been and who and where we are currently, but much like talk therapy, Tarot can help us to re-examine that which we think we already know, and expose hidden layers of our circumstances and personalities, perhaps even dragging long-buried memories back up to the surface. If you prescribe to the notion of free will over

preordination, Tarot cards may be better at revealing the truths of your past and present because the future is not yet set in stone. Ideally, if the cards do their job well, they'll be able to guide you to make wise and healthy choices for your future. But remember, these are still choices, not just the predetermined choreography of fate.

That being said, there are some common forms of query that will often leave both the querent and the cartomancer disappointed. One common issue that comes up in card readings is the issue of specificity with time or numbers. Cards of the Major Arcana are often associated with times or speeds, but they usually reference seasons or types of action (spontaneously, gradually, during the month of the Cancer Zodiac sign) rather than specific dates (within two years, next week, on Friday the 13th). Therefore, the cards may fall short if you pose a question like: "By what date will my boyfriend propose marriage to me?" Or: "In what year will I give birth to my first child?" There's also no guarantee that the reader will pull any cards from the Major Arcana at all; if they're performing a three-card past, present, and future spread (which I'll explain further in the next chapter), they'll only have one card (in the future position) to offer guidance on that timing, and if it turns out to be from the Minor Arcana, it will be very difficult to interpret accurately.

It's also tough to predict specific numbers or amounts. Questions about exactly how much money the querent will gain or lose can fall flat with the cards. Instead, you might opt to translate these curiosities into yes-or-no questions, or either-or, such as:

"Will I get engaged to my current lover someday?"

"Will I be able to have children?"

"Should I go for that promotion?"

"Should I stick with this career, or quit my current job and try something new?"

"Should I stay where I am, or think about moving to a new city soon?"

Generally speaking, though, open-ended and general questions will be able to offer you a more entertaining and illuminating experience with the Tarot deck. They also have a better chance of providing accuracy because, as I mentioned previously, the truest answers to your questions might be surprising, out-of-left-field, and unfathomable, even in your wildest dreams.

"I'm planning to move across the country next month. What will that experience have in store for me?"

"I recently started a new relationship, and so far, it seems great. What kind of romance will we have together?"

"I've been dealing with lots of past traumas and current anxieties in therapy lately, but I wonder if the Tarot can offer some additional insight into my healing process? Or maybe illuminate some repressed issues from the past that I haven't been able to face?"

"I have a bad relationship with my parents, and I worry that if I have my own children, I'll repeat their past mistakes. What kind of parent do you think I would be?"

These open-ended queries also don't have to be phrased specifically in the form of a question. It's perfectly acceptable to give your cartomancer a brief explanation of your current mood, mindset, or lifestyle and simply ask if the cards have any general advice to offer. Here are some examples:

"I've been working like mad lately, juggling multiple projects at once and making good money, but I still feel unfulfilled, like something is missing. What do the cards have to say about that?"

"My head's been full of irrational fears and anxieties this month. I really don't know what's causing this or what to do about it."

"I've been on so many bad dates this year that I think I might be losing faith in love. It seems easier just to go it alone these days. Thoughts?"

"I have absolutely no clue what to do with my career. Help!"

If all else fails, ask the card reader for some inspiration or guidelines. Every cartomancer has their own unique style; some might refuse to work with yes-or-no queries; some will only work with the cards of the Major Arcana; some will recommend that you prepare multiple questions for your session together. Aim to be collaborative and cooperative in order to get the most out of the experience.

Preparing to Perform a Tarot Reading

Whether you're planning to perform a divinatory spread for your own personal benefit or for another querent, it's important to work on clearing and opening your mind first, just as you would before receiving a Tarot reading. Many cartomancers develop their own rituals that allow them to dissociate from whatever stressors or emotional issues they might be handling in their day-to-day lives. These rituals may involve the activities mentioned earlier in this chapter, but they can also be more elaborate, involving smudge sticks, candles, or incense; breathing exercises; drinking a particular type of tea; cleansing by water, internally and externally; scrying; prayer; performing a self-induced hypnosis or trance; crystal healing; chakra alignment; and so on. The possibilities are endless, but most cartomancers develop rituals that involve clearing and centering the mind, as well as cleansing or exercising the hands.

It's also a good idea to have a ritual space and setting prepared for your reading. If you have the resources at your disposal, you might choose a corner of your home in which to create a Tarot table, which is essentially an altar with some open space for the card spreads and two or more seats facing each other. If you can't make this a permanent fixture in your home, though, do not worry. Lots of cartomancers purchase Tarot cloths, which are basically decorated tablecloths, which they roll out every time they need to perform a reading. These are wonderfully useful, as they can travel with you on trips or to parties, and they can be washed.

It's very common to light a candle or incense stick to mark the start point of a reading. This helps the querent and reader to focus and alerts the divine powers, asking them to pay attention. You can also work to hold the attention of the divine powers by spreading healing crystals, relics, or items that represent each of the four natural elements (salt for Earth, a bowl of water for Water, an Athame or feather for Air, and a lava rock or candle for fire, among many other possible options) across your table.

Furthermore, a great many cartomancers begin, after lighting a candle, by asking the querent to close their eyes and hold both of their hands for a minute or two. The point of this is to encourage collaborative energy and get it flowing through both bodies in a cyclical manner. If you're performing a reading for yourself, you might just close your eyes and sit with your hands folded in a prayer position.

If you plan to perform multiple readings in a day, you'll want to devise a method of card cleansing that isn't too time-consuming and doesn't require the presence of a full moon. Smudging may be the easiest way to cleanse the deck between each and every reading with a new querent. If you eschew this practice, you'll likely find that your readings become more and more confusing and less accurate as the day progresses since the cards will pick up and retain energy from each successive querent, and eventually become scattered or overloaded. This is one reason that many cartomancers don't allow querents to touch the deck.

It's a common practice to shuffle your deck after receiving a query while meditating on the nature of the question. Some cartomancers use ritual here, too, shuffling a certain number of times before each pull, using a lucky number, like seven perhaps. Others prefer to simply shuffle until they feel that the cards have absorbed the energy of the query adequately. Many then allow the querent to determine when and where to cut the deck, usually by asking them to say "when," though some will allow the querent a chance to shuffle or cut the deck themselves.

Finally, as the card reader, it's a good idea to prepare some boundaries for yourself. What kinds of queries are you prepared to answer? Are there any you can think of that you wouldn't be comfortable speaking to? How much time are you prepared to devote to this reading? How will you respond if you feel the querent's negativity or skepticism is corrupting the reading? What if you start to get the sense that a nefarious spirit has entered the space? Unexpected situations will no doubt arise, sooner or later, but the more comfortable you are with recognizing and defining your own boundaries, the easier it will be to communicate and enforce them when push comes to shove.

How to Enhance Your Intuitive Sensitivities

There is no simple, one-size-fits-all guide to awakening your intuitive or clairvoyant sensibilities. Everyone starts at a different jumping-off point, as some of us are more naturally intuitive than others, and many of us experience intuition through different senses. Some find intuitive guidance through sight or touch, while others might rely on that feeling of gut instinct, literally rooted in the stomach.

Generally speaking, though, to awaken your intuition for the sake of Tarot readings, the best way to get started is to work with the cards as frequently as possible. This might simply mean handling them frequently or practicing readings every single day.

Many cartomancers recommend sleeping with your Tarot deck under your pillow in order to forge a deeper intuitive connection with the cards. While this advice holds some merit, it's also a good way to increase your chances of bending or damaging the cards. Furthermore, there are some conflicting views on which cards are safe to include in such a practice; some believe it is dangerous to sleep with a deck that includes the Devil card, while others argue that Death or the Tower or the Nine of Swords need to be removed from the deck before you hit the hay.

Perhaps a safer and more reliable way to use the power of your dreaming, subconscious mind to improve your divination skills is to get into the habit of performing quick card readings, single card pulls, or simply shuffling through your deck, every night just before going to sleep. That way, you can keep your cards safe from damage in a silk bag or protective box while still guaranteeing that your dreaming mind will continue to work on the imagery, correspondences, connectivity, and universal themes of the deck while you are asleep.

It's also important to be sure you're getting enough good quality sleep in order to reap these benefits. The dreaming mind works to cleanse the brain, extracting and disposing of superfluous information, frustrations, and confusions while also building new connections between parts of the brain that normally never communicate while we are awake. It cannot do this effectively if your sleep patterns are consistently disrupted by elements like light and noise (which means no more sleeping in front of the television!), intoxicants and stimulants (alcohol, drugs, cigarettes, or even too much coffee during the day can interfere with sleep cycles), or waking interruptions (the frequent urge to urinate, or the need to wake every few hours to respond to an infant's cries, will short circuit your sleep cycle, preventing you from reaching the point of restorative, or REM, sleep, which begins hours after you first lose consciousness). Furthermore, the same elements that disrupt your sleep cycles will also typically prevent you from being able to remember your dreams upon waking or stop you from having notable dreams at all.

If you are able to improve your sleeping habits and achieve restorative sleep, though, your subconscious mind will work every night to open you up to possibilities that your waking mind could never even fathom. In dreams, most of us let our guard down; we do not necessarily lose sight of the ego, but it takes a backseat to other concerns. This is the perfect circumstance in which to strengthen your intuitive capacity. In dreams, when we encounter a nefarious character, we don't feel the need to justify or explain our feelings about them; we simply know, viscerally, that they are up to no good or mean to cause us harm, and our dreaming bodies want to immediately act upon that instinct by fighting or fleeing. By exposing the mind to Tarot just before falling asleep, we can work to develop the same attitudes about the cards, learning not to trust too heavily or exclusively in the opinions of others, even the experts.

In order to get the best possible quality sleep and increase your chances of remembering your dreams, you can do the following.

- Turn your bedroom into a sanctuary, with all light sources and external noises blocked out.

- Stop using screens (phones, tablets, TVs, electronic games) at least half an hour before you plan to go to sleep.
- Drink plenty of water during the day, especially if you are also consuming caffeine.
- Curb your caffeine intake and stop drinking it after two o'clock in the afternoon.
- Quit smoking to make sure nicotine cravings aren't waking you up in the middle of the night.
- Watch your consumption of alcohol.
- If you struggle with anxiety, you might want to consider investing in a weighted blanket, or maybe try gripping a stress ball or similar tool as you drift off.
- Avoid spicy foods two hours before bedtime unless you're hoping for a stressful dream or nightmare.
- If possible, use natural sleep aids (chamomile tea, melatonin supplements) rather than prescription drugs to induce sleep.

With practice, you may eventually find that you start having recurring or progressive dreams, wherein you get closer and closer to some mysterious destination, echelon, or hidden knowledge with each passing night. You may even begin lucid dreaming, a practice where the sleeping mind is able to control the trajectory of dreams, making informed choices in order to get more enjoyment out of the experience and lessen the impact of negative factors in dreams, such as tension, anxiety, frustration, or fear.

In waking life, it is more challenging to stay in touch with your intuition, but not impossible. One way to ease the process is through regular meditation, which helps us to learn how to distinguish between reactionary impulses and permanent truths. For example, a traffic jam might put you in a foul mood, but does that mean that you're a generally negative or angry person? Probably not. Meditation will also give you greater control over your emotional impulses, allowing you to recognize that your reactions are choices, not automatic reflexes. This can be particularly helpful when you are faced with deceptive personalities or institutions. Most of us automatically respond to smiles with smiles, but through meditation, you'll get into the practice of questioning this impulse, asking yourself: Am I smiling because I'm actually happy or because I like this person? Or, do I just feel pressured, maybe even manipulated, to reflect their surface-level attitude because of social conventions?

As I mentioned earlier, you can gain a whole lot of insight and perspective by starting a divination journal. This isn't only a place to record your experiences with the Tarot deck; you can also take note of coincidences, connections, and synchronicities whenever you observe them, in any walk of life. It's also a great place to do free writing or free drawing, which both help to awaken and express the subconscious mind through spontaneous manifestation.

Finally, in order to truly embrace your intuitive instinct, it is imperative that you eliminate sources of constant negativity or skepticism from your life. This may be easier said than done. Most of us have a friend or family member whom we love, despite their constant pessimism or base-line anger. Or, perhaps you've been raised in a religious community that condemns the practice of divination, equating it with evil intention or defiance of God. It isn't always a simple choice to turn away from a relationship or community like this. Still, every time these influencers question or deride your abilities, they'll chip away at your confidence and belief in yourself. Learn to create boundaries with these people or institutions, whether that means changing the subject when negative issues come up in conversation, tuning out during certain parts of a sermon, or walking away entirely.

Memory and Intuition

The stronger your intuitive skills grow, the more likely you are to find that your memories become rich, complex, and highly detailed. Memory is strongly linked to the brain's intuitive and emotional synapses. The trouble is that the most detailed memories aren't necessarily the most accurate. We often think of memory like a photo album in the brain that we can flip through and observe whenever we want to access a specific event. In truth, memory is more like an internal game of telephone. Each time we summon a memory, we give our minds an opportunity to alter it, adding nuance and understanding that we didn't have access to at the time of the initial event.

For this reason, I'd highly recommend that you record your Tarot reading results (wherein you are the querent) in writing whenever possible. The brain is so good at making connections—especially when we are purposefully honing the skill of recognizing intuitive synchronicities—that it can sometimes see connections that aren't actually there. By recording your Tarot results, you'll have a better chance, in the long-term, of understanding what the cards are actually trying to tell you, rather than deciphering the messages that you want to see or hear.

Chapter 9: Tarot Spreads

By this point, I hope your fingers are just itching to get started! In this chapter, we'll outline a number of popular Tarot spreads, explaining how to lay them, how to read them, and what queries they'll be best suited to. This is just the tip of the iceberg, though, so I'd highly recommend doing further research through the internet, alternative texts, or by consulting fellow cartomancers for guidance.

One Card Reading

Single card readings are ideal for novices who want to get some foundational practice. However, they are not well-suited to very specific queries. Vague or open-ended questions are preferable. This won't take very long, so it might be a good idea to prepare a list of queries and perform several single-card pulls in a row.

Set up your space and perform any preparatory rituals that suit your style. Shuffle the cards thoroughly and cut the deck in whatever manner you see fit. When you're ready, state your query aloud to the deck, with a bold and purposeful tone. Or, if you're not comfortable speaking to inanimate objects, meditate on the question as you stare at the deck intently.

Close your eyes and take a deep breath before drawing a card from the deck. It is important that you maintain focus on the question at hand throughout the shuffling and card drawing process. Otherwise, you may turn up a result that is purely bewildering.

Place the card face up, and do your best to abandon your rational and analytic mind for a few moments. Focus on the image rather than the formulas or meanings you may have memorized. Take some time to recognize what the colors and shapes mean to you. Does the card seem like a positive or negative answer to your query? Is it specific, or vague? Does it strike you as masculine or feminine? Naive or wise? Open-ended, or firm and closed? If it's a character, does it represent yourself? Or does it seem to be pointing to another figure, group, or institution in your life?

Only after you've considered your visceral reactions should you consult the assigned interpretations you've memorized, or your guidebook of choice, for further clarification. Consider the card's inherent meaning, direction, and various correspondences. Is it upright, or reversed? What are its numerological or astronomical implications? Its elemental connection? How about its role in the story of the Fool's Journey? Its geographic and temporal associations? Aim to consider multiple possibilities before settling on a singular interpretation. Remember that there is no such thing as an incorrect interpretation here; all that matters is whether or not you find it meaningful, inspiring, impactful, or resonant.

Two Card Spread

There are two primary methods of performing a two-card spread.

You'll begin in much the same way as you did with a single card reading. The only real difference in the preparatory stage is the type of query you bring to the deck. Two card spreads are very well-suited to queries about choices, crossroads, dichotomies, or any situation in which the querent needs to compare and contrast two different options.

The first method is to perform a single card reading, but with two cards drawn and laid side by side. Fairly simple, right? Maybe not. Since the cards can represent two different options or paths, you'll want to carefully consider their meanings individually, as well as the impact they might have on each other. The Emperor card carries a far different meaning on its own, as compared to its meaning when laid next to the Wheel of Fortune. Look for contrasts but also for similarities in theme, color, gender, element, and other correspondences.

The second method is to lay both cards face down at first and flip them over one at a time, pausing to evaluate the meaning of the first card before you expose the second. This method may be used for either-or queries, but it may also be used to illustrate cause and effect, like a before-and-after split-screen photo.

Three Card Spread

Again, there are two common ways to interpret the three-card spread. As in the two-card reading, the cards may be laid and exposed all at once or revealed one at a time.

When exposed all at once, this spread may speak to a querent's past, present, and future experience within a single vein of interest (love, career, family, spirituality, etc.). The past will be represented by the card furthest to the left; the present is found in the middle, and the future is glimpsed in the card on the right. If you are performing this reading for someone else, don't hesitate to ask them questions about their lives in order to make more sense of the past and present cards. Once again, look for connective threads in the cards to see how these different chapters of the querent's life journey have impacted each other. Try to think of time as cyclical rather than linear.

Another option is to lay the three cards and expose them one at a time. This style is better suited to a query about choices or comparisons, like the two-card spread. Here, though, the third card offers a glimpse of divine guidance, helping to nudge the querent toward one path or the other. You'll want to look for connections again; which of the first two cards has the most in common with the third? Common suits, characters, colors, numbers, or symbols will often help to clarify which of the two options is recommended by divine powers.

Horseshoe Spread

This seven-card spread has a slightly misleading name, as the cards will be arranged in a V shape, not U. After shuffling and cutting, the cards are laid out all at once, face down, with their corners overlapping, progressively from left to right, with the fourth card at the lowermost point of the spread. It should look symmetrical when all seven cards are placed.

You'll turn the cards over one at a time, being sure to use a consistent turn, so you don't accidentally reverse a card that should be upright.

- The first card, furthest to the left, speaks to the querent's past.
- The second card will speak to the present—specifically, what circumstances led them to seek out this reading.

- The third card will reference hidden influences, such as intuition, repressed memories, secrets, perhaps even biological predispositions or cosmic movements that influence the querent's behavior without their conscious awareness.
- The fourth card is a representation of the querent. It does not sum up their identity in full but will describe their attitudes, motivations, behaviors, and habits as related to the query.
- The fifth card is about external influences. What do the querent's friends, family, lovers, co-workers, fans, or critics think they should do in this situation?
- The sixth card represents divine guidance and offers impartial advice.
- The seventh card is a glimpse at the future; if you heed the message of the sixth card, what will be the most likely outcome or result?

Romany Spread

This spread is also sometimes called a "Gypsy" spread but use that term with caution—some Roma people will find that term offensive. It has been used for centuries and has changed very little over the years. It uses a large number of cards, so you might not want to use this method if you're pressed for time. That being said, it's a very useful spread for complex queries or situations with multiple influential factors.

The Romany spread is similar to a three-card past-present-future reading, but instead of using three cards, it uses three rows of seven cards each. The rows tell progressive stories. The top row will tell the story of the querent's past, though it may add some details or dimensions that the querent was previously unaware of. The center row will describe the querent's present reality. The bottom row will tell the story of the querent's future.

To add another dimension of insight, you can further analyze this spread by examining the three-card columns, which also tell shorter stories of their own.

- The first column, furthest to the left, describes the querent's social and physical life—the realities that influence their day-to-day decisions and define their routines—the Earth element.
- The second column references emotional journeys or intuitive growth—the Water element.
- The third column will speak to matters of the mind—the Air element.
- The fourth column references the querent's core identity as it pertains to manifestation and the manner in which they express their inner self to the external world—the Fire element.
- The fifth column reveals the unknown and hints at secrets or surprises in store for the future—the Spirit element.
- The sixth column offers recommendations for the near future—the next few days, weeks, or months.
- The seventh column is a prediction of the final result or a glimpse into the distant future.

Celtic Cross Spread

Though it uses fewer cards than the Romany spread, the Celtic Cross layout is considered ideal for extremely specific or complex queries. Traditionally, the cards in this spread are laid and exposed one at a time, analyzed gradually.

- The first card you pull and place will be called the Significator. This card will represent the querent's identity, present mindset, status, or circumstance. This card will impact all other cards that are subsequently pulled.
- The second card will be laid atop the first, either creating a cross shape or an X (either way is fine, but some cartomancers prefer to lay the card at an angle rather than perpendicular to the first in order to negate any potential implication of Christian symbolism). This card represents a barrier, obstacle, challenge, or predicament that is currently troubling the querent.
- The third card will be placed directly beneath the first, parallel to it. It will represent the root of the querent's current circumstances or problems. For example, if the querent is frustrated by failed attempts to manage their body weight, this card might provide the hint that their overeating is rooted in past emotional trauma, rather than an inability to control impulses.
- The fourth card can be placed to the left of the Significator. It will represent past realities that have led to or exacerbated the current problem; alternatively, it might describe elements of the querent's current reality that they are starting to outgrow or itching to leave behind.

- The fifth card will be placed above the Significator. By now, you should see the shape of the cross evolving. This card offers hope and advice for the future: a path forward.
- The sixth card completes the shape of the cross, laid to the right of the Significator, and provides guidance for the near future, or concrete advice on the next steps.
- The next four cards will be laid in a straight vertical line to the right side of the cross formation. Start from the bottom and work up toward the top.
- The seventh card pulled can be seen as a gentle wake-up call. It speaks to aspects of the querent's current routine, habits, or mindset that are defining their reality and possibly holding them back.
- The eighth card will describe external factors that are beyond the querent's control but influencing their decisions nonetheless (social connections, politics, laws, physical limitations, etc.).
- The ninth card illuminates the subconscious. It may reference suppressed hopes, irrational fears, repressed memories, unrecognized emotions, inner demons, or unexpressed desires.
- The tenth and final card points to the ultimate result. It usually points to the best path forward rather than predicting the future. The outcome will depend on the querent's ability to learn and grow from the message of the cards.

Chapter 10: Customized Tarot

If you're working with a deck that isn't based on the Rider-Waite Tarot, you may find that a great deal of the information in chapters 2, 3, 4, 5 and 6 isn't precisely applicable to your divination toolbox. The titles, numbers, and images featured on cards can vary greatly from one deck to the next, especially now that Tarot is growing so popular in the world of DIY and independent publishing.

Whatever deck you choose to work with, make sure you're giving equal weight to the opinions of experts and your own impressions. Spend time examining each card in the deck, reflecting on how the imagery makes you feel on a visceral level. Even if all the books and websites you look to for guidance tell you to interpret a card in a certain way, the illustration might convey something entirely different to you. Pay attention to the feelings that the colors, shapes, and even facial expressions of the characters, inspire within you. Perhaps the Empress is meant to be a positive and benevolent maternal figure, but you can't help but see an off-putting smirk on her face whenever you encounter the card—take note of this reaction! Your personal interpretations are valid and just as worthy of consideration as any of the experts' opinions. Divination, after all, is about intuition, so your gut instincts should never be discouraged in a card reading.

As an example, a great number of cartomancers look at the Chariot card and see a clear illustration of defense, rather than forward momentum; in the Rider-Waite deck, the vehicle is at a standstill, and the prince and his sphinx look somewhat defiant, as well as determined. Some decks, however, will illustrate the vehicle in motion, towed behind galloping horses. These contrasting interpretations can have quite an impact on the meaning of any spread, but neither is considered wrong, per se. One is simply more commonly recognized than the other.

Each deck carries its own unique metaphysical energy, so your readings may not be accurate if you apply a one-size-fits-all philosophy to your alternative decks. A change to the classic illustration or standard title of a card *does* impact its meaning in a spread. If your deck bears little resemblance to the Rider-Waite deck, you can use the information in this chapter to draw your own conclusions and formulate your own interpretations of the cards.

Colors in the Tarot Deck

- ***White*** represents the purity of spirit and intent, innocence, cleansing, illumination, enlightenment, peace, and divinity.
- ***Black*** is most often used to delineate the borders of shapes in illustrations, but whenever it is used for shading or filling, it represents absolutism, formality, stability, forcefulness, and rigidity.
- ***Grey*** conveys uncertainty, mystery, severity, indifference, neutrality, or a grim outlook.
- ***Yellow*** represents optimism, joy, creativity, positivity, radiance, and clarity; particularly when it colors the sky on a card, it should call to mind the infamous pop song lyrics: *I can see clearly now, the rain is gone...*
- ***Red*** is a symbol of passion, action, primal urges, animal instincts, vitality, intensity, power, boldness, sensual pleasure, and love. It usually references the traits of the Fire element.
- ***Green*** is used to illustrate youth, growth, the natural world, fresh starts, rebirth, adventure, and nostalgia.
- ***Blue*** references all matters that concern the Third Eye chakra: imagination, spiritual enlightenment, sensitivity, intuition, freedom, inspiration, and cosmic balance.
- ***Brown*** represents the nature of the Earth element: grounding, structure, stability, security, practicality, rationality, materiality, fertility, health, nutrition, and nurturing.

- ***Orange*** is the color of harmony, amity, aspiration, ambition, contentment, and balance. It is a blend of red (passion and action) mixed with yellow (optimism and clarity) and usually represents social connections or personal fulfillment.
- ***Purple*** is a symbol of regality, grandeur, spirituality, idealism, peace, rest, and recuperation.
- ***Indigo*** carries many of the same associations as blue but particularly denotes intuition, emotion, creativity, and the unknown.

Shapes in the Tarot Deck

- ***Circles*** are symbols of constancy, the cycle of life, the Water element, and feminine energy.
- ***Squares*** represent stability, security, and foundational strength. They are associated with the Earth element.
- ***Triangles***, when facing upright, symbolize the Fire element. They are also sometimes used in alternative positions or echoed with extra line crossings to represent the other three earthly elements (Air, Water, and Earth). In some cultures, the upright triangle also represents mankind.
- ***The Lemniscate*** (also known as the infinity symbol) represents infinite potential or limitless possibility, as well as eternity. The sign is usually used to reference power, energy, or life force.
- ***Stars*** can represent hope, divine guidance, renewal, and spiritual wisdom.
- ***The Five-Pointed Star is a Pentagram***; when encircled, it is called a Pentacle (as in the suit). Both can be used to represent the balance between the

five elements (Earth, Air, Fire, Water, and Spirit) and are considered signs of magical energy in Wiccan, Pagan, and occult belief systems.

- ***The Six-Pointed Star is a Hexagram*** but more commonly known as a Star of David. These days, it is best known for its association with Judaism, but it has also been used in several other religious faiths, including Islam, Hinduism, and Buddhism. It represents a divine shield, heroism, and ceremonial magic. It may also reference outdated astrological systems (it was often used to represent the celestial bodies of the solar system before additional planets were discovered) and is sometimes called the talisman of Saturn or the Seal of Solomon.

- ***The Eight-Pointed Star*** is a symbol of hope, rebirth, resurrection, and salvation.

Symbolic Elements in the Tarot Deck

We've already touched on the four earthly elements—fire, water, air, and earth—as they correspond to the four suits. But what about other natural or manmade elements that may show up repeatedly in the Tarot deck's illustrations?

- ***The Sun*** is usually a symbol of all aspects of the divine masculine, as well as optimism, joy, abundance, and success. When the sun is drawn on a card, shining down over the characters, it implies that divine forces approve of their actions or helped to create their current circumstances. If it is seen rising in the distance, it implies a fresh start, a new beginning, and hope for the future.

- ***The Moon*** represents the characteristics of the divine feminine, as well as fluctuation, imagination, mystery, and intuition.
- ***Stars*** are symbols of illumination, hope, inspiration, faith, and the energy that drives life. They can also be a sign of good luck or divine blessings.
- ***Clouds***, when white, often speak to ideas, dreams, emotions, and spiritual matters. Grey clouds, by contrast, signify uncertainty, doubt, mystery, and misery.
- ***Hills*** signify minor challenges or hard work that is done to earn material rewards or to achieve mastery over a skillset.
- ***Mountains***, by contrast, will represent larger challenges or obstacles, as well as fortitude, courage, wisdom, endurance, rigidity, and permanence.
- ***Paths and Roads*** are representations of spiritual or emotional journeys. Crossroads symbolize major choices or dichotomies.
- ***Stone and Rocks*** are usually symbols of security, stability, certainty, or immovability. In large quantities, they can also point to major obstacles or roadblocks.
- ***Bodies of Water*** reference the traits of the Water element, including emotionality, intuitive powers, flux, receptivity, creativity, and the energy of the divine feminine.
- ***Rivers,*** in particular, point to emotional journeys or spiritual growth, as well as momentum and emotional drive.
- ***Trees*** are symbols of masculine energy and virility, as well as growth, strength, stability, and abundance.

- ***Mammalian Animals*** are representations of the self, as it is rooted in material realities and physical impulses, such as hunger, primal fear, or sexual drive. They symbolize deep instincts.

- ***Birds*** signify messages, inspiration, creativity, freedom, peace, and spirit.

- ***Sea Creatures*** represent the subconscious, intuition, psychic abilities, deep emotions, and any feelings that are kept below the surface.

- ***Flowers*** are often symbols of abundance, youth, growth, beauty, material prosperity, luxury, success, sensuality, or fertility.

- ***Fruit*** usually represents sensuality, fertility, temptation, abundance, or material luxury.

- ***Wheat*** is a symbol of health, harvest, prosperity, maternal nurturing, and karmic cycles, as in: "You reap what you sow."

- ***Precious Metals (Gold, Silver, Etc.)*** represent regality, material wealth, power, spiritual enlightenment, and divine blessings.

- ***Nudity*** is a symbol of vulnerability, particularly emotional vulnerability, as well as honesty, openness, receptiveness, trust, dismantled ego, or shedding of material values.

- ***Heavy Clothing or Armor*** symbolizes protection, security, stability, invulnerability, pride, and inflexibility.

Chapter 11: Why It Works

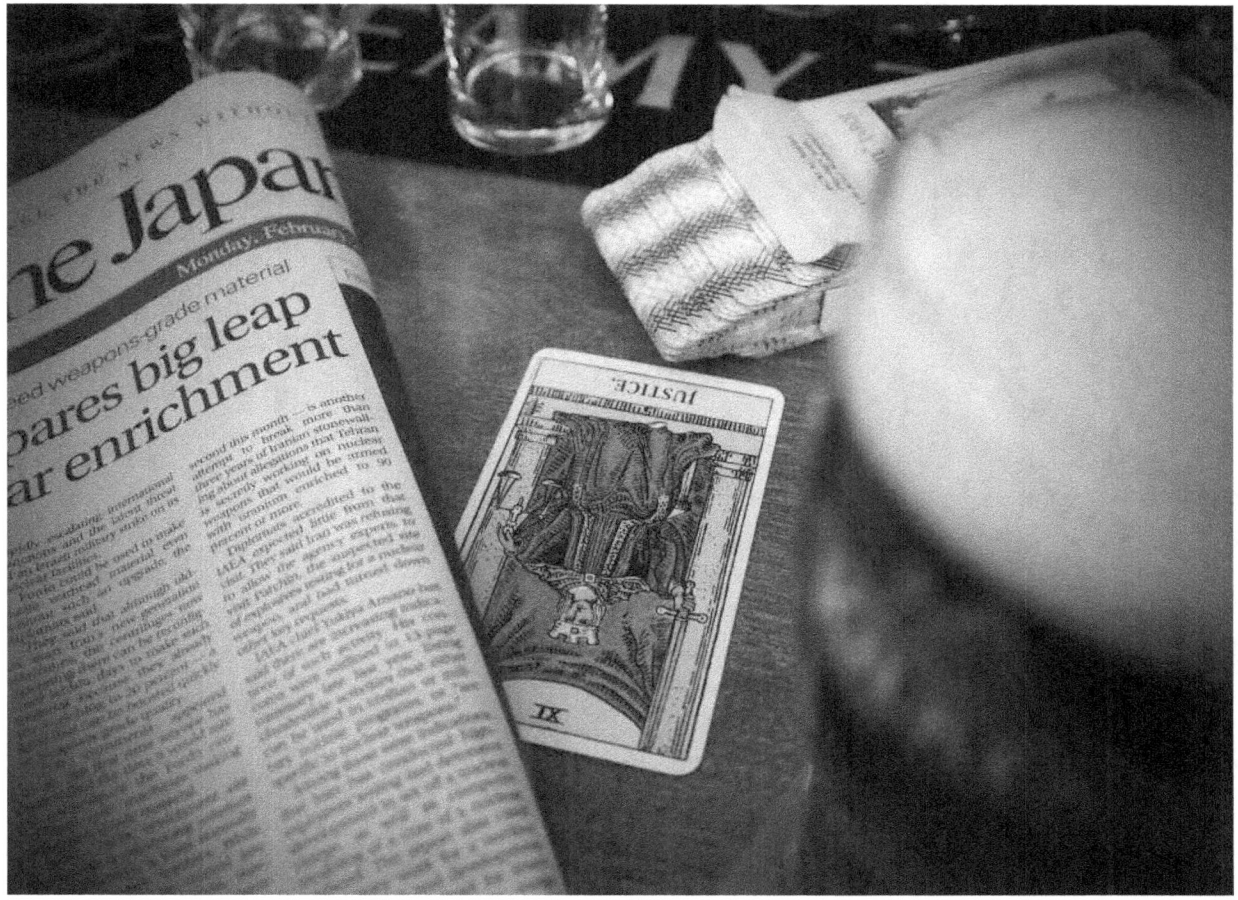

It's all well and good to analyze the beautiful illustrations on Tarot cards and decode their symbolic meanings. But where, exactly, does Tarot stop being a series of beautiful and impactful images and start to become...something more? How can a simple stack of laminated drawings be so powerful and lend us so much insight into the past, present, future, unknown realities, and divine plans? How can a deck of cards, once used for gameplay and frivolity, channel so much magical energy into our everyday lives?

History of Divination

For as long as mankind has been able to look up at the stars, observe the patterns of seasons and cycles of life, and use natural elements as tools, divination has been a central aspect of spiritual life. It predates civilization, and though there are countless divinatory methods in existence, all as varied as the day is long, there are also a great number of overarching, universal themes that we encounter time and time again in different traditions from cultures all over the globe.

It's possible that many of the universal themes we see in various cultures' takes on metaphysical realities are a reflection of the fixed celestial bodies and globally observable astrological movements. No matter where our ancestors may have stood on the globe, they were all exposed to the same patterns in the night sky (though they would have viewed them at different times of the year). Furthermore, cycles of sex, birth, growth, life, and death are also universal, as are the fundamental laws of nature. Together, these concepts may explain why so many cultures, who seem to disagree on almost everything else, share common understandings of the symbolic meanings of shapes, numbers, gender traits, seasons, celestial bodies, animals, and the natural elements.

Before the invention of modern science, fear of the unknown would have dominated the mental landscapes of most individuals; therefore, the desire to get a glimpse at what the future holds in store has been a fundamental part of human nature for millennia. Before television, social media, and the invention of the printing press, divination was used as much for entertainment and amusement as it was for prediction of momentous events, weather patterns or divine will. Divination, or the skill of reading omens, would be used to plan for farming and harvesting activities, to detect oncoming storms or predict the end of the winter season, to decide who to marry or where to wage battles, to devise theories on combating illnesses or healing injuries, and much, much more. Without phones, some cultures trusted in the movements of their hearth fires or bonfires to predict the arrival of guests or determine whether or not departed loved ones would ever return to them from their distant travels. Almost every kind of tool or material you could think of was once used for this purpose; our ancestors read bones and entrails, stones, grains of rice, handfuls of dirt, tea leaves, ashes, wood shavings, tree rings, the flight patterns of birds, movements of clouds, activities of wild animals, and even their own dreams, in addition to the movements of distant celestial bodies. Divination was once a widespread part of everyday life. While Tarot is certainly making a comeback in recent years, it's still fair to say most divination practices have fallen into obscurity, as compared to their former degree of popularity.

Whatever form it takes, divination is a means of manifesting one's faith in the divine. Nowadays, we may presume that it has always been a facet of counterculture, but historically, divination was popularly and openly used by religious and governmental leaders. If you read the Christian Bible closely, there are several methods of divination mentioned, including the use of astrological reading by the Three Wise Men to find their way to the manger in which Jesus Christ was born. Divination methods were essential to the governments and rulers of ancient Egypt, Rome, Greece, China, India, and Mesopotamia, just to name a few, in order to make major decisions that would impact the entirety of their populations. It wasn't until the Middle Ages that the Christian church began to condemn the use of divination throughout Western Europe. Even then, these traditions were so deeply ingrained in the culture that they lived on, behind closed doors and drawn window curtains, or in natural spaces where the arms and eyes of the church could neither reach nor see these supposedly blasphemous acts. These days, many of the most popular historical methods of divination have been all but lost to the ages, but several forms are still thriving, including geomancy, palmistry, tasseomancy, numerology, rune casting, the I Ching, scrying, gastromancy, astrology, and of course, cartomancy.

Why Does Divination Work?

A great many people falsely believe that divination in any form can only work for those who possess innate supernatural gifts, such as clairvoyance or psychic power. In truth, divination is accessible to any person who is willing to suspend disbelief, work to enhance their intuitive sensitivity, and devote some time to the practice.

It's impossible to prove the supernatural element of divination truly exists—that is the nature of the supernatural, after all—but anyone who incorporates a particular practice, such as cartomancy, into their daily routine will, no doubt, find that there are too many uncanny coincidences for the results to be random or illusory. There are some fortune tellers, seers, shamans, and psychics who are indeed con artists, feigning the ability to read the future as clearly as one might read a book, but these characters should be viewed as exceptions to the rule. In truth, we are all born with natural intuition; most of us learn to suppress, deny, or distrust it as we grow into adulthood, but it is always there, just below the surface, ready and waiting to be summoned back up to the forefront of our minds.

Our material senses are highly sensitive, so much so that our brains have to work hard to flush away extraneous and irrelevant information every day. When we look at a landscape, for instance, our eyes can detect every single minute detail, but our brains simplify this information, boiling it down to something more manageable to prevent mental overload. Even after that process, our brains still need to use nightly sleep cycles to process and dispose of any information that doesn't fit into the framework of intel that is necessary for survival.

This means that we are all capable of reading all the signs of the universe—the patterns of the stars, the movements of clouds, the ways in which wind and gravity work to scatter seeds or grains—but we have trained ourselves not to see these details.

Through divination, we put our active brains to rest in order to allow our intuitive brains to process the information that it is usually urged to ignore. Simultaneously, we allow our brains to focus on the one thing that they are designed to do best: notice and analyze patterns. Patterns are how we all make sense of the world. In this sense, divination isn't terribly different from any scientific field. We perform tests, process information, look for patterns, and try to apply them to our material realities. When it doesn't work, we try again.

Divination allows us to tap into our own subconscious energies, as well as the collective subconscious, reading the signs that are always visibles but rarely evaluated. Some like to call it magical, metaphysical, supernatural, or pseudoscientific. Personally, I believe it is one of the most natural and scientific aspects of humanity; and yes, it goes beyond the physical and feels like true magic a great deal of the time. But who's to say that magic can't be real?

Chapter 12: The Sacred Tarot Unveiled

It's not at all uncommon for those who begin dabbling in cartomancy through Tarot to develop an unquenchable thirst for esoteric knowledge. When you begin to incorporate correspondences into your readings and interpretations, it can feel like unwrapping a layered gift that just keeps on giving. By adding astrological analysis, alchemical symbolism, historical context, numerology, and other divinatory schools of thought to your repertoire, you can uncover countless dimensions of truth in just a single Tarot reading. The more you learn, the more empowered you'll feel, gaining a sense of spiritual or universal belonging as you gain the ability to really see the big picture. At the same time, you'll also feel humbled and get closer and closer to the dismantling of the ego and opening of the Third Eye.

Undoubtedly, one of the best ways to further these studies is to enroll yourself in a mystery school.

What Is a Mystery School?

Contemporary mystery schools are a continuation of an ancient esoteric tradition, one which many believe originated in Egypt, though the origins of the tradition are primarily legend, not recorded in any official capacity. Some believe the original masters and teachers of these schools were other-worldly, in one sense or another: survivors of the lost continent of Atlantis, perhaps, or souls who had crossed into the afterlife and somehow managed to return with wisdom gained from the Egyptian Book of the Dead or the Book of Thoth. Perhaps they were demigods, elementals in human form, or immortal beings who survived since the earliest days of man's time on earth. Wherever they hailed from, they possessed ancient knowledge that has since largely been forgotten by the modern world. Luckily for us, their students have worked tirelessly to keep this knowledge intact and continue passing it on to younger generations, ensuring its preservation.

Mystery schools focus on passing on hermetic or arcane teachings through oral transmission; the knowledge they keep is not usually written in books, and the lessons they teach are the kinds that most can only absorb through experience, as opposed to a typical academic study.

In the Middle Ages, mystery schools were often centers of alchemical study, and they were highly exclusive so as to protect their wisdom from the intolerant and destructive arm of the Catholic church. Many aspiring students would have to go through years of tests and trials—sometimes lasting as long as two decades—before being admitted into these institutions officially. Luckily for us, most modern mystery schools have a far less rigorous application and admittance process. There is a lot less fear of persecution, and therefore, the need for secrecy and exclusivity has been replaced by the desire to spread the wealth of knowledge generously and spread enlightenment throughout the world. These days, the biggest hurdles to attendance are the same as they are when enrolling in any institution of higher education: time, funding, distance, and conviction. If you are dedicated and determined, though, there is no reason why you shouldn't be able to gain admittance to the nearest mystery school. Even if you live in the middle of nowhere, hundreds of miles from the closest brick-and-mortar institution, you can still gain access to this esoteric knowledge through mystery classes offered online!

Mystery schools are particularly helpful to those who wish to become prolific in Tarot reading and other forms of divination because they tend to focus on the universal and spiritual language of symbolism. They help to strengthen intuitive reasoning skills by guiding students to observe the intricate interconnectivity of all religious faiths, divination methods, alchemical and magical practices, astrological movements, physiology, psychology, herbology, geology, philosophy, and interpersonal dynamics. Everything in the universe is connected, and mystery schools work to illuminate those connective threads, allowing students to open their eyes to the bigger picture, as well as see below the surface level of life on earth.

Tarot as a Spiritual Practice

There is something uniquely powerful about the Tarot deck, even as compared to other forms of divination. The archetypal imagery is a universal language, allowing us to communicate across divides like language or cultural barriers, differing values, and disparate religious faiths.

Some Tarot enthusiasts will go so far as to call their relationship to the cards a spiritual or religious faith. They may develop daily routines centered on the cards, involving prayer, meditation, trances, a form of communion with spirit, spellcasting, and more.

All religious faiths can be viewed, at their core, as translations of a single universal truth, told through different stories, in different languages or stylistic genres. If that is the case, then Tarot is as good a medium as anyone could devise to consume, understand, analyze, and retell that story. These images, titles, and symbols allow us to see a piece of ourselves, our own lives, and realities reflected in the story of universal truth. The Tarot deck also gives us the opportunity to write our own story of spiritual truth and add it to the cannon, rather than working with a set of limited and outdated words written thousands of years ago. The Tarot deck is constantly evolving, growing, changing to reflect the realities of the modern world while still retaining its ancient wisdom.

There is no official church, temple, or religious sect devoted to the study of the Tarot, but if you feel a strong connection to the deck and wish to find like-minded souls to practice cartomancy with, you probably won't have to look far. There are many people like you who have taken steps to publish their thoughts on this matter, as well as recommendations for spiritual rituals that incorporate the Tarot deck, either in print or online. Consult social media, and you'll find hundreds, maybe thousands, of voices that are eager to speak on this subject. Take their words as inspiration, and reach out to those who share your perspective to forge connections. Who knows; maybe one day soon, you'll be publishing your own piece, offering guidance to novices, or founding your very own Church of Tarot!

Conclusion

Thank you so much for making it through to the end of this book; let's hope it has been deeply informative and able to provide you with all the tools you need to achieve your goals with Tarot and divination, whatever those goals may be. You've taken in a great deal of information here, so go ahead and pat yourself on the back—you should be proud of yourself!

The next step is to keep practicing your card readings while exposing yourself to as much information about Tarot as possible. Continue expanding your knowledge of Tarot and esoteric workings by exploring alternative decks, further researching the symbolism of the cards' illustrations; you might even choose to round out your divination toolbox with additional tools, like metaphysical healing crystals, rune stones, geomancy grids, essential oils, candles, and more. Simultaneously, you'll want to work on developing a regular practice that stokes the intuitive fire, so to speak. Just like the physical body, the subconscious mind needs regular exercise, as well as adequate rest and nourishment, to stay healthy and active in the long-term.

As mentioned in the final chapter, you can also look for a mystery school to enroll in if you're still hungry for more metaphysical awareness and insight. The bottom line, though, is that the more you know and the more you're willing to learn, the more fulfilling your experience with cartomancy is sure to be.

Finally, if you enjoyed reading this book, a review on Amazon is always appreciated, especially if it can help another novice to find their way to the amazing world of Tarot. Best of luck in your divination practice!

Tarot Ultimate Guide

The Supreme Guide for Learning The Art of Tarot Divination and Readings

Serra Night

Introduction

Thank you for your interest in this book. If you are reading this, it is because you are keen on learning more about the Tarot and how this ancient form of divination can be used to gain a deeper perspective on yourself and others around you.

Tarot is an age-old means of learning about the hidden aspects of our lives. It can be used to unveil traits that we might not necessarily be aware of. In addition, it can help us to become consciously aware of the things that make us tick. Indeed, the Tarot in a way in which you can really go down the path of self-discovery.

Yet, the Tarot is often dismissed as quackery as a result of its widespread use by fortune tellers and so-called psychics. There abound self-proclaimed experts who allude to the use of the Tarot as a means of predicting the future. These individuals are commonly found everywhere. Consequently, their inappropriate use of the Tarot has led a vast majority of people to become skeptical about its actual purpose of usefulness.

In this book, you will learn about what the Tarot actually is and what it can be used for. While there is no denying that it is a powerful tool that can be used to reveal general trends about transiting from the present to the future, it should be noted that this book is not about learning how to predict the future. Rather, this book is about learning what the Tarot is about and how you can use it to learn more about yourself and others around you.

Furthermore, this book will help you get a handle on what the individual cards represent and the common archetypes that they are based on. As you will see, each card has a reason for being; they are not merely nice-looking pictures that you can use to "tell the future." Each card speaks to one, or more, aspects of your personality. As such, the meanings attached to each card will help you to hone your senses.

That being said, anyone who is interested in this topic stands to gain from this book. So, whether you are a novice or a seasoned veteran in the Tarot, you will find something useful. You will surely find something that can stimulate your curiosity and take you from a passing curiosity to a serious pursuit of further knowledge. Best of all, you don't actually need to be versed in the Tarot to take advantage of this book. Everything you need to know to get started is right here.

We know that there is a great deal of information out there. Unfortunately, it is scattered all over the internet. In addition, print books are not easy to find on this subject. Therefore, we have incorporated everything you need to know into a single volume. That way, you won't have to go scouring all over the internet, or local bookstores for that matter, in order to find all of the information you have been looking for.

So, do take the time to go over every one of the topics in this book. You will find that they are all interconnected. Thus, it is highly recommended that you read this book in the sequence that it is presented. In this manner, you will be able to fully comprehend the information that we have presented herein.

Moreover, the information contained in this book may lead you down the path to other pursuits. So, we recommend that you keep this volume handy for easy reference down the road. That way, you can always refer back to it any time that you need to do so. Thank you once again for taking the time to read this book. Great care was taken in putting it together. We hope that you will find it both interesting and informative. Now, let's get on with it!

Chapter 1: The History of Tarot

Playing cards are very old and first showed up in Europe sometime around the late 1300s. Playing cards are thought to have been brought to Europe from Egypt and had four suits: batons (or polo sticks), coins (sometimes referred to as disks), swords, and cups. These four suits are very similar to the four suits in modern playing card decks, including tarot, and were the original inspiration for the four common suits that we still use today. Tarot cards have been around for centuries; however, with the oldest known playing card deck that resembled the modern tarot deck was made sometime between the years 1418 and 1425. This was a 60-card deck with 16 cards that featured images of several Greek gods and with four suits, each depicting a different kind of bird. This commissioned deck of playing cards, and others like it, would go on to inspire the first legitimate tarot packs, which were recorded to have been made in the 1440s in Bologna, Ferrara, Florence, and Milan. These decks added trump cards to the typical four suits that many decks contained. These new decks were referred to as "carte da trionfi," with the additional trump cards being called simply as "trionfi," which was later translated to trumps in English. The earliest documented mention of the trionfi was in a written statement in the Florence court records from the year 1440, referring to the transfer of two separate decks to Sigismondo Pandolfo Malatesta at that time. The oldest tarot cards that still survive today are about 15 of the Visconti-Sforza decks, which were painted sometime around the middle of the 15th century. There was also an expanded tarot deck that was commonly used in Florence, which featured 97 separate cards and included things like the four classical elements, astrological symbols, and many of the traditional tarot motifs of that period.

Tarot cards can seem confusing at times, with their ancient iconography and their use of religious imagery, historical events, and various ancient symbols. To those who are not familiar with the cards and their symbolism, they might even seem evil or unholy. A Dominican preacher even talked about the inherent evil of the tarot cards in a sermon during the 15th century, referencing their use in gambling and divinatory practices and spoke out against the use of the tarot. The main use of these cards was entertainment, but some people chose to use them for things like fortune-telling, as well. This is the source of a lot of misconceptions of the nature of the kind of "divination" that is performed with the use of tarot cards, which causes a lot of people to dismiss them as frivolous and foolish; some people even condemned them as "evil." To outsiders and skeptics who dismiss the existence of the "magic" that they believe tarot divination to utilize, the use of these cards can seem silly or pointless. However, the "magic" of the kind of divination that can be performed with the use of tarot cards doesn't come from some mystical force. If you take a closer look at the tarot deck and the meanings of each card, then the true nature of the tarot will become much clearer. Each card represents a different stage of human emotional and mental development and a different aspect of human life. The small, static images that are depicted on each of the tarot cards can be used to reveal many of the most common and complicated struggles or desires that human beings experience and can help us understand our circumstances in order to better understand or shape the outcome of certain events that are happening in our lives or will happen soon. The "magic" of tarot decks comes from simple psychological practices, rather than a mystical force manipulating your fate to show you the cards that you need.

The Meaning of Tarot Cards

The specific meanings of different cards have changed over the years, as well. Divination cards have been altered and changed to reflect the culture of the current era and the needs of their users. This is a large part of why these cards can be so difficult for "outsiders" to understand. Many different tarot decks, especially some of the older ones, contain references or allegories to specific people or events that occurred in the past, sometimes even many centuries earlier. Before the 18th century, a lot of the imagery that exists on the cards of the tarot deck applied to a much larger audience much more directly because they were designed for the people of that time. However, there have been several shifts in the attitudes and mentalities that people carry since then, and as a result, some people find it much more difficult to understand and relate to the meanings on most tarot decks today. Many of the modern tarot cards are either very simple or extremely confusing, still using a number of signs and symbols that most people simply do not recognize immediately unless they have already done some research on the meanings of the cards.

The use of cards for the purposes of this kind of divination goes back to around the 4th century, and many people believe that this practice originated with the cards for a game that was played in Turkey called Mamluk. Sometime around the 1500s, a group of Italian aristocrats had discovered a game called "Tarocchi Appropriati," which had players dealing random cards and using common thematic associations in the meanings of the cards to write simple poetic verses about themselves and the other players, similar to the more modern game "MASH." Even the earliest tarot decks were designed for games, like the "carte da trionfi" decks that were commissioned by several wealthy Italian families to be used in a game that was similar to Bridge. The cards in these decks contained the four suits that we still use today—cups, coins, swords, and sticks (which would later become wands)—as well as face cards, including the king and two male underlings. Tarot cards would later be developed to include a queen, the "trump" cards, and a "fool" card for a total of 78 cards in a single deck.

The artwork that was displayed on the tarot cards' faces was meant to reflect various aspects of the real world that the players of these games lived in at the time. Some people believed that this imagery was also intended to create a realistic narrative within the play of the game that they were created for, which makes sense if you consider the nature of many of the games that have been played with tarot cards throughout the years. This also allows the cards to reflect common archetypes and experiences in a typical human life and led to the use of tarot cards for divination later on as people began to play these games on their own or even applied the games that they played with the cards and the narratives that they created and likely related to themselves or the people they played with.

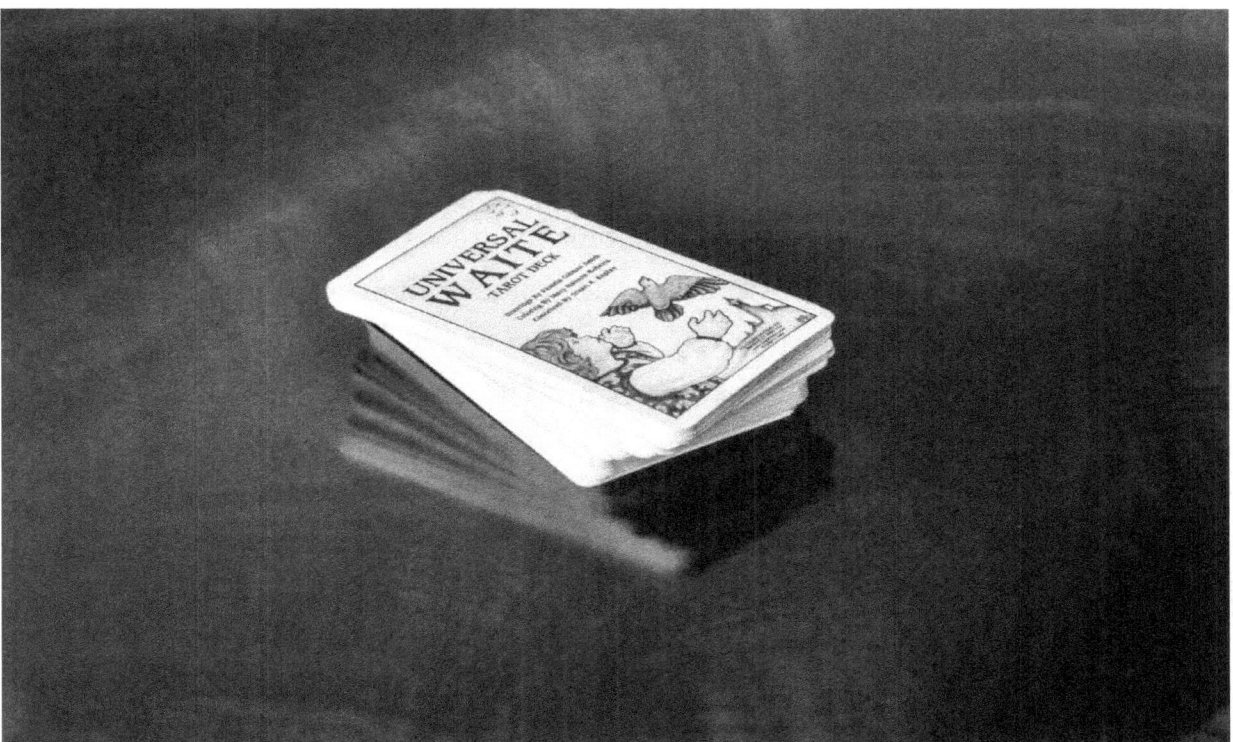

One of the most common tarot decks today is the "Rider-Waite" deck, which has been the most popular version of the tarot deck since the early 1900s. This deck is named after its own publisher William Rider and a popular mystic named A.E. Waite, who had the deck illustrated. The Rider-Waite deck is responsible for bringing the tarot to popularity with modern mystical readers and for divinatory readings. This deck was originally designed to be used for divination, and many decks included a book written by

Waite, which described and explained a lot of the meanings behind all of the imagery and symbolism that the cards contained.

The tarot is definitely one of the most widely known kinds of card decks used for divinatory purposes, but there are other kinds that exist as well. Some of these are the common 52 playing card deck that you will see more commonly or any of the common "oracle decks" that can be purchased outside of the typical tarot, like the Lenormand deck. An interesting fact to note about the tarot, however, is that the original tarot decks that came from Egypt were said to have had a number of Egyptian symbols in their illustrations, which helped in the popularization of this deck over a number of the other kinds of oracle decks. Although the Egyptian system of hieroglyphs had not been deciphered by that point, as the rosetta stone would not be discovered until the year 1799, a large portion of European people in the 18th century thought it was possible that the Egyptian people had a deep insight about the nature of human existence. When the tarot cards were revealed to have a number of Egyptian symbols on their illustrations, a lot of people connected the new tarot cards to the perceived insights of the Egyptian people and began to flock to the tarot over many of the other oracle card decks for the purposes of divination. Additionally, it was also said that the tarot deck was based on the Book of Thoth and was made by Thoth's priests into several gold plates, which served as inspiration for the original tarot decks. They were eventually redesigned as the first card deck that was intended explicitly for divination and cartomancy.

Chapter 2: Tarot and Archetypes

An important thing to learn about tarot is the concept of the Jungian archetypes. Carl Jung is considered to have been one of the founders of analytical psychology, and while he never directly mentioned tarot cards specifically in any of his work, there are very clear connections to the concepts that he helped develop and the concepts and ideas behind the tarot. One of Jung's most influential contributions to the theory of psyche was the introduction of archetypal images and the idea of the collective unconscious, which are significant concepts of the tarot. The concept of the collective unconscious was largely developed and popularized by Jung, who believed that every individual possesses their own personal "conscious" mind, which contains all of the knowledge and all of the memories that a person has experienced in his or her life up to a particular point in time. This is the active mind and what most people commonly think of as the "self." All of the memories and knowledge that you actively draw upon rests within this personal conscious mind. There is also a "personal unconscious" below the personal conscious. The personal unconscious is very similar to the personal conscious; the main difference lies in the fact that it contains the memories and knowledge that a person has forgotten or repressed but have still been experienced in the past. These memories still belong to you and you alone, whether you actively remember it or not. The memories and experiences within the personal unconscious are "hidden away" from the person and were "locked away" or otherwise lost for some reason or another, whether they were traumatic memories or simply unimportant ones that the person did not need. However, while these memories and experiences cannot be recalled, they can still impact the person whom they belong to, in the form of "unexplained" habits or caution that the person takes without an apparent reason for doing so. These repressed or "lost" memories can be revealed or uncovered through therapy, hypnosis, or meditation for a number of reasons, but as they stand in the personal unconscious, the person will not be actively aware of those memories.

Tarot cards can also sometimes reveal the concepts of these unconscious memories or experiences through their imagery. There is another state that people possess that exists outside of the personal conscious and unconscious, which is called the "superconscious." The superconscious is where our "higher self" exists, as well as the experiences and memories from our "past lives" and the things that we learned during those lives. Tarot relates to this concept by using the superconscious and the ways that it will affect the personal unconscious to reveal things about ourselves that we may not have realized or fully understood. The superconscious is also thought to be our primary source of connection to the divine and other universal forces. One of the most common and simplest tarot spreads uses three cards to tell us about our past, present, and future. The idea behind this spread is that we will arrange our tarot deck and choose our cards based on the experiences that we have had that have been hidden within our unconscious mind through the superconscious. Carl Jung believed that we could "tell the future" by examining and evaluating our past and the ways that our past choices have affected the events that followed them, as well as our present situations. This is similar to the concept behind a famous aphorism, which was even adopted by Winston Churchill, "Those who fail to learn from history are condemned to repeat it."

Jungian Archetypes Found in the Tarot

Jung also believed that there was another realm beyond the personal mind, an unconscious mind that every person contributes to and draws from. Jung believed that if you stepped below the personal unconscious, you would find a deeper level, which was called the "collective unconscious." The collective unconscious contained all the general experiences that all of mankind shared since their creation, as well as all the records of mankind's evolution over the years. The memories and experiences that were contained within the collective unconscious are owned collectively by every person in the world.

Every person in the world also has access to the collective unconscious and can draw from it for inspiration or information relating to the common experiences that all or most human people encounter. The collective unconscious is not made up of specific memories or experiences but of common symbols and archetypes. A lot of people believe that the collective unconscious is accessed by people in the form of our dreams. The archetypes, or the models which we use to identify general concepts and ideas, are common or regular patterns of behavior that can be noticed in different kinds of people from different backgrounds or in different situations that we might encounter. There is an archetype, usually multiple archetypes that can be applied to any person or situation that we might encounter in our lives. As humans continue to grow and develop, we find new archetypes to add to the list as we encounter new things or unexpected situations that we cannot explain with ones that already exist. These archetypes can be thought of in a similar way to the tropes that we used to describe film or television characters or stories. As we create new television shows or movies, they will change our perception of existing tropes, and if we encounter a new kind of character or story, we will add it to our list of different kinds of tropes. Similarly, examples of different archetypal concepts can be found in everything and everyone that we come across throughout our lives.

The symbols and archetypes that we use to describe different situations and entities all reside within what we refer to as the collective unconscious. One good example of a common archetype is the "mother" figure from just about every culture around the world. Every person who has ever existed has had a figure that acted as a mother to them or is familiar with the idea of a mother figure. Of course, every person has to be born from their mother, so it would make sense that most cultures share the same or similar ideas of what a mother is. These are figures like Mary or Gaia or any number of deities and characters that act as a "mother" to humankind. This archetype might not manifest itself in the same specific ways for every individual person, but the basic concept of "the mother" is essentially the same, no matter what your personal experiences are. A mother figure is a person who is caring, loving, and nurturing and someone who sees to your physical and emotional growth and well-being.

The theory behind this concept is that all people have relatively consistent connections to these common archetypes and that these archetypal images form the foundation for our perception and affect the ways that we think about and perceive our experiences and tell stories about our lives.

Common Archetypes in the Tarot

Some common archetypes that can be seen in almost every culture are the "anima" and the "animus." These represent two parts of a union that makes up the whole and complete "self." These concepts represent the masculine and feminine parts that every person possesses. These concepts of the masculine and feminine aspects of people and the world exist in most cultures, and an important part of being a well-balanced and mentally healthy person is the ability to understand and accept both the masculine and feminine aspects of yourself and the world. It is also important to understand that while the anima and animus describe traits that are commonly viewed as "masculine" and "feminine," these traits exist in every person regardless of their sex or gender. Every person has aspects and qualities that relate to both the anima and the animus, and whatever way you choose to identify with any of these qualities is absolutely fine. For tarot cards, this means that cards that represent feminine figures can still apply to a man and vice versa. These cards simply use imagery that is easy for us to understand and relate to the archetypes that we probably already know; the masculine and feminine animus and anima are figures that we are familiar with and can help provide us with insight about ourselves with common archetypal symbols.

The lovers are a good representation of the concepts of anima and animus, as they represent a union of masculine and feminine figures. The characters represented on these cards are also typically depicted as having opposing or conflicting natures. Another good card that represents the concepts of the anima and the animus is the world card. This is a card similar to the lovers, but it deals with a larger scale, representing the union of all the different parts of the world.

There are also other important aspects of ourselves that will be important to keep in mind. One is the persona. Carl Jung described the persona as the "masks" that different people show to the world and the people around them. These personas manifest as the ways that we present ourselves and how we would like to be perceived within our societies. These are common archetypes that people will portray to the people around them, like the artist, the scholar, or the leader. Jung also believed that a healthy person would be able to maintain multiple personas and could be much more flexible with the personas that they could align themselves with. It can even be argued that the ability to maintain and align yourself with multiple different personas, along with an understanding of them, is required in order to be mentally and emotionally healthy as a person.

The shadow is also another important concept to understand. Where personas are the parts of ourselves that we project to the people around us and to the world as a whole, the shadow represents the parts of ourselves that we reject. All the aspects of ourselves that we hide from the people around us, and, sometimes, from ourselves are all potential parts that make up our "shadows." For example, you might be kind of rude or malicious sometimes. Everyone can be, at times, but those qualities can be difficult to accept in ourselves. When you reject those qualities, they can become detached and almost like a separate part of ourselves that we try to push away or "brush under the carpet."

Shadows are the archetypal basis for a lot of the monsters and the concepts that make up our perception of "evil." An important part of becoming a healthy and mature human being is being able to understand your "shadows" and accept them as parts of you, instead of simply rejecting them. One card that can be easily related to the concept of the shadow is "the devil." The devil is commonly used to represent the concept of the shadow. Things like addiction and detachment and the ability to come to terms with those qualities and explore them as a part of you are some of the basic concepts of the devil card. Death is also a good card that can be used to relate to the shadow. Death is something that most people fear. Death follows you from the womb throughout the course of your life and is an objective fact regardless of whether you acknowledge it or not. Coming to terms with the concept of death is an important part of developing as a person and will help to shape who you are and the way that you choose to live.

Another common archetype that is related to the concepts of the persona and the shadow is the "self." The concept of the self is a little bit more complicated, but the self can be thought of for the sake of simplicity as the unification of all of the archetypes and all of the different aspects of ourselves. Carl Jung believed that people are usually "whole" as children and become fragmented as they grow up and develop prejudices and insecurities, and the goal of our personal journey, once we reach adulthood, is to become whole again. This idea of the path to becoming whole and healthy can be seen clearly in the "first" (numbered 0) and last cards of the Tarot's major arcana, the fool, and the world. The fool most directly represents the concept of the "self." Each of the numbered major arcana cards represents a step along the "fool's journey" or the path that each person will walk toward becoming "whole." The last numbered major arcana card and the last step on the "fool's journey" is the world. The world represents the unification of all of the various aspects of the self in order to allow us (or the fool) to become whole again. The steps of the fool's journey, the cards that represent them, and their common archetypes are discussed in the following chapter.

Chapter 3: The Major Arcana

In this chapter, we are going to be looking at the Major Arcana in Tarot. Based on the Jungian archetypes discussed earlier, this set of cards represents the large or major archetypes common to virtually all cultures throughout history.

0 – The Fool

The first of the cards that will be described here is the fool. The Fool card most commonly depicts a young man who is carrying a small sack and walking carelessly ahead without paying attention to the dangers along his path. The fool walks forward, toward the edge of a cliff, about to take his final step off and fall off the edge. It is unclear whether he is unaware or if he simply does not care. There is also usually a dog following the fool, sometimes barking at him in an attempt to warn the fool about the dangers that he faces and the traps that he might fall into if he does not become aware of his surroundings. This gives the reader of this card the impression that if the fool does not realize the dangers ahead and act more cautiously, he might not be able to grow as a person and live out the adventures he dreams of. Some of the concepts that the Fool card represents are innocence, opportunities, and wonder. Because of these traits, a common archetype for this card is "the child."

All tarot cards have two meanings—one interpretation for the upright position and one for when the card is drawn upside-down. The fool also applies to this rule. Unlike most of the cards within the tarot deck's major arcana, as well as the minor arcana, the fool does not have a "real" number. The Fool card holds the number 0, which is representative of the fool's potential for growth and development as he walks along the path called the fool's journey. Because of this potential and the number that represents it, the fool is also considered to be a blank slate, without a clear and developed personality. The fool is commonly seen as a symbol of innocence and as a representation of the "broken" state that people find themselves in and need to recover from in order to "build" themselves and become a whole and healthy person again.

Drawing the Fool card, specifically in the upright position, typically represents opportunities. Things like new beginnings or the start of a journey, which will provide us with the opportunity to discover freedom from the typical constraints of mundane life. At the start of his journey, the fool sees each new day as its own adventure in a way that seems almost childish. He sees everything that happens to him as an opportunity and believes that anything is possible in the world. He leads a simple, carefree life and wishes to explore and develop the world, unburdened by any concern for what lies ahead, good or bad. The fool inspires courage among those around him, as he understands that each new day is an opportunity to discover new doors. Drawing the fool card is also sometimes interpreted as a "call to action," telling the recipient of this card that they should begin to embrace risks and new opportunities that present themselves. The fool carries the lesson in his mind that you can never know what lies ahead and that sometimes the only way to find out is to take a leap of faith. Good or bad, you will often find adventure.

However, when the fool is presented in the reversed or upside-down position, he shows some of his more "negative" or undesirable qualities to the recipient of this card. Presented in the reversed position, the Fool card warns us to be cautious and careful and that they might even be acting "like a fool" by ignoring the consequences of our actions. Much like the careless figure that is depicted on this card, you might not be aware of a hazardous position that you are in or will find yourself in unless you can learn to be more aware of your actions and your surroundings. The reversed fool card might be warning the recipient to take more care in planning for the future and being aware of the consequences of their actions, instead of simply "living in the moment." Much like the dog that is commonly depicted on this card, the reversed fool card warns the recipient against acting recklessly or allowing themselves to be taken advantage of. Some things are simply too good to be true, and the reversed fool card acts as a reminder of that fact.

1 – The Magician

The actual first numbered card of the major arcana is the magician. The magician card commonly depicts a figure with one hand pointing toward the heavens and one hand pointing to the ground. One common interpretation of the directions of the magician's hands is a connection to the phrase "as above, so below," which states that the earth reflects the heavens or that the "microcosm" is inspired by the "macrocosm." Another common interpretation is that the magician's hands are representative of his nature as a bridge between the heavens and the earth. The magician typically stands behind a table, which holds one item representative of each of the four symbols of the minor arcana's suits: swords, wands, pentacles, and cups, with an "infinity" symbol above his head, representing the infinite possibilities of creation with the will. For reasons that will most likely seem obvious, the magician is commonly connected to the concepts of power and magic, and a common archetype for the magician card is "the trickster."

When drawn upright, the magician represents the willpower of the recipient, as well as the concepts of creation, desire, and manifestation. With the power of the elements that he wields, the magician is capable of moving forward with the potential that is represented by the fool, molding himself and his desires in order to manifest them and realize his potential. The magician uses his willpower to realize his desires and acts as the link between the heavens and the earth by inciting change on earth to mirror the heavens. The upright magician tells his recipient to remember that they have the power to manifest their desires and realize their potential. Drawing the magician in the upright position can tell you that it might be time to stop hesitating and move forward in order to realize your full potential. This can relate to our lives in the form of new opportunities, which we will need to take in order to grow and develop. Where the fool presents the possibility of new doors along our paths, the magician tells us that it's time to open those doors and begin to take action to mold our world into the one that we desire the most.

Drawing this card in the reversed position, however, represents a version of the magician who more closely embodies the "trickster" archetype. Where the upright magician represents action and power, the reversed magician is a being who is out of touch and uses trickery and illusions to get what he wants. The reversed magician is a warning to its recipient that they might need to make some changes in your life. This might take the form of a friend or another person in your life who pretends as if they have your interests in mind while simultaneously acting against you, or someone who will lure you in with their showmanship and charm in order to manipulate you for their personal gain. Drawing this card in the reversed position means that it might be time for you to evaluate yourself and the people around you. Maybe there is a person close to you who craves power and will manipulate you in order to achieve it, or it might even be possible that you have become obsessed with that power. In order to move forward and grow as a person, you will need to take care to avoid making careless choices that might lead to negative consequences for you and the people around you.

2 – The High Priestess

The second card representing a step along the fool's journey is the high priestess. The high priestess card commonly depicts a woman who sits with her hands in her lap on a cube-shaped stone placed between the pillars in Solomon's Temple—Boaz and Jachin. The pillar to the left of the empress, Jachin, is commonly seen as a symbol of establishment and order, whereas Boaz is representative of the concept of strength. A common interpretation of the meanings of these pillars is that they represent a number of different dual opposing concepts within nature, like the masculine and the feminine or good and evil. The high priestess and her position between these two pillars and on the porch of Solomon's Temple hint at her role as the mediator for fundamental opposing aspects of life and nature, even acting as the "third pillar." The high priestess understands the importance of opposing forces and represents the union of those forces. The high priestess is also very commonly shown with a crown, a cross, and a crescent moon at her feet. These items show her connection to the elements, nature, and emotional awareness. The high priestess is commonly connected to the concepts of intuition and emotion, and a common archetype for the magician card is "the Anima."

When drawn upright, the high priestess represents the inner voice and intuition of the recipient, as well as the unconscious mind and inner knowledge. The magician card leans on the use of passion and desire to actively try to mold the world and manifest their desires. The high priestess suggests to her recipient that they should begin listening more closely to their intuition, as opposed to the conscious mind. The high priestess card most commonly depicts a dark, nighttime scene, representing a time when many people delve into introspection and self-growth. The high priestess instructs us to look within one's own self, instead of outward like the magician, for wisdom. The answers that you seek lie within your personal unconscious, and you will need to look there in order to move forward.

When the high priestess is drawn in the reversed position, she represents a lack or loss of center or your inner voice. You might be having trouble being able to find your center or to hear your inner voice. If this is the case, she advises you to meditate and look inside yourself for a new approach and ultimately trust in your intuition. Sometimes, your situation can be stressful, or you may find yourself being forced to make a difficult decision. Underestimating the value of looking within for the answers to our problems can lead us astray and cause us to "lose ourselves," acting discordantly. This can cause a sort of cognitive dissonance and is the cause of the kinds of actions and decisions that we come to regret with hindsight.

3 – The Empress

The third card representing a step along the fool's journey is the empress. The empress card commonly depicts a woman who sits on a throne in a field, surrounded by a large forest with a river flowing through it. The lush forest around the Empress' throne represents her connection to nature and the earth and is commonly thought to represent the Earth Mother. The empress is also commonly associated with the concepts of fertility, harmony, and love. The empress has a crown of stars on her head, showing a deep connection with the divine. She is typically depicted wearing a robe patterned with pomegranates, which are representative of fertility and sits on cushions that show the symbol of Venus. The empress blesses the earth and the life within it with abundance and love. The empress is commonly connected to the concepts of nature, fertility, and motherhood, and a common archetype for the magician card is "the mother." The anima, which was mentioned earlier, is also a very good archetype for this card.

When drawn upright, the empress represents the feminine aspects of the recipient, as well as things like expression, creativity, and nurturing. The empress suggests to her recipient that they should begin to reach out and embrace an aspect of themselves that they might have neglected or might still be neglecting, leaning on the feminine aspects of themselves in order to foster growth and become a happier, well-adjusted person. The Empress card pushes its recipient to begin to understand themselves on a deeper level and to appreciate and take care of themselves. Drawing the Empress card upright might indicate motherhood or nurturing tendencies, possibly even pregnancy. She can also represent symbolic birth, such as a new idea or a new stage in your life, presenting you with opportunities for abundance and growth. Embrace these new opportunities and nurture them, and they are sure to bring you happiness and fortune.

When the empress is drawn in the reversed position, however, she acts as a warning to her recipient that they have begun to focus too heavily on other people or things and might be neglecting themselves as a result. While the empress is devoted to nurturing and caring for her loved ones, she can sometimes go too far and begin to overwhelm herself, or she might mean well in her actions to help the people around her but end up causing harm in the long run by solving everyone's problems for them. However, the empress simply represents an over-nurturing relationship. Being presented with the reversed empress card might not necessarily mean that you are too caring, or you would go too far trying to help others. You might find yourself on the other side of that coin, relying on other people to solve all of your problems for you or make decisions for you. If this is the case, the reversed empress pushes you to work toward finding your own action and being able to solve problems on your own.

4 – The Emperor

The fourth card representing a step along the fool's journey is the emperor. The emperor card commonly depicts a man in a position of power, most likely an emperor, sitting at his throne. This throne usually has four rams' heads on it at the top of the arm and the headrests, drawing a connection to his zodiac sign, Aries. In each hand, he typically holds a symbol of his power. His right hand holds a scepter, representing his power and right to rule as the emperor, and his left hand holds an orb, representing the lands that he keeps a watch over. The emperor is also most commonly shown to have a long beard, representing his age and experience and the wisdom that comes with them. He is a just and old ruler who learned over time how to rule his lands with power and authority, as well as the importance of order and how to maintain it for the sake of his people. While the empress leans on a kind and caring nature, the emperor relies on strength and power in order to maintain the order that he has worked so hard to achieve. The empress also represents the feminine, and the Emperor mirrors that by being a symbol of the masculine traits that exist within every person. The common concepts that the emperor is used to represent are authority, structure, order, control, and fatherhood.

The most directly apparent archetype for this card is the animus, as it represents the masculine traits of human beings. Other common archetypes that are used to describe the emperor are the father and the hero.

When drawn upright, the emperor represents the masculine aspects of its recipient, as well as concepts such as authority, organization, structure, and fatherhood. The high priestess card leans on the use of intuition and introspection to allow herself to make the right decisions with confidence and without regret. The empress and the emperor balance the ideas of the high priestess by championing active choices and philosophies for the benefit of those around them. The emperor is a strategist who lays plans before enforcing those plans until they have been completed. The emperor is the most direct depiction of the concept of the animus, acting as a paternal figure for the people around him, creating structure and order, and imparting knowledge. He guides his people with a firm hand, performing his role as a source of order above everything else. He rules by serving his people and acting rationally and logically.

Drawing the emperor card in the upright position represents a chance to follow the goals and plans that you have set for yourself, which will allow you to grow and progress as a person. The upright emperor represents to its user a successful and healthy future, as long as they can remember to set goals for themselves and pursue those goals in the same way that the emperor himself does. Another interpretation for the drawing of the emperor card is a current or upcoming position of leadership. This could represent a new position at work or even literal fatherhood. You will need to act as the emperor would, using order and decisiveness, in order to bring clarity and structure to your surroundings.

When the emperor is drawn in the reversed position, however, he represents the abuse of a position of power or authority. This might be something that you have done or will do, or it could be someone close to you. This could be a father figure, possessive partner, or a superior at work who oversteps their role or is performing the role of the emperor inadequately or in a way that betrays the philosophy of the emperor. Regardless of the specifics of your actions, the reversed emperor tells you that you will need to rely more heavily on structure and order in order to find success.

5 – The Hierophant

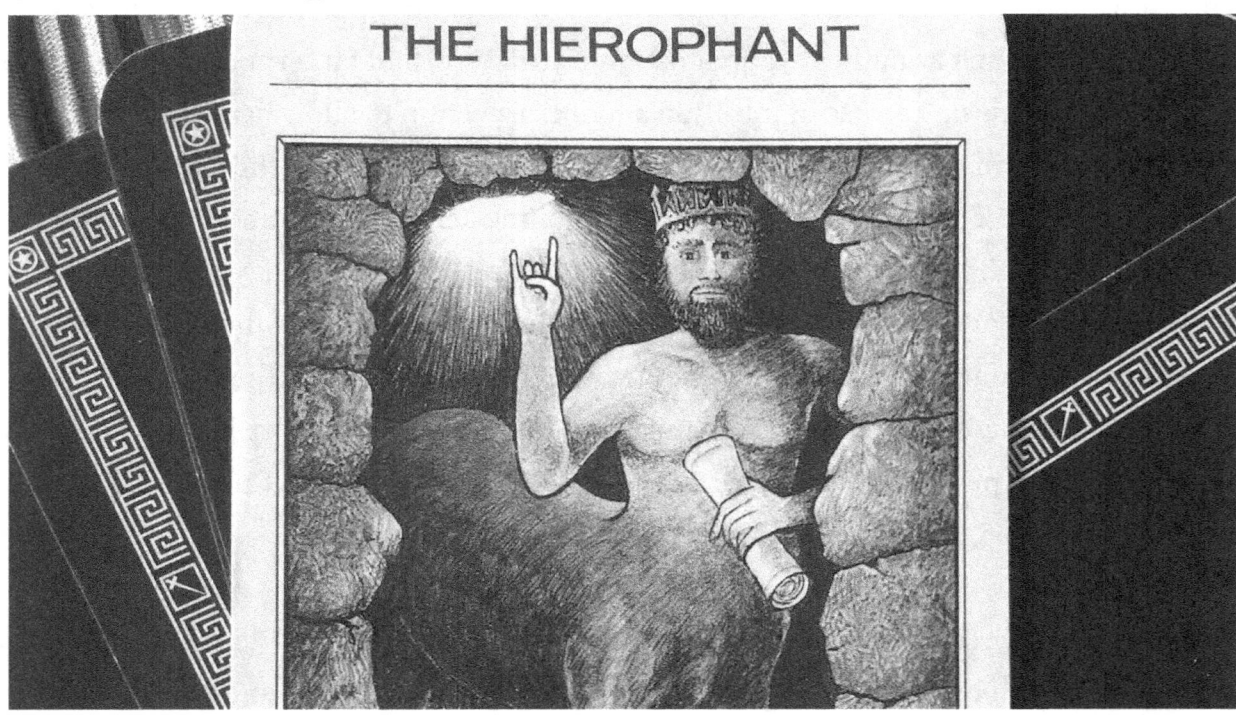

The fifth card representing another step along the fool's journey is the hierophant. The Hierophant card commonly depicts some sort of religious figure sitting within a church, wearing elaborate vestments in three parts, which are meant to represent three different worlds. The hierophant's right hand is raised upward, likely in the middle of some sort of blessing. This is also the same hand that the magician has raised. In their other hand, the hierophant holds a triple cross, which is a symbol often associated with the pope. The three horizontal bars on the triple cross are thought to represent the Father, the Son, and the Holy Spirit. The hierophant is also commonly depicted along with two acolytes, who represent the transfer of sacred knowledge, and the inclusion of these two acolytes adds to the meaning of the card and draw a line from the hierophant card to the path to gaining knowledge. The hierophant is also called by different names in certain tarot decks, acting as the masculine counterpart to the high priestess. Other names for the hierophant are the high priest and the pope. The hierophant is commonly connected to the role of a guide or a teacher and is commonly associated with the "wise old man" archetype.

When drawn upright, the hierophant represents the embrace of tradition and convention. The hierophant suggests to its recipient that they might want to stay within the conventional path or follow one that has been well-traveled. You might want to stay within certain boundaries of what could be considered normal or typical. Instead of innovating and finding new paths, you will adapt to certain beliefs or certain courses of action that have already been put in place. The hierophant guides people along a typical path. He instructs his recipient that they should "stick to the basics" in order to accomplish their goals. Clichés and tropes exist for a reason, after all. The Hierophant card is typically associated with institutions and their core values. The Hierophant represents the safe and proven routes that will allow you to achieve your goals, as well as moral and ethical norms or traditions.

When the hierophant is drawn in the reversed position, however, he acts as a warning to his recipient that they might be feeling a little bit too restricted or constrained, held down by structures and rules. The reversed Hierophant warns the recipient that they might have lost some of their own action and cannot reach their full potential if they continue on their current path. You might have a strong will and require freedom and the ability to act in your own way. Breaking away from tradition and trying new or unorthodox approaches to your problems will allow you to achieve your goals. The reversed Hierophant, more than anything, instructs their recipient to take action and to challenge tradition in order to act in the ways that suit them and allow them to realize their potential.

6 – The Lovers

The sixth card representing another step along the fool's journey is the lovers. The lovers card commonly depicts a man and a woman being guarded by an angel above them. They are also sometimes depicted as similar to Adam and Eve. Both of the lovers typically appear to be content and secure and standing in the Garden of Eden. The fruit tree with the snake from the story of Adam and Eve stands behind the woman and acts as a hint toward the fall of humanity into the realm of temptation, as per the story of Adam and Eve. The angel that stands behind the couple is Raphael, the angel of the air. There are also other connections to the air within this card. The zodiac sign which this card is representative of is Gemini, the twins, which is also connected to the element of air. The air is commonly associated with the mind and with communication, which is also considered to be a vital and basic aspect of a healthy relationship with another person. The lovers are commonly associated with the concepts of balance, harmony, partnerships, and union between two opposing forces. This union is also significant since a majority of the cards that come before the lovers in the fool's journey are originally presented in pairs; the Emperor and Empress and the high pope and high priest. The lovers are representative of the union of the concepts that have been presented in the other cards so far. The lovers are also commonly connected to the concepts of duality and balance, and the common archetypes that this card represents are the soul or the combination of the anima and animus.

When drawn upright, the lovers symbolize attraction, harmony, and balance in a current or future relationship. The bond of the lovers and the trust that they have in each other is a source of strength for each of them and allow them to empower each other. The lovers' bond is a strong one and can be indicative of a strong and close relationship that you have with someone close to you. Another common interpretation of the upright lovers card is the idea of duality, presenting the recipient with a choice between two opposing and mutually exclusive options. This could represent a very important decision that you will need to make, and which will change your current situation based on the choice that you make.

When the lovers card is drawn in the reversed position, however, they can represent a source of imbalance or discord that exists within your life. These harmful forces can make life incredibly difficult and can even begin to place unnecessary pressure on your relationships with the people around you. You might be struggling with a particular event or choice that you have made and need to let go of. You should take your own personal values into account in order to understand the problems that you are facing and how to find peace for yourself. The lovers presented in reverse can also represent a relationship that has been broken or cut off, or it can be a source of imbalance between you and the people around you. These problems need to be addressed in order for you to achieve a sense of balance again.

7 – The Chariot

The next card representing another step along the fool's journey is the chariot. The chariot card typically depicts a figure who sits within a vehicle, usually a chariot, which is being pulled by two sphinxes—one black and one white. The chariot is commonly topped with a blue canopy patterned with white stars and wearing armor with lunar symbols on his person. The chariot represents the spiritual guidance that he receives and is influenced by. He typically wears some sort of crown, as well, showing that he has been "enlightened" and that his intentions are pure. The sphinxes that pull the chariot are black and white, representing two opposing forces that the recipient will need to learn to control. The two sphinxes will often try to move in opposing directions, and the chariot will need to guide them forward in order to arrive at his desired destination. The chariot is commonly associated with concepts like hard work, determination, and willpower, as well as control and direction. He is commonly associated with the "warrior" archetype.

The chariot accomplishes his goals and overcomes obstacles that lie in his way by gaining control of the world around him. He maintains confidence in his ability to control his situation and manipulate the forces around him in order to achieve victory. To the recipient, this card being drawn upright might represent opposing or otherwise chaotic or discordant forces around you that you will need to handle with confidence and determination, maintaining focus on manipulating those forces in order to stay on the path that you have set. If you have a particular course of action in mind, you will need to pursue that plan with determination and a strong plan of action in order to reach your goals. It will be important for you to have a strong will in order to achieve your goals, but if you can stay focused, you will be able to succeed. You might even need to discover new qualities within yourself in order to find this success. Anger can often be seen as a negative quality, but the chariot attempts to remind us that it can also be helpful and even synonymous with willpower and drive. It can even be beneficial to those who are able to contain and focus their anger toward a specific goal.

When drawn in reverse, however, the chariot instructs the recipient to do just that. The recipient of the reversed chariot might have a strong will but too little focus to wield it effectively. The reversed chariot represents the sphinxes running out of control and warns the recipient of similarly discordant forces around them, preventing them from finding success. You will need to focus these forces in order to gain control of your surroundings and reach the goals that you are struggling to achieve.

8 – Strength

The next card representing another step along the fool's journey is referred to as "strength." The Strength card usually depicts a woman who stands above a male lion, holding its jaws, appearing to be calming the lion and having some sort of power over the beast. A common thing that people will notice regarding the woman depicted on the Strength card is how calmly she seems to be handling this fearsome beast. The strength card represents the ability to remain calm and controlled in the face of adversity. She also represents the ideas of bravery and courage, as well as compassion. A common archetype that is associated with strength is "endurance."

The strength card, when drawn in the upright position, shows the strength and fortitude of the recipient, as well as their ability to maintain calmness in stressful or difficult situations. The strength card represents this ability in its recipient and tells them that if they are able to maintain this calmness, they will be able to come out of stressful situations unharmed. The strength card also tells its recipient about the importance of compassion and consideration for the people and things around you. You should always be able to make time for other people. The strength card also represents the patience of the recipient and their ability to come out on top by utilizing this patience, as well as their fortitude to ensure their safety. The strength that this card refers to is not literal physical strength but inner strength and the ability to persevere or endure. You should also have no issue speaking your mind when you feel strongly about something. You are a passionate person, and you should never attempt to hide that.

When drawn in reverse, however, the strength card indicates that you are currently in some sort of intense anger or fear in your life. Or, it could mean that you will soon encounter a similar challenge. The reversed strength card tells its recipient that they lack the inner strength that this card represents. You might also be lacking in happiness or passion and will need to discover or even rediscover your passion in order to move forward. The reversed strength card might also indicate that you are experiencing depression for any number of different reasons, and you will need to move past it in order to find happiness. You will need to become a more confident and fulfilled person in order to rediscover your strength and become "whole" again.

9 – The Hermit

The next card representing another step along the fool's journey is referred to as the hermit. The hermit card usually depicts an old man standing alone at the top of a mountain, holding a staff in his left hand and a lantern in the right. The mountain is commonly accepted as a representation of the development and success that the hermit has achieved throughout his years. The hermit has gained a large amount of spiritual wisdom throughout his long life and is willing to share that knowledge with others in order to help them grow. The hermit is also deeply committed to the path that he is taking toward his goals. Inside his lantern is also another symbol of wisdom, a six-point star known as the Seal of Solomon. The hermit seeks knowledge and wisdom that comes from within, and he wanders at night searching for that wisdom through prolonged periods of solitude and introspection. In order to understand this path and his goals, the hermit separates himself from others to avoid influences that could possibly affect the words of his inner voice and his ability to hear those words. The hermit represents the exploration of the unconscious for the sake of understanding oneself. Common concepts that are associated with the hermit are contemplation, introspection, and isolation, as well as the search for truth. Similar to the hierophant or high priest, the hermit is representative of the "wise old man" archetype.

The hermit seeks knowledge and wisdom through introspection. He searches through his unconscious for his inner voice, which will tell him about himself and his truths. Drawing the hermit card in the upright position might mean that you need to be alone for a period of time in order to look inward. Introspection is important to your personal growth and development. You should never be afraid to spend some time alone and clear your mind of all of the struggles and distractions that come with normal, everyday life. The hermit instructs his recipient that they should also try to be "authentic" and act according to their "true self." The hermit might represent a search for guidance or help with a decision that you do not understand. In some contexts, the hermit might represent the appearance of a person who will act as a mentor to you and provide guidance.

When drawn in reverse, however, the hermit will represent your desire to be alone; maybe you are constantly surrounded by others and need some time to be alone and do some introspection. You should not feel bad about that; everyone needs to take some time for themselves and recover from time to time. However, you should also be careful, as too much "alone time" can become harmful and detrimental to your growth, stunting you in some ways. Isolation can lead to boredom or even madness, causing you to dwell on past events and "losing yourself" or becoming out of touch with reality. The reversed hermit warns against these extremes and reminds the recipient that it is important to maintain a good balance in order to grow and develop as a person.

10 – The Wheel of Fortune

The card holding the number ten, which, of course, represents the tenth step in the fool's journey through the major arcana, is the wheel of fortune. The wheel of fortune is very commonly considered to be one of the most symbolically charged cards within the major arcana and even in the tarot deck as a whole. The image on this card primarily features a large wheel at its center, which is also covered in a number of different symbols and icons. There are also four creatures that are commonly represented on the face of this card, resting on clouds that surround the wheel of fortune at each of the four corners of the card. These creatures are typically the angel, the bull, the eagle, and the lion. These creatures are related to and representative of four of the twelve astrological signs. These are the "fixed" signs, which are Taurus, Leo, Scorpio, and Aquarius. These four beings are also often used to represent the four evangelists within Christianity, which is why they all have wings as well. The books that each being holds in their hands are used to represent the Torah, which is a collection of the laws of the Lord as they were presented to Moses and recorded as the first five books of the Tanakh, which is the collection of 24 books that make up all of the canonical Hebrew scriptures. The Torah communicates concepts related to wisdom and understanding, and provide the groundwork for the rest of the teachings of the Lord. There is also a snake that is typically depicted on the face of this card, which represents a descent into the "material world," a sphinx, which sits on the top of the wheel holding a sword, as well as a creature that is usually depicted as either a devil or as the Egyptian god Anubis, who is rising up from the bottom of the card. The sphinx and Anubis are used to represent the wisdom of kings and of the gods, as well as the underworld in the case of Anubis. These two entities rotate eternally as the wheel of fortune spins, carrying them along with it, suggesting a fluctuating and opposing relationship between the two beings and the concepts and ideas that they represent. As the sphinx rises to the top of the wheel, Anubis is forced to descend, and vice versa. They cannot rise to the top at the same time, and the rising of one means the descent of the other.

The wheel of fortune is always turning, carrying these two opposing entities along with it at opposite ends, which is representative of the way that life is made up of a variety of different experiences that come and go in phases that exist in a mutually exclusive and alternating pattern. This is true for all living beings. The wheel of fortune represents this duality. When this card is presented in the upright position with the sphinx at the tip of the wheel, it reminds its recipient to make sure to take advantage of the "good times" when they present themselves because they will eventually fall away to make room for "negative" experiences in order to restore balance and continue the eternal turning of the wheel of fortune. Of course, the same is true of the opposite; when you are experiencing the "bad times," it is important to recognize that these experiences will not last forever and that you will need to continue to endure in order to reach the more positive phase of the wheel's turning again. These phases can also be thought of as similar to the turning of the earth and the seasons that come with it. Some people might not particularly like winter and will look forward to spring and summer when they can enjoy the warm weather again. The forces that turn the wheel of fortune are the same forces that govern the passage of time and the seasons, as well as the cycle of day and night.

When the wheel of fortune card is presented in the reversed position, it represents the "bad" phase of the wheel's turning. Luck has not been on your side recently. You are very likely in the middle of the negative phase of the wheel, and it will be important for you to continue to maintain your endurance, waiting for the dawn to come again when the wheel begins to shine in your favor during its next phase. The reversed wheel of fortune instructs its recipient to avoid pretending that they have control over their "luck." The lesson that this card attempts to teach its recipient is that it is best to "let go" and coast during these low points, saving their energy to make the most of the next phase of the wheel's spin when fortune favors them again. If you continue to try to maintain control, reversing, or advancing the spin of the wheel of fortune, it will only bring you more suffering. It might negatively affect the situation that you currently find yourself in. By learning to accept your current situation, you can begin to "move on" in the same way that the wheel does, moving forward in your life and on your path to growth and development.

11 – Justice

The 11th step along the fool's journey through the major arcana is represented by the justice card. This is also the 11th numbered major arcana card. The justice card is representative of the concepts of fairness and law, as well as truth and facts. The truth card most commonly depicts an image on its face of a woman sitting in a chair and holding a set of scales in her left hand, which is used to symbolize the justice system and the way that logic should be balanced by intuition. The concepts of logic and intuition can also be thought of as the personal conscious and unconscious minds as well; these two aspects of the mind will need to be balanced for "the fool" to continue to grow and develop and unlock his potential, becoming a unified, whole person again. Justice also carries a double-edged sword in her right hand held up in the air. This represents the duality and the "double-edged" nature of justice and the concepts that she embodies. She also wears a crown atop her head with a square on it, drawing a connection to the element of earth and to clarity, grounded nature, and rigidity that are commonly associated with the element of earth.

When the justice card is drawn in the upright position, she represents the laws of justice. Every decision that you make and every action that you choose to take will have some sort of consequences, whether those consequences are positive or negative. If you have been wronged or you might believe that you are at fault for someone else having been wronged, then the upright justice card tells you that you will not be "punished" for the actions that you have taken or that you will receive some sort of relief. Another common interpretation of the justice card is that it represents the truth. In a situation when the truth might be obfuscated or otherwise concealed or hidden, the truth card tells you that the truth will eventually be revealed or that it needs to be revealed for the situation to be resolved. The truth is based on facts, and you should always be aware of the objective facts that are relevant to your decision before you pass any sort of judgment regarding that situation. You will need to take care and actively seek out the truth in order to maintain fairness in any judgment that you pass. Regardless of the specifics, the truth card presented in the upright position tells its recipient of the importance of objectivity and fairness.

When the justice card is presented in the reversed position, however, it serves to warn its recipient that they are ignoring the truth or "living a lie" in some form or another. This means that you might be thinking objectively or judging someone or something based on your feelings while ignoring the facts of the matter. You might be unwilling to accept the consequences of your actions, falsely believing yourself to be innocent or "running from your guilt." You will need to remember that all actions have consequences and that people make errors sometimes. In order to move forward, you will need to accept the consequences of the actions that you have taken, and you will need to realize that those actions are in the past and learn from the mistakes that you have made. Every new moment presents new opportunities for change and growth, and you can tip the "scales" of justice back in your favor by keeping these lessons in mind. The most significant change that this card advises you to take is to stop unfairly judging yourself, whether you are judging too harshly or not harshly enough. Let yourself be judged by fate. Instead, accept the consequences of your actions, and use those consequences to learn and grow as a person, allowing yourself to move forward.

12 – The Hanged Man

The 12th card and the 12th step along the fool's journey through the major arcana is called the "hanged man." The hanged man card most commonly depicts a man who has been suspended upside down from his foot from the world tree. The world tree is typically thought to support the heavens themselves and is rooted in the "underworld," providing a structure for the mortal world. Some versions of the tarot will show the hanged man being suspended upside-down on an inverted cross, in the same way that Saint Peter requested to be hanged, not believing himself to be worthy of the same method of hanging as Jesus Christ. Supporting this interpretation of the hanged man card, many people believe that the hanged man has been placed in the position of his own free will, partially because of the calm and serene expression that he carries on his face. This would make sense if the hanged man were used to represent Saint Peter, as he himself requested to be hanged upside-down and would have accepted his fate by that point. The hanged man is also commonly shown to be bound by only one food, with his right foot being held to the branches of the tree (or to his cross), and the left foot is left free. The hanged man also holds his hands behind his back, possibly also bound, in a triangular shape. He wears red pants, which are symbolic of passion and the physical body, and a blue shirt that represents the seemingly opposed and contrasted concept of peace and calmness. This color combination is also commonly worn by saints, and this would also support the theory that the hanged man represents Saint Peter, or at least that he is a saint. The hanged man also has yellow hair, a yellow halo, and yellow shoes in the most common depictions, representing a high level of intelligence. The hanged man is commonly used to symbolize concepts, such as sacrifice, and is also connected to the archetype of "sacrifice."

The hanged man understands and accepts his situation and recognized that his sacrifice is one that needs to be made in order for him to move forward. The hanged man has likely been sentenced to this fate as a result of wrongs that he has committed in the past or is a calculated sacrifice that he has made in order to allow himself to move forward once his sentence has been completed. While it might seem like his progress has not been halted, the time that is spent on this "step" along his journey is not going to waste. The "hanged man" stage of the fool's journey is a necessary part of his progression. It will allow him to repent for the wrongs that he might have committed or reevaluate his path in order to recalculate and correct himself. This stage comes directly after the "justice" stage, representing this repentance, as well. The hanged man can also be used to represent a "new perspective," as the hanged man is literally upside down and will have an opportunity to begin to view the world through a different lens, gaining a new sense of perspective regarding the world around them. Other people around the hanged man who is close to him might not understand this part of his journey or the sacrifice that he needs to make. They might even protest against his sentence, but the hanged man will be able to view his situation differently and accept that his sacrifice is necessary for his own growth, as well as the growth of his peers, in some cases. When the hanged man is presented in the upright position, he might tell his recipient of the need to suspend or stop a certain course of action or to reevaluate the current path that they are taking. Certain actions or plans might need to be put off for a while or even stopped altogether for you to progress successfully. The hanged man will instruct his recipient to stop and reflect on their current plans or actions, adopting a new method in order to achieve success. Another important lesson that the hanged man can teach is to wait. Stopping to understand your situation and the outcomes of your actions, waiting until the optimal moment to act will allow you to find success much more easily. In some situations, taking action at the first opportunity might even have negative consequences and prevent you from reaching your goals, and waiting can sometimes be more beneficial.

In the reversed position, the hanged man might represent the failure to listen to his lessons. You might be acting relentlessly and without hesitation, failing to understand the consequences of your actions later on, or you might be pushing toward a goal that is unattainable, at least with the method that you are currently using. You might be doing a lot of work for little to no reward, and it will be important for you to stop and evaluate your situation in order to think of a new approach.

13 – Death

The 13th card and step along the fool's journey through the major arcana is the death card. Death is commonly depicted as the entity known as "death," one of the four horsemen of the apocalypse, resembling an armored skeleton riding a horse and carrying a flag in his hand through what appears to be a battlefield. The figure that is portrayed on the death card is depicted as a skeleton representing his role, as the bones are the last part of the human body to continue existing after they have died. Death also wears armor in a lot of common versions of the tarot, which is symbolic of his invulnerability. He is protected against attacks, unlike most of the other figures portrayed within the tarot. This is connected to death's role in the cycle of life as a concept that will always be following us throughout our lives. Nobody can kill death; it is simply a fact. The white horse that death rides also represents the concept of purity, which is closely related to death as a "purifying" force that will eventually affect every living thing. In one hand, he carries a flag with a black base and a white pattern, usually drawn as a flower of some sort. Death rides his horse through a battlefield filled with dead or dying humans in the dirt. Most versions of this card will show both a king and a pauper in the dirt at death's mercy, representing his objectivity and the way that he does not judge anyone based on their race, class, gender, or any other fabricated symbol of superiority or inferiority that humans and other animals tend to judge each other by. Death eventually comes for all living things when their time has come. Some common concepts that are associated with the death card are change, transition, and rebirth. Death is also associated with the "rebirth" archetype, as well.

Many people tend to misunderstand or even fear death as a result of their perspective coming from the point of view of a creature that has not yet experienced it. Similarly, the death card is also considered "bad" or "unlucky," and its number of 13 certainly does not help with the way it is perceived. A lot of people might even avoid mentioning this card because of their fear of the concept of death and the way that most people will interpret this card, representing literal death. This is false, however. Death can sometimes have one of the most positive meanings of the major arcana cards and even the tarot deck as a whole. The death card, when it is presented in the upright position, represents that one phase of your life is ending and that a new one is about to begin. This is the "halfway point" along the fool's journey, and it might even be represented in the "hero's journey" as the climax of the story. This is the point after which the "hero" would have suffered a massive defeat against the villain and would have found a new drive, being inspired again to finally defeat the antagonist. In terms of typical human life and experiences, this card might manifest as a new job or finishing your time at school in order to move on to begin your career in your chosen field of work. It can also be the end of a long-term relationship that will make room for your "true love" if this change or transition occurs within your romantic life. Regardless of the specifics, the death card represents the end of one phase and the transition to another, similar to the transition from life to death in the journey of human existence. You will need to "let go" of the phase of your life that is coming to an end in order to recognize and embrace the new one that is or will be presenting itself to you.

Another common interpretation of the death card is that the transformation or transition that it represents will be within yourself. You might be undergoing some sort of transformation or "metamorphosis," and you will need to allow your "old self" to "die" in order to make room within yourself for the "new you" to develop. This can often be a scary or daunting period and is usually the cause of some sort of significant life event, but it is usually for the better, allowing you to become a "new person" in order to grow and develop in this "new path" that you will be traveling in the next phase of your life. You will need to embrace this new phase and let go of unhealthy attachments that you might have developed previously in order to move on. This is a very important part of life and will likely occur multiple times throughout a person's journey as they learn and develop throughout their life.

When the death card is presented in the reversed position, it still represents change. However, it might warn you that you have been resisting a significant change in your life, and you will need to begin to embrace it in order to move forward. You might be worried about letting go of your past due to an attachment to aspects of your past that you are still hanging on to, or you might even be unsure or ignorant of the new phase of your life and the opportunities that have been presenting themselves to you. You will need to take time to evaluate and assess the aspects of your past that you are trying to hang on to and begin to let them go so that you can continue to grow and develop. Much like the wheel of fortune, life is constantly moving forward, and any attempt to stop that progress or move backward along the wheel will only be detrimental to you in the long run.

14 – Temperance

The 14th card and step along the fool's journey through the major arcana is the "temperance" card. The temperance card commonly depicts an image of a winged angel, with no obvious gender, which is used to represent a balance between the sexes. The angel stands with one foot in the water of a pond, which symbolizes their unconscious mind, while their left foot rests on dry land as a representation of their connection to their conscious mind and to the material world. The angel wears a white robe with the image of a triangle inside a square, drawing another connection between the physical, material world and the divine or the holy trinity. Temperance also holds two cups, mixing water between the two cups. A lot of people will also believe these two cups to be representative of the conscious and unconscious minds. Balance is an important theme in this card, and it represents the harmony that comes from the union of dual opposed forces, similar to the forces that have been represented in a number of the cards of the major arcana up to this point in the fool's journey. Common concepts that are associated with the temperance card are balance, moderation, and the union of opposites.

When the temperance card is presented in the upright position, it tells its recipient that they might have a good handle on the lessons that they teach. You might be able to maintain balance well and even maintain control and calmness in times of stress. Being able to remain calm in stressful situations, maintain control, and not let the "little things" bother you can be extremely valuable skills that will help you in achieving any goals that you set for yourself. Temperance instructs their recipients to maintain balance in all aspects of life. Moving toward the extreme in any situation, especially in sensitive situations, should be avoided if possible. The temperance card also suggests that its recipient likely has a clear drive and a specific vision, understanding exactly what they are aiming for. This is important in achieving your goals, as you will be able to understand each of the steps that need to be taken in order to reach them. Understanding the temperance card's lessons will be useful in helping you to find "peace" within yourself and situations that you might find yourself in. The temperance card might also be telling you that it is time to reevaluate and assess the situation and your priorities. Being able to find some sort of balance between your inner self and the outside world will allow you to find a much greater purpose and live a much more fulfilling and satisfying life.

When the temperance card is presented in reversed order, it might represent some kind of imbalance somewhere in your life that is causing you some sort of stress or anxiety. The specifics of this imbalance will often be revealed through the other cards in your spread. Temperance can also serve as a warning against a specific path or course of action. That will force you to lean on an extreme and will cause an imbalance in your life in the near future. You might also be in danger of suffering from a lack of drive or purpose. The primary lesson that temperance teaches is that balance and moderation should be maintained at all times and that it is important to stop and consider our actions and our lives to make sure to maintain that balance as much as we can.

15 – The Devil

The 15th card and 15th step along the fool's journey through the major arcana is the devil card. The devil card most commonly depicts a demon or an evil in a very satyr-like form. It is commonly thought that the creature represented on this card is Baphomet. He is half-goat and half-man and has two unsettling bat wings, as well as an inverted pentagram on his forehead. He stands on top of a pedestal behind a nude man and woman who are chained to the pedestal, showing that he has some sort of control over these two people. Both the man and the woman also have horns, which are representative of their sinful and sub-human nature, which they have adopted after a long period of time spent in service of the devil. The chains that bind them give the impression that they have been imprisoned or otherwise taken captive by the devil. Both of these people also have a tail, as well. The man's tail has a flame at its end, while the woman's tail has a cluster of grapes at the end of her tail, representing their respective addictions to power and the "finer" things in life. Of course, if you look at the expression of the man and the woman's faces, you would see that they look very displeased because they have been stripped of their power and status when they were taken hostage by the devil and left exposed and naked as a sign of shame.

The devil card is very different from the rest of the cards that have led up to it so far in that its meanings are reversed. The upright devil's appearance in your reading might reveal feelings of entrapment or restriction that you are experiencing or even lacking satisfaction or fulfillment within your life. You might also be distracted by materialism and drawn from your path by greed or similar struggles in a similar manner to the man and the woman shown on the face of the devil card. You might even be aware that the path that you walk on is a sinful and dangerous one, but you do not seem to have control over your hunger or greed. This card can often be used to represent a struggle with addiction to substances like drugs, alcohol, or even food, as well as greed and materialism. In these kinds of situations, you might feel a lack of control or that you are unable to control your impulses, directing yourself toward anything other than these impure desires. Drawing the devil card in your reading might mean that you need to break free from these bonds and begin to walk a pure path again, or you might risk becoming a "slave" to these desires like the man and woman on this card.

Drawing the devil card in its reversed position is also somewhat "backward," holding the "positive" interpretation of this card, unlike the rest of the cards of the major arcana, which represent positive lessons when they are presented in the upright position and negative lessons when they are drawn reversed, requiring some form of adjustment or change from the recipient in order to move forward on their path to growth and development. Drawing the devil card in its reversed position, however, represents the moment when an individual is able to recognize their addictions and break free of the bonds that hold them captive. This might represent something like overcoming an addiction to drugs or alcohol or even something like breaking "bad habits" that you might have formed over time and beginning to recover from the damage that those things have caused to you.

Usually, this turn comes from a moment of self-awareness or becoming exhausted with the way you have been moving, recognizing that the path you walk is harmful to your growth or that you have been turned around and begun to walk backward and will need to turn around again in order to move forward again. Regardless of the specifics of your situation, being able to break your "bonds" and let go of your addictions or vices is always difficult, and you will need to be able to make all of the changes that are necessary, regardless of how scary or painful they are in order to continue walking on the "correct path." While the reversed death card still instructs its recipient that they will need to make some sort of change in their life, it is the more "positive" orientation of this card and presents an opportunity to change their negative habits and recover from them, as opposed to simply being a warning against a negative course of action that will need to be corrected.

16 – The Tower

The next step along the fool's journey along the major arcana is the 16th numbered card, which is referred to as the tower. The tower card commonly depicts a tall tower that rests at the top of a high mountain. The tower is also usually shown being struck by lightning, which also sets the tower on fire, causing panic in the people inside the tower. The windows of this tower burst with flames, including the people who used to be inside the tower, who have jumped, at this point, out of the windows. These people are likely the same people who can be seen in the other cards of the major arcana, like the devil or the lovers, and possibly the people in the paired cards, like the emperor and empress.

The people are jumping from the windows of their tower in an act of desperation, wishing to escape the destruction of the tower and the chaos that is caused by it. The tower card is most often used to represent ambition that is built on shaky or unstable foundations, as well as things like change or destruction as a form of creation. The tower needs to be destroyed and broken down for it to be cleared out to make room for new things to exist in its place. It is also likely going to serve as part of the foundation for whatever ends up being built in its place. The tower card is commonly associated with concepts like forceful change or a sudden upheaval, or some sort of chaos or disaster that is unexpected or unwanted. A common archetype for this card is "chaos."

The tower card represents extreme change. This card is specifically designed to be very dark and to look very differently from a lot of the cards that have come earlier in the journey of the fool. Its design primarily features an object, as opposed to a person or creature, that is being attacked in a very dark background. The tower is the first card in the major arcana that illustrates an event, especially one so violent and destructive, as well. The crown that calls from the top of the tower is meant to paint the tower as some sort of a symbol of power, and as it is being destroyed, that symbol and that power go with it, enforcing the theory that the man and the woman featured in the image on this card are the same man and woman featured in the devil card. This card represents change much more directly than any of the other cards in the major arcana and even in the tarot deck as a whole. This card very directly represents a deep, foundational change to the person who draws it in their tarot reading. However, this event does not necessarily need to be a destructive, unpleasant, or terrible disaster like lightning and fire, which are featured on the face of this card. It is usually violent or extreme, however. Despite change being such a very important part of life that all people and things experience, many people do not handle change very well and will rather cling to the normalcy that is provided by the lives that they are used to, even if the change that is occurring in their life is a positive one or will provide benefits to that person. Even if the change that they are experiencing is positive, they might respond with fear because of reasons similar to those that are mentioned in the section on the death card. You will need to abandon your previous situation or truths, or "abandoning the tower," in order to embrace your new situation, but whether this change is positive or negative, it will be beneficial in the long run. Life only moves forward, and embracing change will allow you to move forward as a person and grow in the way that the fool's journey is intended to represent.

When the tower card is presented in the upright position, it tells you that you might be experiencing a significant change in your life soon or at the current time with positivity and eagerness. This period of change might create some sort of tension between you and the people who are involved with you. Because of this, you will need to remain calm in order to maintain control and transition smoothly to this new stage. In the context of work or interpersonal relationships, this might mean that you will need to be objective and calm, making sure not to lose your temper or be heavily emotionally affected. You need to meditate to prevent inadvertently hurting the people around you during this stressful or unfamiliar time.

When the tower is presented in the reversed position, this might mean that a significant change will be coming soon. This change is commonly interpreted as negative, taking the form of a stressful or unwanted crisis that will cause trouble for you or those around you. You might want to try to delay this event, but you should, instead, try to embrace the change that comes; even if they are unpleasant, painful, or harmful to you at the moment, these kinds of events can be incredibly beneficial to you in the long run. More often than not, these changes will serve to destroy or break negative habits or reliance on habits or things that are detrimental to your personal development. The "tower" or this reliance is built on weak foundations, and it will need to fall in order to be rebuilt as something more stable.

17 – The Star

The 17th card and the 17th step along the fool's journey through the major arcana is referred to as the star. The star card commonly depicts a nude blonde woman kneeling at the edge of a small pond, which is similar to the pond that the figure in the temperance card stands above. The woman on the star card is also similar to the woman on the face of the temperance card, as she also holds two containers with water in them. Instead of cups, however, the woman holds two much larger vessels, which more closely resemble jugs. One of these jugs is pouring its contents out onto the land, filling it with water, and nourishing the dry land in order to encourage fertility and growth. The land that surrounds the star seems to indicate that pouring water into the soil seems to be working, judging by the healthy field that surrounds her. In a similar manner to temperance, the star also has one foot immersed in the water of her pond, representing her spiritual abilities and her inner strength. The other food is firmly planted on the land to represent her connection with the material world. Behind the woman, there is a large star that is also surrounded by seven smaller white stars. Each of these stars represents a different chakra or "spiritual center" that exists within the body, with the largest likely being used to represent the star herself. Far behind the star in the field stands a single tree, with a bird perched on top of it. This bird is meant to represent the wisdom of Thoth. Some common concepts that are associated with the star card are faith and hope, and an archetype that is connected to this card is, of course, referred to as "the star."

The star represents hope, faith, and inner strength when it is drawn in the upright position. This card follows the trauma and the change that is presented in the tower card, and it represents the strength that is needed in order to handle the change that is described in that card's meaning. Following that significant period of change or trauma, it might not necessarily be immediately apparent, but the star card lets you know that you have not been forgotten by "the universe" and that you will need to endure difficulty in this trying time. When you come out of this period, you will come out much stronger than before and with all of the tools that you need in order to reach your goals. The star also tries to instruct its recipient that they will need to have faith and be courageous in these difficult times, and the universe will bless them with the strength that they need in order to succeed. When you draw this card in a tarot reading, it represents some sort of challenge or difficult experience that you have had recently in your life. It also means that you have managed to go through it without losing your hope. While you very likely suffered in some way or another because of this event, you managed to come out of it relatively okay. You might have even learned that you are stronger than you thought yourself to be, and this traumatic event has helped you to understand your inner strength and potential.

If you draw the star card in the reversed position, however, this might represent a loss of faith regarding a recent traumatic or otherwise stressful or trying situation. You might be feeling like everything is hopeless or that you do not have the strength that you need. These challenges might normally be something that you would look forward to, but for some reason, you have lost faith and begun to second-guess yourself. This loss of faith or "strength" has most likely been caused by a change in your perception of either yourself or of something that you hold dear and which is a large part of your inner strength. When you lose faith in something that is so important to you and who you are, it becomes incredibly difficult to continue to move forward or find the motivation to do anything at all. Sometimes, this might manifest as anxiety, depression, or any other number of psychological disorders that occur as a result of trauma. In order to begin to move past this difficult or traumatic event, you need to evaluate your feelings and understand them. You need to understand why you might be experiencing this defeat or why you are experiencing this loss of faith. The reversed star instructs its recipient to take care of their mental health and nurture it in a healthy way that allows them to find their faith and rebuild their strength.

18 – The Moon

The next step along the fool's journey through the major arcana is the 18th card, which is referred to as "the moon." The moon card most commonly depicts a scene that features the literal moon. The moon rests at the top of the image on this card, above a path that leads off into the horizon. On each side of this path, at the center of the card, are a wolf and a dog. These two animals represent the nature of human beings, split between one part that is civilized and domesticated and one that is wild and feral. The path comes from a pond at the bottom of this card's image, and a crawfish is also shown to be coming out of that pond. Off in the distance, the scene also shows two towers set at the opposite ends of the path, drawing another connection to duality and opposing forces. Everything in this card seems to be a mirror image of its other side, in the same way that the moon reflects the light of the sun. These mirrored images also represent choices between two divergent paths, which is a quite common theme with the tarot's major arcana. Walking the path that is depicted in this card requires us to maintain a balance between the conscious and the unconscious mind, or between the wild and civilized aspects of ourselves, as they are represented by the wolf and the dog, respectively. Additionally, the towers on either side of the moon's path are also representative of the forces of good and evil. Which tower is meant to represent which concept is intentionally left unclear, and this is likely in an effort to obfuscate the differences between these forces at a surface level and highlighting the similarities between the two. These two forces can often be difficult to tell apart since good and evil are largely subjective concepts, with morality being a large grey area. The line between the two is a very thin one, which might be represented by the path between these two towers. The moon card is commonly associated with feelings and emotions.

When the moon card is presented in an upright position, it can be symbolic of the imagination. It might mean that your imagination is running out of control and getting the better of you; similarly to when you are walking along a dark path at night, you might be unsure of your surroundings, wary of the danger that lurks in the shadows and stalks you, waiting for an opportune moment to lunge and attack you. In this situation, you will be represented by the crawfish, which is rising up out of the water and is at the beginning of the moon card's path. To you, the crawfish, the moon will be a source of light and will bring you a sense of clarity and understanding. You should follow the moon or your intuition, allowing it to guide you through this darkness and carry you to safety. You will also need to consider the fear or unease that you are experiencing and keep them in mind. More often than not, these feelings are based on input from the outside world or from our unconscious minds trying to tell us something about our surroundings or our situation. Another common interpretation of the moon card is that it represents illusions or deception. You will need to look past the shadows or unpleasant feelings that you might have in order to discover the truth.

When the moon card is drawn in the reversed position, it can be interpreted as a representation of the dark, negative aspects of the moon, which represents your intuition or unconscious mind. The reversed moon card might be representative of feelings of unease or confusion that you might be feeling. You might want to move forward, but you are unsure of which direction to move or which path to take. You will need to move past these unpleasant feelings and look past the shadows along your path in order to discover the truth along the "correct" path. Another common interpretation of the reversed moon card is that the forces of the night bringing you confusion are starting to dissipate. You have started managing your fears and anxiety. Whatever negative energies you have been facing are slowly fading away. It presents a liberating experience as you discover the positive side of things.

19 – The Sun

The next stage of the fool's journey through the major arcana is the 19th numbered card, which is referred to as the sun. The sun card is used to represent feelings like optimism and fulfillment. This card also represents the dawn, which follows the darkest of nights, both in a literal sense and a symbolic one. The sun is the source of all life on our planet; we would not exist without its energy and light. The sun card commonly depicts a child in the image on its surface. This child is shown to be playing in the foreground of this image and is a representation of innocence. This child and its innocence are also symbolic of the happiness that can be felt when you are in alignment with your "true self." The child is also naked, but unlike some other figures that are shown to be naked, like the man and woman in the devil card, this child does not seem to mind. This is representative of the fact that this child is pure and innocent and that there's nothing to hide; this child does not care to hide anything about themselves. This child does not have any shame and simply exists to enjoy their life. This child also rides on the back of a white horse, similar to the one in the Death card. Like the horse that death rides on, this horse is used to represent the concept of purity, as well as the strength and nobility in the context of this card. Common concepts that are associated with this card are joy and positivity, as well as success and achievement.

When the sun card is presented in an upright position, it can be used to represent things like abundance, success, and radiance. Much like the literal celestial body of the sun, the sun card is a symbol of strength and vitality, pouring life into all the people and things that fall within reach of the sun. This is an incredibly positive card, telling its recipient that they will be experiencing easy times of joy and happiness in the very near future. At the time when the fool comes to the sun card's stage of his journey, he would have experienced a great deal of hardship, and the sun card is where the fool will begin to experience the benefits of those hardships much more directly. You have accomplished a lot and grown as a person, and because of your own personal fulfillment, you will often provide other people around you with inspiration and joy as well. A lot of people will be almost magnetically drawn or attracted to you because of the warm and beautiful energy that you bring into their lives with your drive and ambition, as well as your positivity and your kindness. You will also be able to help other people by shifting some of that light and leading it in their direction in order to allow them to grow and flourish, much like plants or animals, as they experience the warmth of the real sun. This card represents a significant amount of confidence that you have achieved through hard work and perseverance, enduring all the difficulties and overcoming all the obstacles that fell along your path in order to continue growing. Your life will be particularly pleasant and easy. The sun shines on you and will allow you to easily reach the goals that you have set for yourself. While the devil card was singled out as a very unpleasant card for a number of different reasons, the sun card would represent the opposite. The sun card is one of the most positive cards in the tarot, and finding this card in a reading can almost always represent a similar positivity that you carry with you at all times.

In the reversed position, the sun indicates that you might have significant difficulties in finding positive aspects in certain situations. The clouds might be blocking out the warmth and light that you need to progress. This might be preventing you from feeling confident and powerful. You may experience certain setbacks, which are damaging your optimism and enthusiasm. On the other hand, the sun reversed might be indicative that you are unrealistic. It might be a sign that you have an overly optimistic perception of certain situations. These are things that you need to take into account in order to ensure that you are on the right track and your successes continue as they do.

20 – Judgment

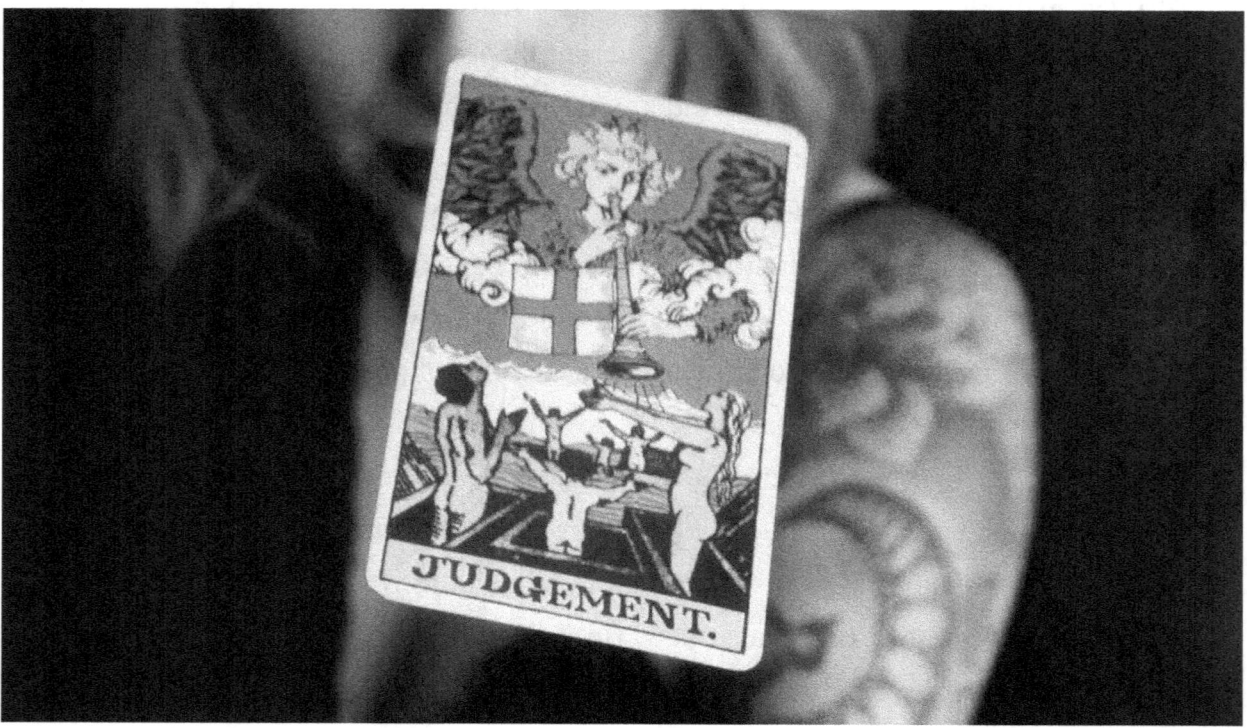

The next step along the fool's journey through the major arcana is the 20th numbered card, which is referred to as "judgment." The judgment card commonly depicts an angel, Gabriel, who sits in the sky playing the trumpet. There are several people who are shown on this card to be rising up from their graves to greet Gabriel, reaching their arms out to show that they are prepared to be judged by the universe or by their gods. These people are likely being pulled from their graves as part of the rapture to have their actions weighed in order to be judged by the universe and find out where they will live for the rest of eternity—in the heavens up above or in hell below. The judgment card also commonly features a large tidal wave coming from the horizon, which is meant to represent a catastrophic event that will eventually come for all the people who still wait for their judgment. That judgment is unavoidable and cannot be changed. The judgment card has a similar meaning as the death card, in the sense that it represents the end of one phase of existence to allow us to move on to the next. The primary difference between the judgment and death cards is the context. Many of the people portrayed in this card or versions of this card have already died and risen from their graves to receive judgment. This card also presents (at least) two paths: heaven and hell. These two paths represent the result of the actions that we have taken and the consequences that those actions will have. Additionally, this card is different from death and most of the other cards in the major arcana because it does not describe an event that is happening or about to happen to its recipient. The judgment card acts as more of a warning, letting its recipient know that they will eventually be judged for their actions and their intentions and that they should keep that in mind when they act. Judgment mentions the transitions that we experience going from life to death, but those transitions are not its main focus; judgment intends to let its recipients know that their actions will have consequences, regardless of the intent behind them. Some common concepts that are associated with the judgment card are awareness, awakening, reflection, completion, and consequences.

The judgment card's original meaning was to help its recipient to begin to reflect on themselves and the actions that they take through this reflection and self-awareness. In order to understand how we will be judged, we will need to gain a clear and objective understanding of where we are now and the ways that our actions will be judged when the time comes. For a lot of people, this understanding will largely come from a moment when we become self-aware and begin to evaluate the actions that we have taken, changing the path where we travel in order to become "better people." This is a common archetype in film and television and will be easy to understand with the context of characters like Ebenezer Scrooge. The judgment card refers to the moment when we begin to reflect on the paths that we have chosen and the actions that we have taken. This card is used to represent that you might be coming close to "awakening" or that you are in the middle of awakening in your life. It follows that you might soon begin evaluating yourself and your intentions, judging yourself in order to understand what you might need to change and how you might need to alter your path in life. If you are already going through this period of awakening, you might need to move forward and make those changes in your life in order to continue growing and become a better, more spiritually, or mentally healthy person. Not only will this course correction affect you positively in the long run, but the people around you might also end up benefiting from your new outlook.

Ultimately, the judgment card represents moments of clarity that present us with choices that we will need to make in our lives, deciding the direction that we will end up taking toward the future. Sometimes, these moments are irreversible and cannot be altered or changed once they have been made, so it is important to understand all the details and the consequences of these choices in order to make the "correct" one. You will be judged for these actions later on, so it is important to choose your path wisely, but you must choose a path and accept the consequences of that choice either way. It is important to judge yourself and your actions in order to be self-aware and to understand the choices that you make and why those choices are made, but it is also important to judge yourself accurately. When the judgment card is drawn in the reversed position, it can act as a warning that you might not be judging yourself accurately. You might be too loose with your judgments, not accurately weighing your actions and intentions, or you might even be judging yourself too harshly. This might be causing you to miss out on opportunities that are waiting for you or that have presented themselves to you while you spend too much of your time worrying about the actions that you have taken and the consequences of those actions. This lost momentum can sometimes cause you to fall behind your plans and make it much more difficult to reach the goals that you have set for yourself. You might need to worry less about the consequences of your actions in order to continue moving forward. Of course, you should still be keeping those actions in mind, but you should also remember that if you focus all of your attention on worrying about the past, you will not be able to focus on the present as effectively. You should be able to move onward proudly and confidently in order to act in a way that is true to yourself.

21 – The World

The last step on the path of the fool's journey through the major arcana is the card with the number 21, referred to as the world. The world card commonly depicts a woman in the center of the image on its face. This woman seems to be dancing, with one leg crossed behind the other as if she were walking or dancing. She holds one wand in each of her hands, placed down at her sides. She is surrounded by a green wreath of flowers that symbolizes her success, and the wreath is wrapped in red ribbons that are meant to appear similar to the infinity symbol. There are also usually four beings in the four corners of this card, which are the same beings that can be seen on the wheel of fortune card. These creatures are representations of a number of different aspects of our universe and our world. Connections can be drawn from these four creatures to the four evangelicals, the four classical elements, the four corners of our universe, and even to astrological symbols. Regardless of the specific interpretation of what these four creatures are, they represent harmony and unification of their energies. These four vastly different beings all exist together and work in harmony to support the figure depicted in the center of this card. There are a number of different concepts that are commonly associated with the world card, as it represents the unification of all of the lessons and the different aspects of the self that have been discovered and understood by the fool throughout his journey through the major arcana, but some of these concepts include completion, harmony, fulfillment, satisfaction, and wholeness.

Drawing the world card in the upright position often represents a sense of unity and completion in your life, whether that unity is occurring at the time of the reading or will be coming to you in the near future. This card is representative of the inner and outer worlds coming together to become a single entity. In terms of personal growth, this can be thought of as the bridge between the conscious and unconscious minds or your connection with the world around you. In some traditions, people will refer to this state as "enlightenment" or "nirvana." This is the final stage of your journey, at least mentally and emotionally speaking. This is when you will have recognized that you and all other living things are linked with each other and that we all serve as individual parts of the universe as a whole. Being able to recognize and understand the nature of human existence and life as a whole means that you have completed your spiritual journey and that you are able to be a part of the greater whole that makes up the universe. At this point, you can be considered "whole" again, and you have all the strength and the tools that you will need in order to handle any challenge that might come your way. This card also represents joy, fulfillment, and accomplishment. All the efforts that you have been putting in place are finally beginning to pay off. You have completed a very significant milestone in your life and have gained all the tools that you need in order to move forward.

When the world card is drawn in the reversed position, it can represent the end of a particular journey or era. You may have many accomplishments that have lined your path, but there is a strange emptiness that fills you when you look back upon it as if you have all the pieces, but they are not coming together. In order to continue to move onward, you will need to evaluate yourself and your personal growth in order to understand what is missing or what is preventing you from experiencing the satisfaction that you should be feeling right now. Something is missing and needs to be recovered before you can complete your journey.

Chapter 4: Tarot and the Unconscious

As was discussed briefly in the last chapter of this book, divinatory tarot readings are based on the concepts of Jungian psychology, rather than from magic or some other mystical force that manipulates the cards. The personal and collective unconscious play a large role in the outcomes of tarot readings. When you read or receive a tarot reading, the cards themselves are not the tool that will provide you with the answers you are looking for. The cards simply act as catalysts, pushing you to look within your unconscious mind by presenting you with concepts from the "collective unconscious," which can be thought of as a level deeper than the "personal unconscious" mind, where all the experiences and archetypes common to all people or to large groups of people can be held. The collective unconscious is simply made up of all the experiences and concepts that are common to many or all people and is more of a metaphysical space rather than a real location or part of the mind.

Being able to access the personal unconscious can sometimes be difficult for different people, depending on how closely they are connected to their unconscious minds. This is because, over time, we have "lost touch" with our inner selves. It could also be because of the way that people have evolved. Modern people tend to ignore their unconscious minds, neglecting the development of these parts of ourselves and, instead, favoring the conscious mind and turning to logic and reasoning in order to help us solve our problems. Most people will tend to look outside themselves and even reach out to other people for the answers and solutions to their problems, which can be harmful to their growth within their unconscious minds. When we fall sick, we will usually go to a doctor or purchase medications that can treat the symptoms of those diseases instead of simply searching for the original cause or source of the issue, like our environment or habits. A large part of our personalities and the things that make us ourselves lie in our unconscious minds. It contains all the information that we do not actively remember but affect us, which can often be more important to our identities than the conscious mind. The unconscious mind forms our "unexplained" habits, our likes and dislikes, and even our dreams. It is said that we experience our unconscious minds and the experiences and thoughts within them through our dreams. This is because when we sleep, our conscious mind also "sleeps" and lets its guard down to allow the unconscious mind to surface.

A lot of people will rely too much on their conscious mind to help them make their decisions and guide them through their everyday lives. Modern-day people rely heavily on their physical senses, focusing primarily on the world around them. When we think of an object, the way we think of that object is primarily influenced by the physical senses that we use to perceive or experience that object, rather than the experiences that we have with that object. Usually, the first method by which we consider specific objects is our sight. Most of the time, this is the first sense that we use to experience a particular object. Before we can feel, smell, or taste something, we will usually see it. There are some exceptions, like objects with strong odors or very loud machines, but normally, we will judge an item based on its physical appearance. However, most of these objects also make some sort of impact on our unconscious minds based on the experiences that we have involving those objects. This is the source of a lot of our fears or habits that we form. Most people have begun to lean more heavily on the outside world and their physical senses and have become imbalanced and unhealthy after losing touch with their unconscious minds as they have developed. Tarot cards, when used for divinatory purposes, push us to try to become closer with our unconscious minds in order to better understand how we function as people and how to solve the issues that we face in our lives.

Some people may be more in tune with their unconscious minds and more aware of when it is "trying to tell them something." Usually, these people will rely much more heavily on intuition than a lot of other people, or they will be a little bit more self-aware, having the ability to acknowledge their quirks and the origins of the aspects of their personalities that they might not otherwise be aware of. Every person has moments throughout their lives when they might be more in tune with their unconscious minds, however. And they simply need to be aware of the messages that they are receiving from their unconscious mind in order to recognize them and understand themselves as a person. Usually, these messages will manifest in the form of "intuition" when you encounter a new person who gives you a creepy or unsettling feeling. For example, one might be trying to make an important decision and feel inexplicably compelled to choose one option over another. When people say to "listen to your gut," this is usually referring to intuition and the unconscious mind. In this sense, it is true that people only use part of their brain's full capacity because many people fail to recognize that their "gut sense" or "intuition" is a real part of their brain and mind and can provide incredibly valuable insight in times of stress or difficulty, even if we do not completely understand the *why* part at that time.

Tarot cards are designed in a way to rely on imagery and concepts that exist within the "collective unconscious" in order to encourage readers or people who are receiving readings about themselves to reach out to their unconscious mind for guidance. It encourages people to develop a stronger connection to their unconscious mind so that they can learn to rely on it more often and begin to understand themselves better. This will help the reader or recipient of the reading to grow and develop more and become a "whole" person, as Carl Jung believed that every person has the opportunity to do so.

Chapter 5: Tarot and Numerology

Another very important part of the symbolism of tarot cards is the number that is on each card. The major arcana cards each have a number ranging from 0 to 21, and the minor arcana have four suits of 1-10 numbered cards with four cards that do not have numbers. The numbers on the cards can help you to understand various archetypes and aspects of human life, as well as serve as a little bit of a shortcut when performing tarot readings once you know what each number means. Tarot cards have been carefully designed with their numbers in mind. These numbers and their cards were discussed briefly earlier in this book, as well as the concept of the "fool's journey," which outlines the path to mental and emotional growth that the "fool" takes throughout his life. However, the numbers on the minor arcana cards are also helpful and allow us to understand ourselves better in a similar way to the major arcana cards.

Minor Arcana

The minor arcana has a total of 56 cards, split into four groups—swords, coins, cups, and wands. Each of these groups has 10 numbered cards and four "court" cards. These are the king, queen, knight, and page. Most of the time, however, some decks have different variations on the specific roles that the court cards play. Some decks might change out the knight and page cards to be the prince and princess, the jack and knave, or even add two extra cards, the maid and the mounted lady, to act as foils to the knight and page. Again, while there are a lot of cards in the tarot deck, with the most well-known decks containing 78 cards, they can all be split up into much smaller sections with consistent rules. The meanings of the minor arcana's numbered cards are listed here.

1 — This is also known as the ace. The ace card of any suit is the beginning of the numbered progression of that suit's ideals and concepts. As such, the ace cards represent beginnings, new opportunities, and potential. This is the first step in the path to the shorter, simpler journey to the "minor secrets" that the minor arcana holds. These are shorter than the major arcana but still very important, as they represent the paths to understanding the more specific ideals of the four suits of the minor arcana. The ace can be thought of like the introduction to the concepts and ideals of the four suits. This introduction might come in the form of inspiration regarding a particular art or field of study, or even as something like recognizing your career goals or receiving an opportunity to move into your desired field of work or study. This first step is all about beginnings and new opportunities.

2 — The second step along this journey is the 2 cards. These cards represent concepts like balance, duality, and even partnership. These concepts can also be seen in some of the major arcana cards, such as the emperor and empress, the lovers, and the chariot's two sphinxes. Sometimes, the two cards will represent a choice that you have to make between two opposing or mutually exclusive options. Another common interpretation is the union of two opposing forces or options for the purpose of moving forward, similarly to the chariot card of the major arcana.

3 — The third step along this journey is the 3 cards. These cards represent concepts like creativity, growth, or completion. Some of these concepts can be seen within the major arcana as well, but the most common interpretation for the three cards is that they represent a particular phase of a person's life, or the pursuit of a specific goal is coming to an end. This might be manifested in the form of finishing college in order to move on to your true career or completing a large artistic project that has taken up a large amount of time. Maybe you've accomplished a specific part of an overall goal, and it is time to move on to the next. Regardless of the specific details involved, the 3 cards are representative of the completion of a particular phase.

4 — The fourth step along this journey is the 4 cards. These cards represent concepts like manifestation, stability, and structure. These concepts are an organic and natural step to come to after the third. With the example of finishing college in pursuit of a particular field of work, this is the time when you would be out of school and need to find real work in order to manifest those goals and provide structure for yourself while

you do so. This stage is also very representative of the concepts of foundation and endurance. This will likely be a difficult time for you, and it might even take some time for you to adjust. However, once you do, you will be able to move on easily to the next stage of your life. It is important to continue to motivate yourself, however. Endurance will be a very large part of this step and even the ones that follow.

5 — The fifth step along this journey is represented by the 5 cards. These cards commonly represent concepts like change and instability or even conflict. Cards like death and the Tower from the major arcana can represent these concepts very well. In terms of a career path or the pursuit of a specific goal, this might manifest in the form of a difficult time in your life that could distract you from your work or even as a loss of inspiration or motivation. You might be in the process of beginning a new job, and change can be difficult to handle. Your situation could fluctuate frequently, and you will need to continue to maintain stability and conquer the challenges and the obstacles in your path.

6 — The sixth step along this journey is represented by the 6 cards. These cards commonly represent concepts like communication and cooperation, as well as adjustment and alignment. Continuing with the example of a specific career path or personal goal, this will be the step when you need to learn how to overcome the difficulty and inconsistency that you encountered in the fifth card's step. You will need to learn how to communicate effectively with other people and understand the issues that you are facing more accurately in order to allow you to adjust and be able to consider your situation.

7 — The seventh step along this journey is represented by the 7 cards. These cards commonly represent concepts like assessment, reflection, and understanding. This will require you to look within and perform some introspection or meditation regarding your current situation in order to understand how to handle that situation as effectively as possible. You might need to reevaluate the way that you perceive your situation in order to be able to understand it.

8 — The eighth step along this journey is represented by the 8 cards of the minor arcana. These cards most commonly represent concepts, such as action, accomplishment, and mastery. These concepts are also represented well by some of the major arcana cards, like death and the tower, similar to the third step. This eighth step describes the unification of the lessons you would have learned in the previous cards' steps in order to master the skills that you need in order to enable you to handle your current situation and master it, allowing yourself to be "reborn" in a similar way to the end of a phase that is described by the third card. These cards also function as a gateway to the next portion of your journey through the minor arcana, allowing you to realize your goals and move onward.

9 — The ninth step along this journey is represented by the 9 cards of the minor arcana. These cards most commonly represent concepts like attainment or a period of transition where you are close to achieving your goals. This is the stage that leads up to your ultimate success regarding the goal that this journey refers to. During this stage, you will need to keep your goals in mind and avoid slowing down and losing your drive. You will need to remember to "follow-through" in order to reach those goals.

10 — The tenth and final step along this journey is represented by the 10 cards of the minor arcana. These cards most commonly represent concepts such as completion, endings, and progress. During this stage, you will be completing your goals and realizing your potential. You will have "completed your journey" and will be able to begin with new things.

Additionally, each of the four suits of the minor arcana also carries its own meanings. Each one represents its own aspect of life that will be incredibly important to the development of every person. The suit of cups is the first of these. This suit represents the element of water, as well as the astrological signs that are connected to that element. This suit commonly represents concepts like emotions, intuition, creativity, and relationships with people and things. The second suit is represented by pentacles or coins. This suit is connected to the element of earth and all of its astrological signs. This suit is most commonly used to represent concepts like materials, money, manifestation, and personal goals. The third suit is represented by swords; it is connected to the element of air, as well as the air's astrological signs. This suit is most commonly associated with concepts such as communication, intelligence, thoughts, and the truth. The fourth and final suit is represented by the wand or the stick. This suit is connected to the element of fire, as well as its astrological signs. This suit is most commonly associated with concepts like enthusiasm and energy, as well as inspiration and spirit. Each of the suits' numbered cards represents the journey to mastering the concepts and ideals of their suit. Once you know the four "domains" of each of the four suits and the linear journeys represented by their numbered cards, you will be able to understand a large majority of the tarot deck's cards much more easily.

Major Arcana

The numbers of the cards in the major arcana are also significant. These cards and their numbers were discussed in the first chapter of this book but will be recapped here in a more simplistic manner for the purpose of understanding the significance of their numbers on a deeper level.

Of course, the Fool card is the "first" of the major arcana's cards, given the number 0 to represent his potential and position as the "avatar" of the recipient along their own "fool's journey." The final card is numbered 21 and is called "the world." This card represents the unification of the concepts and the various steps of the major arcana, which will allow the "fool" or the recipient to become a "whole" person again, mentally and emotionally healthy. Each of the cards between these two, from 1 to 20, has its own numerological associations, which you can apply to gain a better understanding of where it stands along the fool's journey.

The major arcana cards go above the 10-card structure of the minor arcana's numbered cards but can still be applied to those steps even beyond the number 10 at a basic level. For example, the tower card is labeled with the number 16, as the 16th step in the fool's journey. The numbers 1 and 6 can be added together to create a sum of 7, which is about assessment and evaluation. These are particularly important parts of the tower's emphasis on change and new beginnings. This is not the most comprehensive explanation of the tower card but can still serve to help in explaining the tower card or whichever card you might want to understand better. However, double-digit numerology will be much more effective and helpful in allowing you to understand the meanings of the major arcana cards and their numbers. A great example of this concept would be the death card, which is labeled with the number 13. The number 13 is typically considered an "unlucky" or "evil" number because of its connection to concepts like death or karmic debt. These associations will be especially important in understanding the death card.

Master Numbers in Numerology

Another interesting concept that is important to the major arcana is the "master number." This is another term that comes from numerology. There are three different "master numbers," which are 11, 22, and 33. Some sources might include 44, 55, and 66 as additional master numbers, but this is false. Not just any number with repeating twinned digits is a master number; the master numbers are specific to the numbers 1, 2, and 3 because of the "triangle of enlightenment" that they form. The master numbers are connected to numerology and numerological life paths, as well. Other numbers like the master numbers that are made from a pair of the same digit are referred to as power numbers in the field of numerology; however, this section will be focusing on only the master numbers.

The first master number is 11. This is the most intuitive of the master numbers, and it represents a connection with the unconscious mind. The 11 represents concepts like insight, emotional and mental sensitivity, and intuition. The number 11 is charged with charismatic energy and the ability to lead and inspire other people. It also represents duality in all of its positive and negative aspects, which can manifest as harmony or as discord and conflict. The potential of this number is largely dependent on the amount of direction that it has and the amount of focus that it is given toward its goals. Much like the magician or justice, the 11 walks a thin line between greatness and self-destruction at all times, and it will need to balance dreams with discipline.

The second master number is called the master builder, which has the potential to be the most successful of the master numbers. The 22 has the ability to transform dreams into reality, both of its own and others when it is supported by the other numbers around it. The number 22 is similar to 11 but differs in its focus on practicality and logic. It faces an opposite problem to the 11 in the sense that it can lean too heavily on logic and reasoning and needs to pair them with dreams, goals, and ambition in order to reach its full potential.

The third master number is 33. This number is often referred to as the master teacher and is the most spiritually inclined of the three master numbers. The number 33 is the most influential of all numbers; it combines the numbers 11 and 22, boosting their potential to another level. It is also important to note, however, that the weakness of 33 is its inability to reach its potential on its own. Instead of taking its own action, 33 devotes itself to lifting up those around it with an extremely high level of devotion.

These three numbers relate to numerology and life paths, which are calculated by adding up the separate digits of the day that you were born on. For example, if your birthday was on February second of 1980, then you would add the month, day, and the four digits from the year. These numbers would be 2, 2, 1, 9, 8, and 0 and would add up to 22, which would align you with the master number 22. Most of the time, numbers with multiple digits are added together to get a single-digit value, but the master numbers stay how they are. If you were born on December 25, 1995, then you would need to add together 1 and 2 for the month, 2 and 5 for the day, and 1, 9, 9, and 5 for the year to get 34, which you would then add together to get 7.

Of course, these master numbers and other concepts from numerology also relate to the tarot. The single-digit numbers and 10 each have their own meanings within numerology and connect to the tarot's minor arcana, and the master numbers can be connected to the major arcana. The master builder, 22, is more directly associated with the major arcana than the other two. The major arcana has 22 cards in total, possibly because of the nature of the number's significance and its potential, which mirror the fool's potential as he completes his journey through the major arcana's numbered cards.

The number 22 can be associated with either the fool or the world, as both can be considered the "last" or 22nd card in the major arcana, which is fitting for the number and the duality and potential that it represents so strongly. The fool represents the dangers of acting carelessly and the importance of understanding your potential in order to grow and become "whole," while the world represents the realization of your potential and the act of achieving your goals. These two seemingly opposite cards are very fitting for the master-builder number, as they represent the seemingly unlimited potential that this number carries while also highlighting the dangers of acting carelessly and without direction in the same way that the fool does before he begins his journey in the narrative of the major arcana's fool's journey. The fool needs to open his eyes to the world around him and have a clear path, or he will risk stepping carelessly and obliviously off a cliff.

Chapter 6: Tarot and the Zodiac

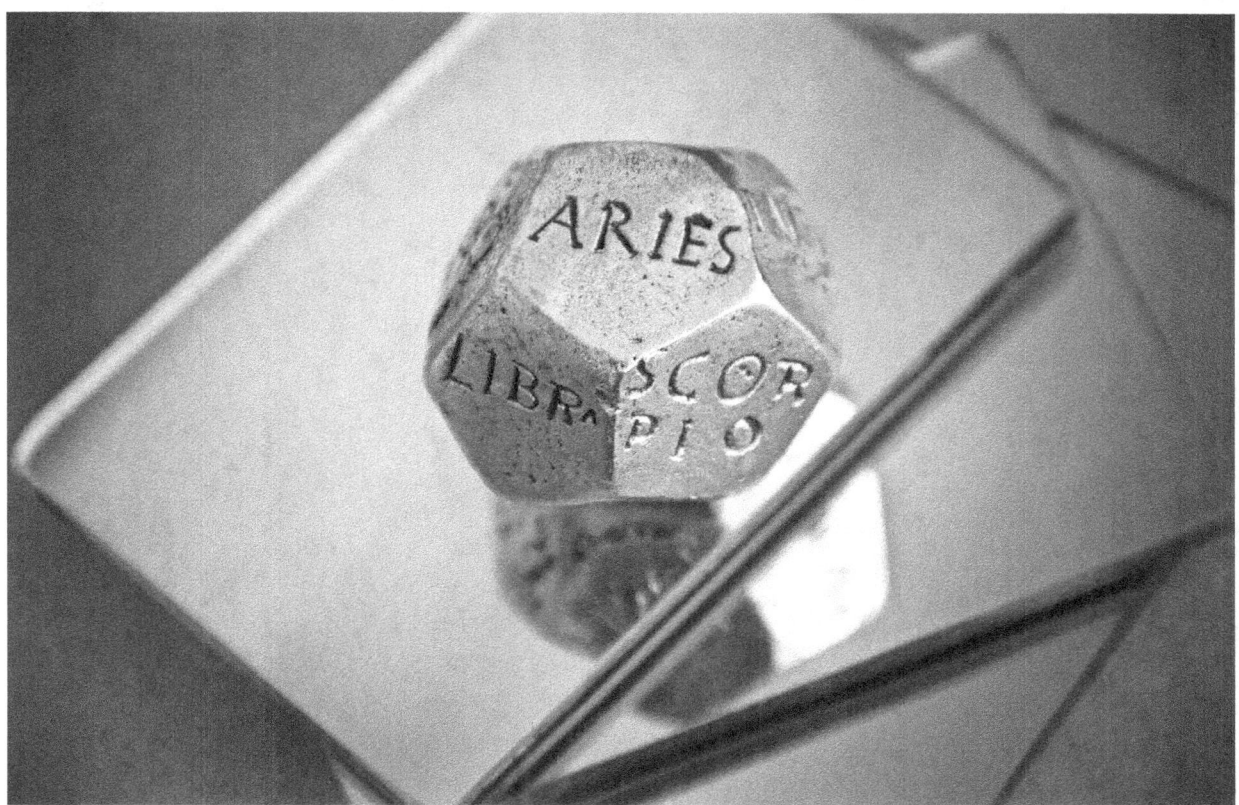

Numerology is not the only study that tarot cards are connected to. Each of the cards and the different suits is associated with one of the four classical elements and the three astrological signs that are represented by that element. Once you are able to understand and remember which elements and which astrological signs are connected to each of the suits and individual cards in your tarot deck, you will have a much easier time understanding the meanings of each of the cards in that deck and be able to perform readings much more easily than you would otherwise be able to do. This chapter will be discussing these associations between the tarot and astrology.

The Suits and Their Corresponding Signs

The first suit that will be discussed here is the suit of cups. The cups represent the element of water, which comes from the cup's own connection to the water in a number of different religions and practices. Cups are literally used to hold liquids and can act as a vessel for the water that is represented by this suit. Modern playing card decks often replace the suit of cups with a symbol that represents a heart. This is because the cups are most commonly associated with concepts like feelings and emotions, as well as love, romance, and other kinds of relationships with other people or objects. This can be thought of as similar to the way that the cup is connected to the water it holds. The flexibility and fluidity of water are also important, as the water is able to adapt to its environment, being calm or active to fit its surroundings. The astrological signs that are represented by the element of water and its tarot suit of cups are Cancer, Pisces, and Scorpio.

The second suit is called the coins or pentacles. The coins represent the element of earth, which comes from the coin's literal connection to the earth, having originally come from the earth itself, as well as "earthly desires" such as money or wealth, personal goals, and manifestation, as well as the body. In modern playing card decks, the suit of coins or pentacles has been replaced with diamonds, which represent the same or similar concepts to the original coin suit. The suit of coins can be thought of as a simple representation of our desires and goals, as modern life is largely fueled by financial goals and desires, or in the form of the pentacles that can represent our nature as beings that came from the earth and are supported by it. The astrological signs that are represented by the element of earth and the suit of coins or pentacles are Capricorn, Taurus, and Virgo.

The third suit that will be discussed here is called the swords. This suit is often considered to be the most logical of the four suits, having a connection to concepts, such as intelligence, as well as ideas, thoughts, and order and the communication that is required in order to convey those thoughts and concepts and the truth. In most modern playing card decks, the sword is replaced by a symbol representing a spade. The suit of swords can be thought of as a simple representation of the logic and thoughts that are required of a successful swordsman. This suit is represented by the astrological signs of Gemini, Libra, and Aquarius.

The fourth and last suit of the tarot's minor arcana is the wands. This suit was originally referred to as the sticks but was changed to wands in order to more accurately embody the element of fire. Similar to the more mundane objects that are used to represent the other elements, the element of fire is perceived as much more mystical than the other three elements. Fire has allowed humankind to develop much further than they were able to before its discovery as a tool that we have access to. It allowed us to create machines and shape the world, and it is arguably one of the most versatile tools that humans have at their disposal while simultaneously damaging us if we come too close to it, burning our skin. As a result, we have to maintain a safe distance and take care when working with this element. Additionally, the other three classical elements all exist on their own as physical objects. The water and earth exist on their own, and the air exists as all of the particles that rise and are captured within the sky. Fire stands out as a unique case as it is not a physical object. This element exists as a force, being made up of excited particles filled with energy. The wand is similar, in the sense that it represents a much more mystical and uncommon object that the other three suits. The suit of wands, in more modern playing card decks, has been replaced by a number of different symbols like clubs, clovers, flowers, sticks or batons, and the cross. The suit of wands can be seen as a representation of our connection to magic or to the divine, as the wand or cross would suggest, and to forces like the element of fire, which we might not completely understand yet, but which can help us to grow and develop once we are able to form a stronger understanding of them. The astrological signs that the suit of wands is connected to are the three fire signs, which are Aries, Leo, and Sagittarius.

Court Cards

In addition to each of the suits, the court cards of each suit also have an element that it is associated with, meaning each of the court cards can be used to represent two different elements, with one from its suit and one from its title. The suit's element represents the forces and concepts that the card works in, while the court card's role represents the approach or the method that each court card takes in their actions and in dealing with its suit element. For example, queens are represented by water and are usually gifted with wisdom or inner knowledge and empathy for other people or things. The queen of coins, which is the suit representative of the earth, would be helpful and generous to others in their financial or otherwise personal goals and will usually have a great amount of wisdom to share with those around her.

The page is the first and the least experienced of the court cards. Pages represent the element of earth, and they embody curiosity more than anything else. They are eager to learn and willing to explore all of the possibilities that their suit presents. This represents eagerness, almost bordering on greed, for the different opportunities that they will find in their suit. They also crave representations of the suit that they belong to, especially physical ones that can be held or felt in some way. For the Page of air, they might want to learn or study the theory of certain disciplines.

The knight is the second court card, one rank up from the page. Knights are representative of the element of fire, and they embody concepts like passion or energy. The knights are eager for action, always trying to find something that will keep them busy in some way or another. The knight would be very eager to prove themselves, and it might even need to keep that eagerness in check, or they might risk falling out of control. This can sometimes manifest as impatience. The knight of air might throw themselves wholeheartedly into their studies, always looking for some new area of study to branch into or might focus on one area relentlessly. The knight of earth, on the other hand, might throw themselves into their work in a similar way, always looking for something to do and excelling in their work, often going above and beyond even when they do not necessarily need to. These are the people who will become masters in their field of study or work or expert strategists, provided that they are able to reign in their eagerness and focus on finding direction, applying their skills toward a specific goal, as opposed to constantly looking for new skills to master.

The queen is the third court card, only one rank lower than the king. The queen is also considered the counterpart to the king, both in title and function. She represents the element of water and embodies the pursuit of knowledge that comes from within, as opposed to learning new skills based on the world around them, like the knight and page. The queen is a source of wisdom, seeking to grow her inner knowledge. She is quieter than the court members below her and much more reserved. She focuses on inspiring and helping others through their pursuit of her own self-improvement. The queen or air or earth, for example, might excel in her work through her pursuit of excellence, but her own skills are not the area in which she shines. The queen would serve as a source of inspiration, possibly even to the knight or page. Her quiet, disciplined brand of enthusiasm for her craft would serve to inspire the people who witness it, motivating them to develop their own skills in her footsteps. The queen, while likely more capable than her peers, chooses to adopt a leadership role in order to elevate the potential of the people around her or in her "court."

The fourth, final, and highest-ranking court card is the king. The king is considered to be the embodiment of their suit and the element that it is associated with. The king represents the element of air, and as such, he is level-headed and intellectual, approaching their goals with ambition and drive. The king would need to be able to think strategically and have clear goals, as well as the ability to communicate those goals effectively to other people. The king is a leader, much like the queen, but leads using their own excellence to guide others instead of motivating them to take their own action.

Cardinal, Fixed, and Mutable Signs

While these sets of associations between the suits and court cards to their respective elements and astrological signs are very helpful methods of dissecting and understanding the different cards and their meanings, there is also another approach that can be helpful. If you've ever looked into your zodiac sign or astrology, then you might have noticed a label of "cardinal, fixed, or mutable" on each sign. These labels are connected to the tarot as well. The cardinal signs are representative of the queen; the fixed signs represent the knight, and the mutable signs represent the kings.

The cardinal signs, or the signs aligned with the queens, are considered to be more assertive and aggressive. They take their own action and act in order to motivate others and allow others to shine with the element that they are associated with. Each of the signs represents the earliest stage of their season, as well. Aries is the cardinal fire sign associated with the beginning of the spring. Cancer is the cardinal water sign commonly associated with the beginning of the summer. Libra is the cardinal air sign associated with the beginning of the fall. Capricorn is the cardinal earth sign associated with the beginning of the winter season.

The fixed signs, or the signs aligned with the knights, are considered to be more focused and driven. The fixed signs are reliable and determined, sometimes even to the point of stubbornness. Each of these signs represents the height of their season. Taurus is the fixed earth sign associated with the spring. Leo is the fixed fire sign commonly associated with the summer. Scorpio is the fixed water sign associated with the fall. Aquarius is the fixed air sign associated with the winter season.

The mutable signs, the signs aligned with the kings, are considered to be more adaptable and flexible. The kings are excellent communicators and can sometimes even be rebellious or difficult to deal with. Each of these signs represents the final portion of their season. The Gemini is the mutable air sign associated with the end of the spring season. Virgo is the mutable earth sign commonly associated with the end of the summer season. Sagittarius is the mutable fire sign associated with the end of the fall season. Pisces is the mutable water sign associated with the end of the winter season. The page is not assigned to any of the astrological signs, as the ranks of each of the signs and their roles come from a tradition that excludes the page from this list. The reason for this is that the page is still "undeveloped" and has the potential to move on to any of the three court titles.

Chapter 7: Tarot and the Chakras

Another very useful thing that you can learn in order to help you understand the tarot a little better is the concept of chakras, as well as how those chakras work and how they relate to the tarot. The chakras, in simple terms, are the seven "centers" of energy within the human body, and most people choose to visualize the chakras as "wheels" of energy that exist within the body, roughly along the spine. There are seven chakras within the human body, existing in a more spiritual or metaphysical sense rather than literally being organs within the body. However, the chakras can be thought of as similar to the organs in the sense that while our physical organs keep our physical bodies running and ideally in good shape, the chakras serve the same purpose for a person's soul and allow it to continue to be healthy if they are maintained and able to function properly. These chakras serve different purposes that all relate to the emotional aspect and well-being of a person. In order for a person to live a happy and successful life, it is important for them to maintain their chakras, the same way that a physically healthy person will take care of their body.

The Importance of Balance of the Chakras

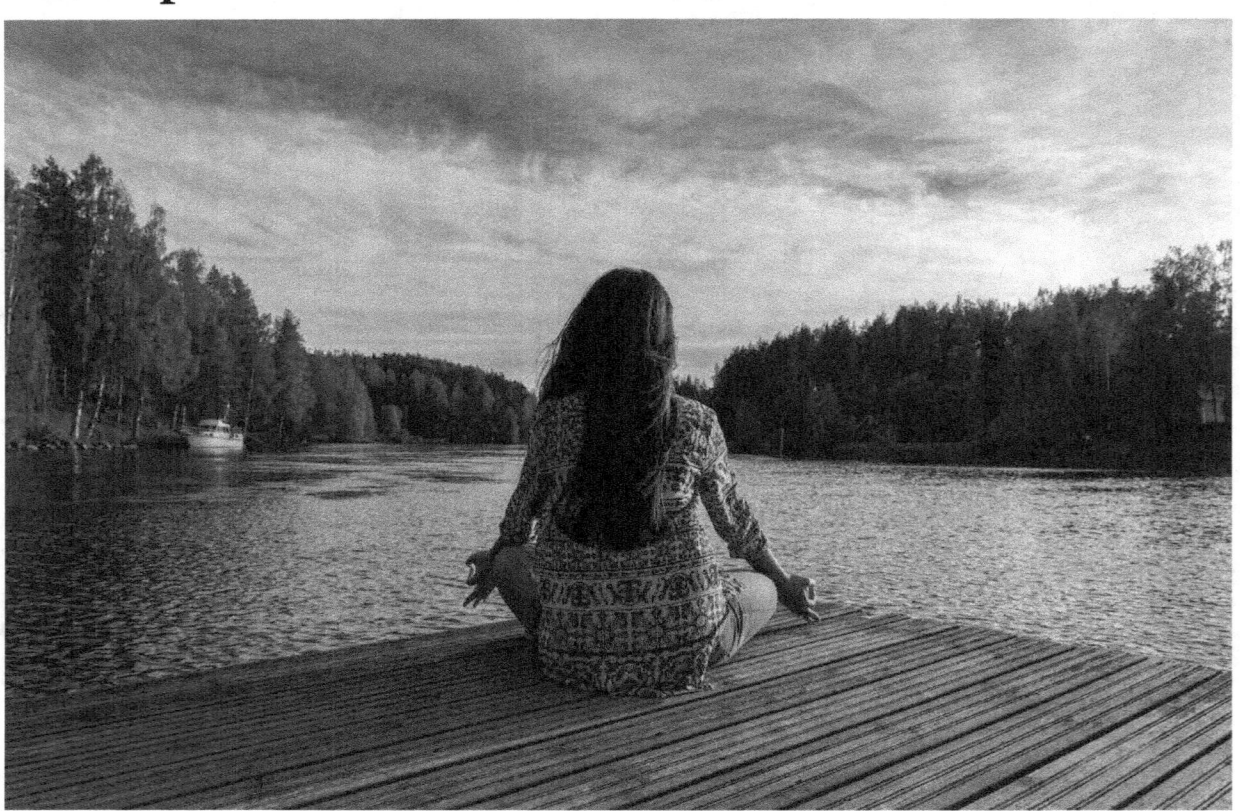

Most people experience some sort of disturbance or imbalance in their chakras at some point throughout their life. You might wake up one morning and feel a little off-center or unusual, somehow different from how you normally feel, but you just can't place it. It is more than likely that this disturbance was caused by an imbalance in your chakras and will possibly be solved with a little care of those chakras. This can be helpful in one's day-to-day life to help you to be "at your best" and understand and handle your problems much more confidently. Most commonly, these problems are caused by significant events or changes in a person's life that they are unable to handle mentally and emotionally at the time that the event occurs. You might have had a serious physical illness and be forced to focus on physical or financial recovery or some sort of emotional disturbance, like the end of a significant long-term relationship. In these cases, it can be incredibly helpful for you to understand which chakras relate to these different aspects of yourself in order to deal with them as effectively as you can and continue to be healthy and happy. You could even choose to perform daily "maintenance" for your chakras in order to keep your emotional, mental, and spiritual health in good shape. In some cases, they can also help your physical body to function more smoothly since the body and spirit are connected and part of every person.

There are a number of methods that you can use in order to realign your chakras and get them to work properly or simply to keep them that way, thereby avoiding a lot of potential unnecessary imbalance within you. One of these methods is meditation. Meditation is a helpful tool that can help you to understand a lot of different issues that you might experience, and this applies just as well to spiritual matters. Another method, of course, is by using divination to help you to understand your issues and how to resolve them. This chapter will be about the use of the tarot cards and divinatory tarot readings for the purpose of aligning your chakras and keeping your spirit healthy.

There are different kinds of divination tools that can help you with this, but the practice of tarot reading is one of the most effective tools. For one, it can help you pin down the specific problem that you might be facing if you do not already understand it, as well as the areas that need attention because of that issue. Tarot is a much more direct and specific kind of tool for divination in a very detailed way, especially when compared to other kinds of divinatory methods because of the nature of how tarot cards reveal information about the reader or the recipient of the reading.

When you are performing a tarot reading for this purpose, you will want to start out by shuffling your tarot deck. Think about the different chakras and the states that they are in, as well as why this might be the case. You should have a specific question in mind, performing the reading to help you to understand that question. Your seven chakras and their health would be a great topic to focus on to help you to understand each of the chakras within your body. Once your deck has been shuffled, you will need to draw seven cards from your deck, drawing one card for each chakra. You will also need to remember the order you drew these cards, so it will be important to remember that when you draw and lay your cards on the table. Additionally, there are different ways that different people will use to draw their cards. Some people will simply pull from the top of their deck, while some people might split or cut their deck and draw their cards from one or both halves of the deck, some people will fan their decks out and choose the cards that speak out to them, and some people might even choose to simply go down the stack and pull cards out either at random or with a specific system that speaks to them. It is important that when you are drawing your cards, you use whatever method feels "right" to you and pull out the cards that you feel are the "correct" cards for yourself. Choose your seven cards and lay your spread. For a reading regarding your chakras, you will want to lay your cards out in the same arrangement as your seven chakras, which are in a vertical line. The first card that you draw will go at the bottom, representing your root chakra, and the seventh card that you draw will go to the top to represent your crown chakra. The cards should not make contact with any of the other cards but spaced out separately. The reasoning for this is simply to allow you to remember which card corresponds to the chakras more easily, but it is also meant to represent the separate locations of the chakras along your spine and your perception of them and the situation that you find yourself in.

Your cards should be on your table or a similar flat surface, facing downward so that you cannot read them yet at this point, but they should be arranged in such a way that you can flip them and read them when you are ready. But before you do so, you should try to stop for a moment and consider the cards that lay in front of you. Take a moment to think about what you feel before you read the cards in front of you. What are your thoughts regarding those seven cards? You should be listening to your "gut" or your intuition for the answer, as well as any significant signs that your body might be sending to you or any messages that might be coming from your unconscious mind. You might begin to feel pressure in a certain part of your body or some other form of discomfort or anxiety. These kinds of signals can serve to help you to understand the state of your chakras on a deeper level before you begin your reading. You might even notice that a specific card or multiple cards might seem different from the others. They might be shifted in slightly different positions from the rest of your cards, and you might even literally begin to see certain cards as darker or "blurred," making it harder for you to focus on that card or cards. These can be signs that those chakras are blocked and need to be cleared, or you might need to take more care of those chakras in comparison to the others. On the other hand, "brighter" cards or the ones that you find you can focus on much more clearly will act as signs that those chakras are functioning especially well, or at least better than some of the others. Intuition can be an especially useful tool, and it can be important to reach out to your intuition and your unconscious mind for guidance from time to time. Taking a moment to actively reach out to them before a tarot reading can prime you for that tendency and strengthen your connection to those parts of yourself and even to the chakras that you are focusing on. You might even find that you have already answered your initial question to some degree. Do not stop there, though. You should still continue on with the reading, looking to the cards to confirm any suspicions that you might have or pointing you in the correct direction if those suspicions are not completely true.

Why You Need to Read Your Tarot Cards

The last thing that you will need to do during this reading, of course, is to read your cards. At this step in the process, you will need to understand the meanings of the cards within the tarot deck. The various cards and the meanings of those cards are discussed in this book, and information on those cards can be found in the first chapter for the major arcana, the fourth and fifth chapters for the minor arcana (the numbered cards in the fourth chapter and the court cards in the fifth chapter), and the history and theory of the tarot in the second and third chapters. Additionally, most tarot decks will also include a short book about the different cards and how to read them; you can use this to help you interpret the reading. However, chakra readings are usually much easier than most other spreads because the cards that you have drawn and laid out already have a specific meaning and relate to a specific question almost inherently.

Each card will be read with regards to the specific chakra that it represents in the order that you have laid them out on the surface. You will want to be looking for specific information about the chakra that the card relates to. Each of the seven chakras has its own rules and relates to its own areas of your life and your well-being. Each chakra can also be blocked by specific kinds of events that might happen throughout your life or experiences that you might be having at the moment. Additionally, you will need to understand the seven chakras, as well as the different kinds of experiences or circumstances that can block them. Read on to know more about the chakras and the ways that they work.

The Chakras and the Tarot

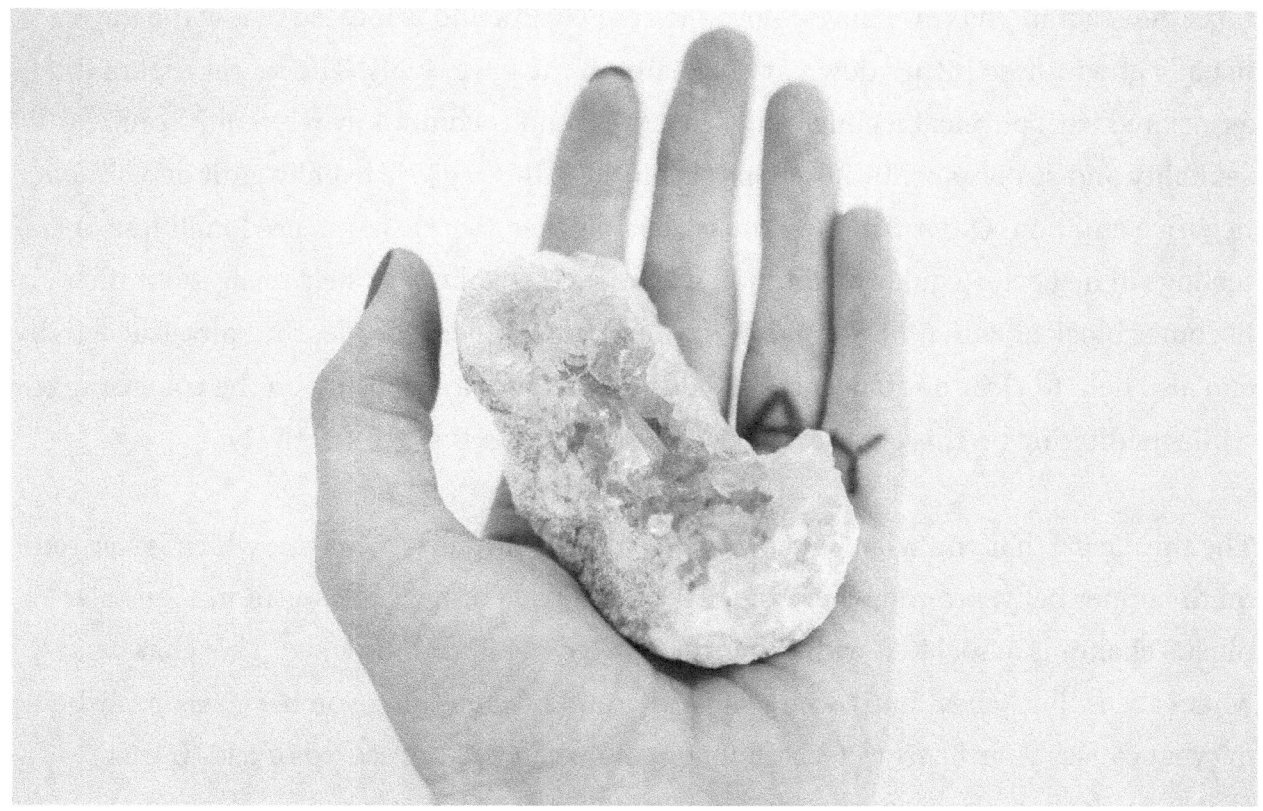

As mentioned earlier, the seven chakras are arranged along the spine, starting from the base going to the top of the head or the crown. The first one is at the base of the spine and is called the root chakra. The root chakra is the first you will need to draw and read a card for. The root chakra affects all of your basic survival functions and needs. The card that you drew for this chakra will let you know about the condition of this chakra and if its basic needs are being met. If it is in good shape, then you are healthy, at least with regards to your root chakra and the parts of yourself that it governs. If it is in a particularly poor condition, then it is likely that this chakra is blocked, and its basic needs are not being met. This will typically require some level of "chakra work," usually in the form of meditation. The root chakra is very commonly associated with the red color, and focusing on this color and the needs or the root chakra while you meditate on that chakra can be helpful in healing or "unblocking" it.

The second card that you will be reading is also for the second chakra, which is referred to as the "sacral" chakra. This is above the root chakra and is located below the navel, usually about three inches down at the center of the lower belly. The sacral chakra is associated with physical feelings and sensations and is commonly related to your sexuality and sex organs. If this chakra is blocked, the cause is usually guilt or a similar negative emotion. Other common causes of a blocked sacral chakra are loneliness or feelings of neglect. Regular meditation on the sacral chakra can help clear it out if it becomes blocked, and other things like adopting healthier lifestyles and physical activity can also help to clear out blockages in your sacral chakra. Focusing on the color orange while meditating on this chakra can also help clear it out more effectively.

The third card that you will be reading is for the "solar plexus" chakra, which is located on the upper belly, around where the diaphragm rests or near the sternum. The solar plexus chakra is associated with things like willpower and confidence. This chakra is what causes that "chest puff" when you are proud of something you have accomplished or what causes your heart to feel empty or cold when you are scared or sad. If this chakra is blocked, the reason is usually something similar to shame or a lack of accomplishment. Regular meditation on the solar plexus chakra can help clear it out if it becomes blocked or is underperforming. Other things like "getting a win," accomplishing goals, following through a task, or performing a job that you are proud of can help improve the flow of energy in the solar plexus chakra. Focusing on the yellow color while meditating on this chakra can also help clear it out more effectively.

The fourth card that you will be reading is for the "heart" chakra. This is located in the middle of the chest, above the solar plexus. The heart chakra is associated with things like love, compassion, and relationships with other people. This is where you will feel, most heavily, the weight of a wrong that has been committed against you. You can also notice this weight when you forgive someone or accept a situation that you have been struggling with, especially for a long time. If this chakra is blocked, the cause is usually something similar to a grudge that you might be holding or another kind of unresolved trauma or experience that affected you deeply. Regular meditation on the heart chakra can help clear it out if it becomes blocked. Other ways to improve the state of your heart chakra are giving forgiveness or letting go of your unresolved issues. Focusing on the color green while you meditate on this chakra can also help clear it out better.

The fifth card that you will be reading is for the "throat" chakra. This is located in the middle of the neck or throat, and it is associated with things like your ability to "speak out" and general communication, including your voice. If this chakra is blocked, it could mean that you are not receiving the whole truth, or you are haunted by the feeling of guilt for lying to or deceiving someone else. Regular meditation on the throat chakra can help clear its negative energy. Being more honest and open and trying to encourage openness and honesty in others, can effectively unblock this chakra. Remember that open communication is the cure to a blocked throat chakra. Focusing on the color blue while you meditate on this chakra can also help clear it out.

The sixth card that you will be reading is for the "third eye" chakra. This is located between the eyes on your forehead, where the third eye is believed to exist. The third eye chakra is associated with things like the "sixth sense" or things that you might not be able to physically see with your "real eyes." This sixth sense is based on intuition and insight, similar to the concept of the personal unconscious, and it shapes the way that you perceive certain things that have a strong impact on you. Some people are especially more sensitive or aware of their "sixth sense" or their personal unconscious and might experience a blockage of this chakra in the form of a headache. Regular meditation on the third eye chakra can help clear it out if it becomes blocked or inactive. Focusing on the color indigo while you meditate on this chakra can also help clear it out better.

The seventh and last card that you will be reading is for the "crown" chakra. This is located at the top of your head or the crown. This is also the "last" chakra on the list. The crown chakra is associated with things like your connection to the divine or the universe, depending on your religious practice or belief. A healthy crown chakra represents a healthy connection to your deity or deities or a strong sense of faith in the general sense if you do not worship a deity. If this chakra is blocked, the cause is usually something similar to "spiritual greed," or focusing more on yourself rather than on what you put out into the world. Regular meditation on the crown chakra can help clear it out if it becomes blocked. Also, strengthening your connection to your faith or the divine will improve the energy surrounding this chakra. Focusing on the colors of violet or white while you meditate on this chakra can also help clear the negative energy affecting the crown.

Chapter 8: Tarot and Religion

Another important thing to consider with regards to tarot and the use of tarot cards for divinatory purposes is religion. A big question that might come up when considering its use to perform divination is: "Is this okay with my religion?" This is, of course, a very important point to consider, especially for people who are devoted to their religion and religious practices. Christianity is likely one of the most significant religions to consider since it is one of the most popular religions practiced in the world and one that has the strongest prejudice against practices like divination. Many Christians will cite Bible verses or other similar sources with regards to these kinds of "occult" practices like divination, claiming that they are sinful, even satanic in nature. Some of the most common Bible verses that are used to condemn the use of practices like these are as follows:

<u>Here is Leviticus 19:31, which is stated in the King James Version:</u>
"Regard not them that have familiar spirits, neither seek after wizards, to be defiled by them: I [am] the LORD your God."

<u>Here is Leviticus 20:27, also from the King James Version:</u>
"A man also or woman that hath a familiar spirit, or that is a wizard, shall surely be put to death: they shall stone them with stones: their blood [shall be] upon them."

<u>Deuteronomy 18:10, 18:11, and 18:12, from the King James Version:</u>
"There shall not be found among you [any one] that maketh his son or his daughter to pass through the fire, [or] that useth divination, [or] an observer of times, or an enchanter, or a witch. Or a charmer, or a consulter with familiar spirits, or a wizard, or a necromancer. For all that do these things [are] an abomination unto the LORD: and because of these abominations, the LORD thy God doth drive them out from before thee."

<u>Jeremiah 27:9 and 27:10, from the King James Version:</u>
"Therefore, hearken not ye to your prophets, nor to your diviners, nor to your dreamers, nor to your enchanters, nor to your sorcerers, which speak unto you, saying, Ye shall not serve the king of Babylon: For they prophesy a lie unto you, to remove you far from your land; and that I should drive you out, and ye should perish."

As you can see, these verses essentially state that faithful Christians should not allow themselves to be persuaded by "those with familiar spirits" or "wizards," which, in this context, refers to those who practice witchcraft, divination, or other magical traditions, specifically ones that require the user to act in ways that go against the word of the Lord. They also condemn the use of prophecy from sources other than the Lord or agents of the Lord, as well as divination or enchanters. It would seem, at a surface level, that the word of the Bible and the Lord, by extension, would condemn the use of divinatory practices, like the tarot readings that are described in this book. However, the divination that is referred to in the Bible, while it wears the same name, is not the same kind of "divination" that is performed in tarot readings at all. Yes, the Bible does literally use the word divination, as do tarot readings, but only for lack of a more accurate term for the practice. The kind of divination referred to in these verses is specific to magical divination that relies on the use of "familiar spirits," which essentially means that in order for these "rules" or "laws" to apply based on "the spirit of the law," the divinatory practices in question would need to be the sort that relies on "familiar spirits" from religions that defy the word of the Christian God or the Lord, such as those who devoutly practiced religions that were being encountered for the first time or had recently been encountered for the first time when the Bible was recorded.

The practice of performing divinatory tarot readings absolutely does NOT apply to any of these verses, nor do they apply to similar verses condemning the use of magic, witchcraft, or any other sort of unholy practices unless the cards themselves are made from materials that should not be combined according to the word of the Bible. As has been mentioned in this book, the use of tarot cards for divinatory purposes relies more heavily on psychology rather than unexplained magic, and unless a version of the Bible is released that condemns the use of tarot cards specifically or the use of psychology, then any Christian person should be relatively "safe." It is, however, important to consider these verses (if you are a Christian) and any other sources that might be relevant to your own religion, as it is always better to be safe than sorry.

Indeed, it is worth considering what your specific religion has to say about this practice as your religion may frown upon the Tarot or even outright ban it. If you have any specific questions, it would be wise to consult with your religious leaders so that they may be to give you proper guidance and counsel on what is permitted and what is not. The last thing we want to do is to give you advice that may contradict your faith. Everything here is present in good faith. As such, please take it as an exercise in the use of psychology rather than engaging in inappropriate practices.

Conclusion

Thank you very much for having taken the time to read this book. By now, we hope that you have gotten a good sense of what the Tarot is and what it can be used for. In addition, we hope that you have gained a different perspective on it. We sincerely hope that if you had ever believed it to be quackery or even a means of fooling people out of their money, you have now gained a different perception of it.

At this point, please go over any parts or chapters, which you feel you need to brush up on. In doing so, you will be able to improve your overall understanding of the subject matter. Furthermore, you will be able to interpret each of the cards based on sound fundamentals rather than apparent mystical or supernatural powers.

Additionally, do take the time to reflect on the discoveries which you have made about yourself or even human nature for that matter. We are confident that you have gained a newfound sense of understanding of the underlying motivations of the people around you. As you begin to see the archetypes we have discussed in action, you will begin to really see how and why people act the way they do. This will help you to avoid feeling confused by seemingly erratic behavior. As a matter of fact, your understanding of human nature will lead you to become far more insightful and wiser.

The fact of the matter is that by learning more about yourself and your feelings, you will not only grow spiritually but also intellectually. Consequently, you have a great deal to gain from using the Tarot to further your journey of self-discovery and personal development. We hope that this book will be able to give you just the boost you need along this path.

Thanks again for choosing this book. We feel that with the number of options out there. It can be hard to tell which sources of information are legit and which ones are just a bunch of baloney. Great care was taken in ensuring that the information in this book is forthcoming and honest. The last thing we want to do is to give you false or otherwise misleading information about the Tarot and how it can be used to improve your outlook on life and yourself.

If you have found this book to be useful and informative, by all means tell your friends, family, and colleagues about it. We hope that they, too, will find it to be useful and informative. If you feel compelled to share your knowledge with others who might be interested in this topic, then you can certainly use this book as a reference to guide you. We are sure that plenty of folks out there would be interested to know more about the Tarot in a truthful and honest manner. Plus, it can make a great topic of conversation at a dinner party when spending time with friends and family.

See you next time!

www.ingramcontent.com/pod-product-compliance
Lightning Source LLC
Chambersburg PA
CBHW081343070526
44578CB00005B/700